The Complete Book of
DESSERTS

The Complete Book of
DESSERTS

Edited by Linda Doeser

NEWNES BOOKS

House Editor: Sally Taylor
Designer: Caroline Dewing

Published by Newnes Books, a division
of The Hamlyn Publishing Group Limited,
84–88 The Centre, Feltham, Middlesex, England
and distributed for them by
Hamlyn Distribution Services Limited,
Sanders Lodge Estate, Rushden, Northants,
England

© Marshall Cavendish Limited 1985

ISBN 0 600 35898 4

Any editorial queries should be addressed to
Marshall Cavendish Books Limited.
Any trade queries should be
addressed to Newnes Books

Phototypeset by Quadraset Limited,
Midsomer Norton, Bath, Avon.

Printed and bound in Italy by
New Interlitho SpA.

Introduction

A dessert is undoubtedly the highlight of a meal. Whether a light-as-air concoction served after a hearty main course or a warming sponge pudding which ensures a lazy afternoon, it is something to look forward to, something to give the final feeling of well-being. The desserts in this book cater for every possible taste and occasion, and range from tingling fresh sorbets to serve at the end of a summer dinner party, to creamy milk puddings that will always receive a welcome from the family.

Chapter One is all about Ices—Ice-creams, Sorbets, Water Ices, Granitas and Bombes. Home-made ice-creams are a different—and vastly superior—experience to commercial varieties and none are difficult to make. Useful as a freezer stand-by, remember that they also have a role to play as a 'planned' dessert.

The Mousses, Creams and Jellies that follow are all-occasion favourites, too. Included here are some old-fashioned recipes—Blancmange and a Tansy, for example—that along with home-made jellies are due for a revival. Next come Soufflés and Meringues which are special-occasion desserts—easy to make but spectacular in appearance. A cooked soufflé can be all ready to assemble before guests arrive, and then popped into the oven while you are eating the main course. Cold soufflés, made to look like their risen cooked counterparts, can be prepared well in advance, as can melt-in-the-mouth meringue confections.

The chapter on Fruit has versions of popular favourites as well as some appealing new ideas. The same is true for the next chapter—Pies, Flans and Tarts. Here, traditional fruit pies, elegant flans and wonderful puff-pastry creations share the pages. The cheesecakes that follow lose none of their popularity as they become part of every cook's dessert repertoire. The ones here pander to all tastes—from those who like the rich full flavour of cooked cheesecakes to those who like the lighter 'mousse-like' types. They lead into a chapter on Gâteaux and Cakes— creative masterpieces that really demand an audience to appreciate their extravagantly embellished appearance.

Pancakes, Crêpes and Batter Puddings are too often neglected—all the more surprising when one realises the full extent of their versatility. Pancakes and Crêpes can be rolled round all sorts of fillings as well as stacked into high-rise treats interleaved with a variety of delicious flavourings, or, of course, simply eaten with sugar and lemon. Any way and all ways—they find favour every time.

No book of desserts could ignore the Traditional Puddings—Steamed Sponges and Suets, Jam Roll, Rice Pudding, Trifles and the like. They are all here, ready to bring a smile to the faces of your family. After their calorie-laden wickedness, come ideas for slimmers, proving that you need not forgo this part of a meal simply because you are watching your waistline. Finally, there is a collection of sauces that can turn even the humblest pudding—admittedly not frequently found in these pages—into a special treat.

Contents

Ice Creams, Sorbets & Bombes

There is a shop in the south of France which is said to sell the best ice-creams in the world. Fortunately, however, you don't have to travel that far! These wonderful recipes are the "real thing"; make them and you will discover the genuine taste of ice-cream. Once you've mastered the art—and it isn't hard—you can combine these richly flavoured ice-creams into bombes, surely the pièce de résistance of the cook's art. In addition, there are mouthwatering recipes for granitas, water ices and that aristocrat of frozen desserts, sorbets.

If ever there was a misnomer, it is ice-*cream*, when applied to commercial mélanges of whipped-up fats and chemical flavourings. However tempting their descriptions sound and their appearances suggest, they are almost invariably disappointing to taste. Genuine ice-creams, however, are the ultimate in luxurious desserts, and they are no more difficult or troublesome to make than any other dessert.

Traditional ice-creams are not the only frozen desserts you can make easily at home. Water ices, granitas and sorbets are just as easy and provide a delightful summer treat for the family or a refreshing, delicate end to a sumptuous dinner party at any time of year.

Bombes are among the most spectacular of all desserts. A shell of ice-cream surrounding a surprise filling looks and tastes wonderful. Step-by-step instructions to a traditional bombe are given on page 11 and a recipe for the basic bombe mixture is on page 20. However, you can give full rein to your imagination and combine whatever flavours appeal to you.

Ice-creams

There are three basic types of ice-creams—simple fruit ice-creams, cream ices and rich ice-cream—and each is made by a different method.

The first method is ideal for ice-creams flavoured with raw, soft fruit, such as raspberries and strawberries. It can also be used for cooked fruits, such as blackcurrants. Whichever fruit you choose, it must be puréed. If this is done in an electric blender, it will add more texture to the final ice-cream; if rubbed through a sieve, the result will be smoother. However, any fruit with pips, such as raspberries and gooseberries, must be sieved. Icing sugar is best for sweetening the purée.

The method for making the ice is exactly the same as for making a custard-based fruit mould (see page 28). The gelatine is usually omitted, although some people feel it gives a better texture to the ice-cream. When the fruit and cream have been combined, the mixture is poured into an ice tray. It is then put in the freezing compartment of the refrigerator until it is partially frozen but still mushy. At this stage, it is thoroughly beaten to break up the ice crystals, then returned to the refrigerator for re-freezing. If possible, it should be beaten a second time to give it a smooth final texture, after which it is frozen until firm.

For cream ices, a sugar syrup is combined with the puréed fruit before freezing and also before cream is added. The proportions of sugar and water in the syrup will vary, according to the type of fruit being used. Equally, the proportion of fruit juices or purée to syrup will vary. Always use the quantities given in the recipes to avoid any difficulties with freezing the ice-cream.

The fruit purée and syrup are combined and frozen until mushy, then the mixture is beaten to break up the ice crystals. Cream, whipped until it forms soft peaks, is added at this stage and the mixture is re-frozen. Once again it is beaten and then returned to the refrigerator until it is frozen and firm.

Rich ice-creams, the most famous of which is, of course, vanilla, are made from a custard base. Instructions for this are given in the steps on page 10; you can, of course, substitute other flavourings such as melted chocolate or coffee, in place of vanilla in step 3. You can also use single cream (not whipped) instead of double, but the texture of the final ice-cream will not be as rich. It is particularly important to include the second beating if using single cream, or the texture tends to be a little granular.

Add flavourings such as chopped fruit or liqueurs at the same time as the cream, when the mixture is partially frozen. If added before, they can inhibit freezing because of their sugar content.

Ice-creams (and bombes, too) should be removed from the freezer before serving. If not, they will be too hard to spoon out, uncomfortably cold on the tongue and lacking their full flavour. Remove soft textured ice-cream 15 minutes before serving. Put firmer ice-creams at the bottom of the refrigerator at the beginning of the meal.

Granitas, Water Ices and Sorbets

Granitas are the easiest of all frozen desserts, consisting simply of a weak sugar syrup flavoured with tea, coffee or fruit juice.

Water ices are made from a stronger syrup, flavoured with fruit juice or purée. They are partially frozen and then a little egg white is beaten in. After freezing until almost firm, they are beaten thoroughly to break up the ice crystals and then re-frozen.

Sorbets are the finest of ices. They are made by the same technique as water ices, but a very strong syrup and more egg white is used.

Freezing

No special freezing equipment, beyond an ordinary domestic refrigerator or a freezer, is necessary. If using the refrigerator, turn it to its lowest setting 1 hour before the mixture is to go in the freezer compartment (the normal temperature of a freezer is cold enough). Once the final freezing has been completed and the ice-cream or sorbet is firm, the refrigerator can be switched back to its normal setting. Ice-creams, water ices, sorbets and bombes can be stored in the frozen food compartment, but use them as quickly as you can for the best flavour. Granitas must be served as soon as they are ready, as storage will destroy the texture.

Other Equipment

An electric sorbetière, or ice-cream maker, while not essential, helps in making ice-creams as it eliminates the need to beat the mixture during freezing. It is not a freezing device, so it must be used inside the freezer or refrigerator. When it is switched on, electrically operated paddles move constantly. If using one, never fill it more than three-quarters full, as the mixture expands during beating.

All other necessary equipment—a heavy-based saucepan, a double boiler or heatproof bowl, mixing bowls, a jug, a balloon or (preferably) electric whisk, aluminium foil, etc—will already exist in a well-equipped kitchen.

For freezing the ice-cream or sorbets, use ice cube trays with the dividers removed, or plastic boxes or bowls.

Ordinary china or glass bowls can be used as bombe moulds, but you will need to allow more time for freezing. Specially made metal bombe moulds fitted with lids can be bought. In either case, chill before using.

Making Rich Vanilla Ice-cream

Serves 4–6
275 ml (½ pint) single cream
1 vanilla pod *or* 2–3 drops vanilla essence
1 egg and 2 egg yolks
50 g (2 oz) caster sugar
275 ml (½ pint) double cream

1 Put single cream and a vanilla pod *(if using)* in a pan over low heat. Bring to just below boiling point. Remove from heat, cover and leave for 15 minutes. Put egg, egg yolks and sugar in the top of a double boiler and beat over a low heat until thick.

2 Take pan from heat and remove vanilla pod. Pour the hot cream on to the beaten egg mixture, stirring. Cook in the double boiler, stirring constantly over a low heat, for about 15 minutes, until the mixture coats the back of the spoon.

3 Remove the mixture from the heat, and, if you are using vanilla essence, add 2–3 drops. Strain the mixture and set aside to cool. Then chill before freezing. When thoroughly chilled, pour the mixture into a chilled container and cover with foil.

4 Freeze the custard mixture for about 45 minutes until it forms a partially frozen mush. Just before removing the container from the freezer compartment, lightly whip the double cream, using a balloon whisk, until it forms soft peaks.

5 Remove the container from the freezer compartment and turn the mixture into a bowl. Beat the mixture thoroughly with a wooden spoon to break up the ice crystals, then fold in whipped cream. Return the mixture to the container, cover again with foil and re-freeze for a further 45 minutes.

6 Remove the container from the freezer, turn the mixture into a bowl and beat thoroughly again. Return it to the container, cover with foil and freeze until firm. It is now ready to serve or store. An ice-cream scoop used for serving gives a professional look to desserts.

Making a Traditional Bombe

Serves 6
425 ml (15 fl oz) ice-cream
150 ml (5 fl oz) basic bombe mixture (*see page 20*)
flavourings of your choice
1 egg white, whisked (optional)
30 ml (2 tablespoons) double cream, lightly whipped (optional)

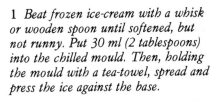

1 *Beat frozen ice-cream with a whisk or wooden spoon until softened, but not runny. Put 30 ml (2 tablespoons) into the chilled mould. Then, holding the mould with a tea-towel, spread and press the ice against the base.*

2 *Working from base to rim, continue adding and spreading the ice-cream until the sides of the mould are lined with a layer 1.2–2.5 cm (¼–1 in) thick. When the lining is even, cover the bombe with grease-proof paper and a lid or foil and return it to the freezer for at least 1 hour.*

3 *When the ice-cream is frozen hard, fold flavourings, egg white or cream, if desired, into the bombe mixture. Spoon it into the bombe cavity and press down firmly, filling until the surface is level. Cover and freeze until firm.*

4 *To serve, remove the lid and wrap the mould in a cloth. Dip it in hot water. Remove the cloth. Invert the bombe on to a plate and remove the mould. Smooth with a palette knife. Refrigerate for 15 minutes before serving to soften slightly.*

Mould Sizes and Quantities

Servings	Mould size	Contents	Servings	Mould size	Contents
Bombes:			**Cassata:**		
6	575 ml (1 pint)	425 ml (15 fl oz) ice-cream 150 ml (5 fl oz) bombe mixture	6	575 ml (1 pint)	200 ml (7 fl oz) ice-cream 200 ml (7 fl oz) sorbet cassata mix (see page 23)
8–9	850 ml (1½ pints)	575 ml (1 pint) ice-cream 212 ml (7½ fl oz) bombe mixture	8–9	850 ml (1½ pints)	350 ml (12 fl oz) ice-cream 275 ml (½ pint) sorbet cassata mix using 125 ml (4 fl oz) cream
10–12	1.1 litres (2 pints)	850 ml (1½ pints) ice-cream 275 ml (½ pint) bombe mixture	10–12	1.1 litres (2 pints)	450 ml (16 fl oz) ice-cream 350 ml (12 fl oz) sorbet cassata mix using 175 ml (6 fl oz) cream

Brown Bread Ice-cream

Serves 8
475 ml (17 fl oz) rich vanilla ice-cream (*see step-by-step recipe, page 10*)
4 small slices brown bread, crusts removed
5 ml (1 teaspoon) ground cinnamon
125 ml (4 fl oz) water
75 g (3 oz) sugar

Break up the ice-cream with a fork and set aside to soften slightly. Crumble the bread and mix together with the cinnamon.

Put the water and sugar in a pan and set over medium heat, stirring constantly, until the sugar has dissolved. Increase the heat to high and bring the mixture to the boil. Boil until the mixture caramelizes and turns golden.

Remove the pan from the heat and stir in the breadcrumbs. Immediately blend the mixture evenly into the softened ice-cream, before the breadcrumbs form large lumps.

Store in the freezer until required. Leave to soften in the refrigerator for 30 minutes before serving.

Apricot Ice-cream

Serves 8
450 g (1 lb) dried apricots
50 g (2 oz) sugar
275 ml (½ pint) single cream
1 vanilla pod
2 egg yolks
50 g (2 oz) caster sugar
275 ml (½ pint) double cream
15 ml (1 tablespoon) apricot brandy

Put the apricots in a measuring jug and make a note of the mark they reach. Then tip them into a saucepan and cover with twice their volume of water. Add the sugar and set the pan over a medium heat. Bring to the boil, cover and simmer for 40 minutes. Remove the pan from the heat and set aside for 5 hours.

Set the refrigerator at its lowest setting (*if necessary —see page 9*) and chill an ice-cream container.

Put the single cream and the vanilla pod in a saucepan over low heat. Bring to just below boiling point. Remove the pan from the heat, cover and set aside for 15 minutes.

Clockwise from top: Brown Bread Ice-cream, Apricot Ice-cream, Blackcurrant Ice-cream, Minted Lemon Ice, Coffee Ice-cream with Chocolate Sauce

Beat together the egg yolks and caster sugar in the top of a double boiler. Remove the vanilla pod from the single cream and pour the hot cream on to the egg yolk mixture in a thin trickle, stirring constantly. Set the top of the boiler over the bottom and put on a low heat. Cook, stirring constantly, for 15 minutes or until the custard is thick enough to coat the back of the spoon.

Remove the custard from the heat, strain and set aside to cool. Then chill in the refrigerator.

Drain the apricots. Rub them through a sieve or blend them in an electric blender to form a smooth purée. Stir this purée into the chilled custard.

Pour the mixture into the ice-cream container, cover with foil and freeze for 2 hours, or until mushy.

Whip the double cream until it forms soft peaks. Remove the ice-cream from the freezer and turn it into a bowl. Beat briskly, then fold in the double cream and the brandy. Return mixture to the ice-cream container, cover and re-freeze for 1½ hours.

Turn out the ice-cream and beat again. Return it to the container, cover and re-freeze until firm.

Blackcurrant Ice-cream

Serves 4–6
150 ml (5 fl oz) water
225 g (8 oz) caster sugar
575 ml (1 pint) blackcurrant purée*
juice of 1 orange
275 ml (½ pint) double cream

Set the refrigerator at its lowest setting (*if necessary— see page 9*) and chill an ice-cream container.

Put the water and sugar in a saucepan over low heat, stirring constantly, until the sugar has dissolved. Bring to the boil. Boil for 5 minutes. Remove the pan from the heat and set aside to cool.

Stir the purée into the syrup. Stir in the orange juice. Turn the mixture into the ice-cream container, cover with foil and freeze for 45 minutes, or until mushy.

Whip the cream until it forms soft peaks. Turn the blackcurrant ice into a bowl and stir vigorously. Beat in the cream.

Return the mixture to the container, cover and re-freeze for 45 minutes.

Turn the mixture into a bowl and beat again. Return it to the container, cover and re-freeze until firm.

*To make blackcurrant purée, simmer 450 g (1 lb) blackcurrants with a little water until soft. Push through a sieve and make up to 575 ml (1 pint) with water or a little blackcurrant syrup if you have any.

Coffee Ice-cream

Serves 4
275 ml (½ pint) milk
45 ml (3 tablespoons) instant coffee powder
3 eggs, separated
100 g (4 oz) soft brown sugar
575 ml (1 pint) double cream

Set the refrigerator at its lowest setting (*if necessary—see page 9*) and chill an ice-cream container.

Put the milk in a pan over low heat. Stir in the coffee powder and bring the mixture to just below boiling point. Remove the pan from the heat and set aside.

Beat together the egg yolks and the sugar in the top of a double boiler. Pour the hot milk mixture on to the egg yolk mixture in a thin trickle, stirring constantly. Set the top of the boiler over the bottom and put on a low heat. Cook, stirring constantly, until the mixture is thick enough to coat the back of the spoon. Remove from the heat, strain and set aside to cool. If time permits, chill the mixture in the refrigerator for an hour or so.

Pour the mixture into the ice-cream container, cover and freeze for 1 hour, or until mushy.

Whip the cream until it forms soft peaks. Turn the ice-cream into a bowl and beat vigorously. Fold in the cream.

Return the mixture to the container, cover and re-freeze for 1 hour.

Whisk the egg whites until they form soft peaks. Turn the ice-cream into a bowl again and stir vigorously. Fold in the egg whites.

Return the mixture to the container, cover and re-freeze for 2–3 hours, or until firm.

Fruit and Nut Ice-cream

Serves 6
275 ml (½ pint) milk
60 ml (4 tablespoons) honey
2 eggs
2 extra egg yolks
7.5 ml (1½ teaspoons) ground nutmeg
275 ml (½ pint) double cream
100 g (4 oz) sultanas
60 ml (4 tablespoons) chopped almonds

Set the refrigerator at its lowest setting (*if necessary—see page 9*) and chill an ice-cream container.

Put the milk and honey in a saucepan over low heat and bring to just below boiling point. Remove the pan from the heat and set aside.

Beat together the eggs and the egg yolks in the top of a double boiler. Pour the hot milk mixture on to the eggs in a thin trickle, stirring constantly. Set the top of the boiler over the bottom and put on a low heat. Cook, stirring constantly, for 15 minutes, or until the custard is thick enough to coat the back of the spoon.

Remove from the heat and strain. Stir in the nutmeg and set aside to cool. Then chill in the refrigerator for an hour or so if time permits.

Pour the cold custard into the ice-cream container, cover with foil and freeze for 45 minutes, or until mushy.

Whip the cream until it forms soft peaks. Turn the ice into a bowl and stir vigorously. Fold in the cream.

Return the mixture to the container, cover and re-freeze for 45 minutes.

Turn the mixture into a bowl and beat again. Stir in the sultanas and almonds. Return the mixture to the container, cover and freeze until firm.

Grand Marnier Ice-cream

Serves 4
5 medium egg yolks
3 sugar lumps
1 medium orange
75 g (3 oz) caster sugar
15 ml (1 tablespoon) water
60 ml (4 tablespoons) Grand Marnier
275 ml (½ pint) double cream, softly whipped
DECORATION:
segments from 1 orange
candied orange or candied peel slices

Set the refrigerator at its lowest setting (*if necessary—see page 9*) and chill an ice-cream container.

Beat the egg yolks until pale and creamy.

Rub the sugar lumps over the peel of the orange so that they absorb the oils from the zest. Put in a small saucepan with the caster sugar and 15 ml (1 tablespoon) water.

Put the pan on a moderate heat and stir until the sugar has dissolved. Bring to the boil, then add the Grand Marnier.

Tip this mixture on to the yolks in a slow stream, beating all the time to keep the mixture creamy. Put over a large bowl of ice and beat until cold.

Fold the egg yolk mixture into the whipped cream and pour into the prepared container. Freeze for 2 hours.

Remove the ice-cream from the freezer, turn into a bowl and beat. Re-freeze.

Remove from the freezer 30 minutes before serving and scoop out into 4 individual glasses. Decorate with fresh orange segments and the candied orange or péel.

Strawberry Ice-cream

Serves 4–6
450 g (1 lb) strawberries, washed, hulled and roughly
chopped
225 g (8 oz) icing sugar, sifted
juice of ½ orange
juice of ½ lemon
275 ml (½ pint) double cream

Set the refrigerator to its lowest setting (*if necessary—
see page 9*) and chill an ice-cream container.

Rub the strawberries through a sieve to form a
smooth purée. Measure 275 ml (½ pint) of the purée
and stir it into the icing sugar. Stir in the orange and
lemon juice. Chill the purée in the refrigerator.

Lightly whip the cream until it forms soft peaks. Fold
the cream into the purée mixture and combine
thoroughly.

Pour the mixture into the ice-cream container, cover
with foil and freeze for 45 minutes, or until mushy.

Turn the mixture into a bowl and beat thoroughly.
Return the ice-cream to the container, cover and re-
freeze for 45 minutes.

Turn out the ice-cream and stir vigorously again.
Return it to the container, cover and re-freeze for a
further 45 minutes, or until firm.

Strawberry Ice-cream

15

Blackcurrant Leaf Water Ice

Serves 4
850 ml (1½ pints) water
thinly pared rind and juice of 3 large lemons
200 g (7 oz) caster sugar .
4 large handfuls blackcurrant leaves, washed and drained
2–3 drops green food colouring
1 small egg white
4 small bunches blackcurrants, washed (for decoration)

Set the refrigerator at its lowest setting (*if necessary—see page 9*) and chill an ice tray.

Put the water, lemon rind, lemon juice and sugar in a saucepan over low heat and stir constantly until the sugar has dissolved. Bring to the boil, still stirring, then lower the heat and simmer for 5 minutes.

Remove the pan from the heat. Reserve a few black-currant leaves for decoration and stir the remainder into the syrup. Cover and leave for 30 minutes to infuse.

Strain the syrup and squeeze the leaves to extract all the liquid. Stir in the green colouring and chill for an hour or so.

Pour the mixture into the tray, cover and freeze for 30 minutes, or until mushy.

Whisk the egg white until it forms soft peaks. Turn the ice into a bowl and stir vigorously. Beat it into the egg white, 15 ml (1 tablespoon) at a time.

Return the ice to the tray, cover and re-freeze for 1½ hours, or until firm.

Turn the ice into a bowl and beat again. Return it to the tray, cover and re-freeze for 1½ hours, or until firm.

Remove the ice from the freezer 30 minutes before serving. Divide it between 4 glasses and top each with the reserved leaves and a bunch of blackcurrants.

*This is an unusual ice with a fresh, delicate taste, ideal for a summer evening. Add sufficient colouring to make it an attractive pale shade of green. Select young fresh leaves, free from any blemish or hint of disease. Use them as quickly as possible after picking to maintain their freshness. Wash them very thoroughly.

Minted Lemon Ice

Serves 8
175 g (6 oz) caster sugar
350 ml (12 fl oz) water
grated rind of 3 lemons
125 ml (4 fl oz) lemon juice, strained
60 ml (4 tablespoons) finely chopped fresh mint
150 ml (5 fl oz) double cream
45 ml (3 tablespoons) single cream

Set the refrigerator at its lowest setting (*if necessary—see page 9*) and chill an ice-cream container.

Put the sugar and water in a saucepan over low heat, stirring constantly, until the sugar has dissolved. Bring to the boil, then remove the pan from the heat and stir in the lemon rind, lemon juice and chopped mint. Set aside to cool.

Pour the mixture into the ice-cream container, cover with foil and freeze for 1 hour, or until just firm.

Whip the creams together until they form stiff peaks. Turn the ice into a bowl and break it up with a fork until it is mushy and smooth. Fold the ice into the cream.

Return the ice to the container, cover and re-freeze until firm.

Peach Brandy Water Ice

(Illustrated on page 8)
Serves 4
850 ml (1½ pints) water
thinly pared rind and juice of 1 lemon
350 g (12 oz) caster sugar
150 ml (5 fl oz) peach brandy
1 small egg white

Set the refrigerator at its lowest setting (*if necessary—see page 9*) and chill an ice tray.

Put the water, lemon rind and sugar in a saucepan over low heat, stirring constantly, until the sugar has dissolved. Bring to the boil, then lower the heat and simmer for 5 minutes.

Remove the pan from the heat and stir in the lemon juice. Set aside to cool and then chill.

Strain the syrup into the ice tray and stir in the brandy. Cover and freeze for 30 minutes, or until mushy.

Whisk the egg white until it forms soft peaks. Turn the ice into a bowl and stir vigorously. Beat the ice into the egg white, 15 ml (1 tablespoon) at a time.

Return the ice to the tray, cover and re-freeze for 1½ hours, or until firm.

Turn the ice into a bowl and beat again. Return it to the tray, cover and re-freeze for 2 hours, or until firm.

Champagne Ice

Serves 4
150 g (5 oz) sugar
125 ml (4 fl oz) water
juice of 2 oranges
finely grated rind of 2 lemons
juice of 3 lemons
575 ml (1 pint) champagne
575 ml (1 pint) double cream
30 ml (2 tablespoons) brandy

Set the refrigerator at its lowest setting (*if necessary—see page* 9) and chill an ice-cream container.

Put the sugar and water in a pan over low heat, stirring constantly, until the sugar has dissolved. Bring to the boil, then remove from the heat and set aside to cool.

Stir in the orange juice, lemon rind and juice and champagne. Pour the mixture into the chilled container, cover with foil and freeze for 1 hour, or until mushy.

Whip the cream until it stands in soft peaks. Turn the ice into a bowl and stir vigorously. Fold in the cream and add the brandy.

Return the mixture to the container, cover and re-freeze for 2−3 hours, or until firm.

Lemon Sorbet

(*Illustrated on page 8*)
Serves 4
5 lemons
225 g (8 oz) caster sugar
1 egg white

Set the refrigerator at its lowest setting (*if necessary—see page* 9) and chill an ice-cream container.

Grate the rind of 1 lemon. Squeeze the juice from all of them and measure it, making it up to 425 ml (15 fl oz) with water.

Put the grated rind, lemon juice and sugar in a saucepan and stir over a gentle heat until the sugar has dissolved. Bring to the boil and boil for 5 minutes. Remove from the heat and leave to cool completely. Pour into the container and freeze for 1 hour.

Turn out the mixture and whisk it with a wire whisk. Whisk the egg white until it forms soft peaks and fold the lemon mixture into it. Pour back into the container and freeze for another hour or so.

Turn out the sorbet and beat thoroughly once more. Freeze until firm.

Pear Sorbet

(*Illustrated on page 8*)
Serves 4
900 g (2 lb) firm pears, peeled and cored
50 g (2 oz) caster sugar
275 ml (½ pint) water
45 ml (3 tablespoons) Poire William liqueur
1 large egg white

Set the refrigerator at its lowest setting (*if necessary—see page* 9) and chill an ice-cream container.

Put the sugar and water in a heavy-bottomed pan and stir over a gentle heat until the sugar has dissolved.

Add the prepared pears to the syrup (prepare them and drop them straight into the syrup to prevent discoloration). Simmer for 15−20 minutes until the pears are tender. Leave to cool in the syrup.

Put the cold pears and syrup in an electric blender with the liqueur and blend to a smooth purée. Rub through a sieve and measure, making up to 1 litre (1¾ pints) with water if necessary. Leave to cool.

Pour the pear purée into the container and freeze for 1 hour. Turn out and beat well with a wire whisk.

Whisk the egg white until it forms soft peaks. Tip the purée into it, return to the container and freeze again.

When the mixture is slushy, turn it out once more and beat thoroughly. Return to the container and freeze until firm.

Coupe Jacques

Serves 6
575 ml (1 pint) assorted fresh fruit*, cut into small pieces
30 ml (2 tablespoons) caster sugar
10 ml (2 teaspoons) lemon juice
125 ml (4 fl oz) Kirsch
575 ml (1 pint) lemon sorbet (*see left*)
575 ml (1 pint) raspberry sorbet (*see page 19*)
50 g (2 oz) blanched almonds, halved

Combine the fruit, sugar, lemon juice and 90 ml (6 tablespoons) of the Kirsch. Stir, cover and chill in the refrigerator for 1 hour.

Put about 15 ml (1 tablespoon) each of lemon and raspberry sorbet in 6 individual serving dishes, leaving a space in between. Pile 15 ml (1 tablespoon) of the fruit mixture in each of the spaces and top with remaining fruit.

Sprinkle over the remaining kirsch and decorate with almonds. Serve immediately.

*Make a choice from whatever fruit is in season.

Apple and Ginger Sorbet

Serves 4–6
275 ml (½ pint) water
thinly pared rind and juice of 3 lemons
225 g (8 oz) caster sugar
2 large ripe dessert apples
40 g (1½ oz) stem ginger, finely chopped
2 large egg whites

Set the refrigerator at its lowest setting (*if necessary—see page 9*) and chill an ice tray.

Put the water, lemon rind and sugar in a saucepan over moderate heat. Bring to the boil, stirring constantly. Reduce the heat to low and simmer for 5 minutes. Remove the pan from the heat and set aside to cool.

Strain the mixture into a jug and add 75 ml (5 table-

Apple and Ginger Sorbet

spoons) of the lemon juice. Chill in the refrigerator.

Meanwhile, peel, quarter and core the apples. Blend them in an electric blender with 15 ml (1 tablespoon) of the remaining lemon juice. Or, pass them through a food mill and add 15 ml (1 tablespoon) lemon juice.

Stir the purée into the chilled syrup and fold in the chopped ginger. Pour the mixture into the tray, cover and freeze for 1½ hours, or until mushy.

Whisk the egg whites until they form soft peaks. Turn the ice into a bowl and beat vigorously. Beat the mixture into the egg whites, a little at a time.

Return the mixture to the tray, cover and re-freeze for 2 hours, or until firm.

Turn the mixture into a bowl and beat again. Return to the tray, cover and freeze until firm.

Orange Sorbet

Serves 4
275 ml (½ pint) water
175 g (6 oz) sugar
finely grated rind and juice of 2 oranges
275 ml (½ pint) fresh orange juice
2 egg whites

Set the refrigerator at its lowest setting (*if necessary—see page 9*) and chill an ice tray.

Put the water and sugar in a saucepan over low heat, stirring constantly, until the sugar has dissolved. Bring to the boil, then remove the pan from the heat and set aside to cool.

Stir the orange rind and juice into the syrup. Pour into the ice tray, cover and freeze for 1 hour, or until mushy.

Turn the mixture into a bowl and beat. Return it to the tray, cover and re-freeze for 1 hour.

Whisk the egg whites until they form soft peaks. Turn the ice into a bowl and beat. Beat the ice into the egg whites, a little at a time. Return the sorbet to the tray, cover and re-freeze for 2–3 hours, or until firm.

Raspberry Sorbet

Serves 4
575 ml (1 pint) water
225 g (8 oz) caster sugar
450 g (1 lb) raspberries, washed
30 ml (2 tablespoons) lemon juice
2 egg whites

Set the refrigerator at its lowest setting (*if necessary—see page 9*) and chill an ice tray.

Put the water and sugar in a saucepan over low heat, stirring constantly, until the sugar has dissolved. Bring to the boil, then lower the heat and simmer for 5 minutes.

Remove the pan from the heat and set aside to cool. Strain and chill in the refrigerator for an hour or so.

Rub the raspberries through a sieve to form a smooth purée. Stir in the lemon juice. Mix together the purée and the syrup. Pour into the ice tray, cover and freeze for 1 hour, or until mushy.

Whisk the egg whites until they form soft peaks. Turn the ice into a bowl and stir vigorously. Beat the ice into the egg white, 15 ml (1 tablespoon) at a time.

Return it to the tray, cover and re-freeze for 1½–2 hours, or until firm.

Turn the ice into a bowl and beat again. Return it to the tray, cover and re-freeze for 1 hour, or until firm.

Tea Granita

Serves 4
1.1 litre (2 pints) water
75 g (3 oz) caster sugar
50 g (2 oz) tea leaves (flavour of your choice)
75 ml (3 fl oz) double cream, stiffly whipped

Set the refrigerator at its lowest setting (*if necessary—see page 9*) and chill an ice-cream container.

Put the water and sugar in a saucepan over low heat, stirring constantly, until the sugar has dissolved. Bring to the boil and boil for 3 minutes. Remove the pan from the heat, stir in the tea leaves and set aside for 15 minutes to infuse. Strain the mixture and let it cool completely.

Pour the mixture into a container, cover and freeze for 1 hour, or until mushy.

Turn the ice into a bowl and beat. Return it to the container, cover and re-freeze for 30 minutes.

Turn the ice into a bowl and beat again. Re-freeze for 30 minutes and then beat again, until a granular slush is formed.

Turn into tall glasses and top with a whirl of cream.

Coffee Granita

Serves 6
200 g (7 oz) sugar
1 litre (1¾ pints) fresh, strong, hot black coffee
150 ml (5 fl oz) double cream,
stiffly whipped
20 ml (4 teaspoons) powdered drinking chocolate

Set the refrigerator at its lowest setting (*if necessary—see page 9*) and chill an ice-cream container.

Stir the sugar into the coffee and set aside to cool. Pour into the ice-cream container, cover and freeze for 1 hour, until it becomes mushy.

Turn the ice into a bowl and beat. Return it to the container, cover and re-freeze for 30 minutes.

Turn the ice into a bowl and beat again. Re-freeze for 30 minutes and then beat again, until a granular slush is formed.

Turn into tall glasses. Top with a little whipped cream and sprinkle the powdered chocolate on top.

Basic Bombe Mixture

Makes 150 ml (5 fl oz)
150 ml (5 fl oz) water
40 g (1½ oz) caster sugar
2 large egg yolks

Fill a large mixing bowl with water and ice cubes and set aside.

Put the water and sugar in a saucepan over low heat and stir constantly, until the sugar has dissolved. Increase the heat to high and bring the mixture to the boil. Simmer for 5 minutes, or until the temperature registers 102°C (217°F) on a sugar thermometer.

Remove the pan from the heat and set in the bowl of water and ice cubes to cool.

Meanwhile, put the egg yolks in the top of a double boiler. Set over the bottom on a low heat and whisk until the yolks are thick, light and creamy.

Whisk in the cooled syrup, 15 ml (1 tablespoon) at a time. Continue whisking over low heat for about 15 minutes, or until the mixture has doubled in bulk.

Remove the top of the boiler from the heat and plunge it into the bowl of water and ice cubes. Continue whisking until the mixture is cold and thick.

The basic bombe mixture is now ready for the addition of flavourings, whipped cream or egg white.

Apricot Bombe

Serves 6
½ quantity apricot ice-cream (*see page 13*)
25 g (1 oz) crystallized apricots, rinsed, patted dry and chopped
25 g (1 oz) slivered almonds
15 ml (1 tablespoon) apricot brandy
150 ml (5 fl oz) basic bombe mixture (*see page 20*)
1 egg white

Beat the ice-cream until it is softened and workable. Line a 575-ml (1-pint) chilled bombe mould with it (*see page 11*). Cover and freeze for 1 hour, or until frozen hard.

Mix together the apricots, almonds and brandy. Stir these into the bombe mixture. Whisk the egg white until it forms stiff peaks and fold into the bombe mixture.

Spoon the bombe mixture into the cavity and smooth the top. Cover and freeze for 1½–2 hours, or until firm.

Turn out the bombe (*see page 11*) 15 minutes before serving and smooth the surface with a palette knife. Decorate with extra crystallized apricots, if you like.

Black Bombe

Serves 8
½ quantity blackcurrant ice-cream (*see page 13*)
150 ml (5 fl oz) basic bombe mixture (*see page 20*)
30 ml (2 tablespoons) blackberries, washed and chopped
5 ml (1 teaspoon) orange juice
5 ml (1 teaspoon) lemon juice
5 ml (1 teaspoon) grated orange rind
30 ml (2 tablespoons) double cream, lightly whipped
DECORATION:
450 g (1 lb) blackberries, washed

Beat the ice-cream until it is softened and workable. Line a 1.2-L (2-pint) chilled bombe mould with it (*see page 11*). Cover and freeze for 1 hour, or until frozen hard.

Put the bombe mixture and the blackberries into a bowl. Add the orange and lemon juice and the orange rind. Stir to combine everything thoroughly.

Lightly whip the cream and fold it into the blackberry bombe mixture.

Spoon this bombe mixture into the cavity and smooth the top. Cover and freeze for 1½–2 hours, or until firm.

Turn the bombe out 15 minutes (*see page 11*) before serving and smooth the sides with a palette knife. Arrange a border of blackberries around it to decorate.

Mocha Bombe

Serves 6
½ quantity chocolate ice-cream (*see page 23*)
30 ml (2 tablespoons) double cream
150 ml (5 fl oz) basic bombe mixture (*see page 20*)
15 ml (1 tablespoon) coffee essence
30 ml (2 tablespoons) rum or
coffee liqueur

Beat the ice-cream until it is softened and workable, then line a 575-ml (1-pint) chilled bombe mould with it (*see page 11*). Cover and freeze for 1 hour, or until frozen hard.

Lightly whip the cream. Fold it into the bombe mixture and stir in the coffee essence.

Spoon the bombe mixture into the cavity and smooth the top. Cover and freeze for 1½–2 hours, or until firm.

Turn out the bombe (*see page 11*) 15 minutes before serving and smooth the sides with a palette knife. Just before serving, trickle over the rum or coffee liqueur.

Black Bombe

Raspberry Bombe

Serves 6
450 g (1 lb) raspberries
225 ml (8 fl oz) double cream
2.5 ml (½ teaspoon) lemon juice
10 ml (2 teaspoons) framboise or kirsch
25 g (1 oz) caster sugar
150 ml (5 fl oz) basic bombe mixture (*see page 20*)
30 ml (2 tablespoons) double cream, lightly whipped
10 ml (2 teaspoons) Grand Marnier
25 g (1 oz) slivered almonds
grated rind of 1 orange
1 large egg white
DECORATION:
225 g (8 oz) raspberries

Make the raspberry ice-cream in advance, as it needs to be frozen for this recipe.

Set the refrigerator to its lowest setting (*if necessary —see page 9*) and chill an ice-cream container.

Push the raspberries through a sieve into a small saucepan. Simmer over a very gentle heat to reduce the purée to 225 ml (8 fl oz). Leave to cool.

Whip the 225 ml (8 fl oz) cream until it forms soft peaks. Gently fold in the lemon juice, framboise or kirsch, caster sugar and cooled purée. Spoon this into the container, cover and freeze for about 1 hour.

Turn into a bowl and beat thoroughly. Return the ice-cream to the container and re-freeze until almost firm.

Turn out the ice-cream and use to line a 575-ml (1-pint) bombe mould (*see page 11*) Freeze for about 1 hour, until hard.

Meanwhile, prepare the bombe mixture. Stir into it the lightly whipped cream, Grand Marnier, slivered almonds and the grated orange rind.

Whisk the egg white until soft peaks form, then fold this into the bombe mixture.

Spoon the mixture into the cavity in the raspberry ice-cream. Cover and freeze until firm.

Turn out the bombe (*see page 11*) 15 minutes before serving and smooth the surface with a palette knife. Arrange the raspberries round the bottom. If you want to give these a slightly frosty look, pop them in the freezer for about 15 minutes.

Coffee Ice-cream Gâteau and Raspberry Bombe

Cassata Napoletana

Serves 6
200 ml (7 fl oz) strawberry ice-cream (*see page 15*)
200 ml (7 fl oz) blackcurrant leaf water ice (*see page 16*)
CASSATA MIX:
75 ml (3 fl oz) double cream
2.5 ml (½ teaspoon) icing sugar
25 g (1 oz) angelica, rinsed in warm water, patted dry and chopped
25 g (1 oz) glacé cherries, rinsed in warm water, patted dry and chopped
40 g (1½ oz) pistachio nuts

Beat the ice-cream until it is softened and workable and line a 575-ml (1-pint) chilled bombe mould with it (*see page 11*). Cover and freeze for 1 hour, or until frozen hard.

Beat the water ice until softened. Spoon it into the mould to make a second layer still leaving a central cavity. Cover and freeze for 45 minutes.

Whip the cream until it will just hold its shape. Fold in the icing sugar, angelica, cherries and nuts. Spoon the mixture into the cavity in the mould. Cover and freeze for 1–2 hours, or until firm.

Turn the cassata out 15 minutes before serving and smooth the surface with a palette knife.

Chocolate and Coffee Ice-cream Gâteau

Serves 12
575 ml (1 pint) single cream
2 eggs
4 extra egg yolks
175 g (6 oz) caster sugar
100 g (4 oz) plain, dark chocolate, broken into pieces
150 ml (5 fl oz) boiling water
40 g (1½ oz) ground coffee
50 g (2 oz) icing sugar
575 ml (1 pint) double cream
30 ml (2 tablespoons) orange-flavoured liqueur
30 ml (2 tablespoons) coffee-flavoured liqueur
DECORATION:
150 ml (5 fl oz) double cream, stiffly whipped
50 g (2 oz) shelled hazelnuts

Set the refrigerator at its lowest setting (*if necessary— see page 9*) and chill two ice-cream containers.

Put the single cream in a saucepan over low heat and bring to just below boiling point. Remove the pan from the heat and set aside.

Beat together the eggs, egg yolks and caster sugar in the top of a double boiler. Pour the hot cream on to the mixture in a thin trickle, stirring constantly. Set the top of the boiler over the bottom and put on a low heat. Cook, stirring constantly, for 15 minutes, or until the custard is thick enough to coat the back of the spoon. Remove from the heat and strain. Divide the custard equally between two mixing bowls and set aside.

Melt the chocolate in a heatproof bowl over a pan of hot water. Stir it into one bowl of custard and set aside to cool.

Pour the boiling water on to the ground coffee and set aside for 15 minutes to infuse. Strain, stir in the icing sugar and set aside to cool. When this coffee mixture is cold, stir it into the second bowl of custard.

Pour each flavoured custard into one of the ice-cream containers. Cover and freeze for 45 minutes, or until mushy.

Divide the double cream in half. Whip each half until it forms soft peaks.

Turn the chocolate-flavoured ice into a bowl and stir vigorously. Beat in half the cream and the orange-flavoured liqueur. Return it to the container, cover and re-freeze for 45 minutes.

Turn out the coffee-flavoured ice and stir vigorously. Beat in the remaining cream and the coffee-flavoured liqueur. Return it to the container, cover and re-freeze for 45 minutes.

Turn the chocolate-flavoured ice-cream into a bowl and beat again. Spoon it into a loose-bottomed cake tin, 18 cm (7 in) in diameter and 7.5 cm (3 in) deep. Smooth the top and put in the freezer.

Turn the coffee-flavoured ice-cream into a bowl and beat again. Spoon this on top of the chocolate ice-cream and level the top. Cover and freeze until firm.

Remove the cake from the freezer 20 minutes before serving. Turn it out on to a serving plate and pipe rosettes of cream around the top. Decorate with the nuts.

*To make the cake shown in the picture opposite, freeze the coffee-flavoured ice-cream only in a cake tin, and the chocolate ice-cream in an ordinary container. Take the chocolate ice-cream out of the freezer about 45 minutes before you want to serve the gâteau. When it has softened slightly, spoon it into a bowl, and soften it still more by beating it with a wooden spoon. Put it into a piping bag with a star nozzle. Turn out the coffee ice-cream on to a plate, and pipe swirls of chocolate ice-cream round the edge. Fill the centre with small meringues (see chapter 3).

Café Liegeoise

Serves 6
275 ml (½ pint) single cream
1 large egg
2 large extra egg yolks
75 g (3 oz) caster sugar
150 ml (5 fl oz) boiling water
40 g (1½ oz) finely ground coffee
50 g (2 oz) icing sugar
275 ml (½ pint) double cream
SYRUP:
100 g (4 oz) caster sugar
275 ml (½ pint) cold water
15 ml (1 tablespoon) instant coffee
60 ml (4 tablespoons) boiling water
DECORATION:
150 ml (5 fl oz) double cream, stiffly whipped
grated rind of 1 large orange*

Set the refrigerator at its lowest setting (*if necessary—see page 9*) and chill an ice-cream container.

Put the single cream in a saucepan over low heat and bring to just below boiling point. Remove the pan from the heat and set aside.

Beat together the egg, egg yolks and caster sugar in the top of a double boiler. Pour the hot cream on to the mixture in a thin trickle, stirring constantly. Set the top of the boiler over the bottom and put on a low heat. Cook, stirring constantly, for 15 minutes, or until the custard is thick enough to coat the back of the spoon. Remove from the heat, strain and set aside.

Pour the boiling water on to the ground coffee and set aside for 15 minutes to infuse.

Strain the coffee and stir in the icing sugar. Stir the coffee mixture into the custard and chill in the refrigerator for an hour or so.

Pour the mixture into the container, cover and freeze for 45 minutes, or until mushy.

Whip the double cream until it will just hold its shape. Turn the ice-cream into a bowl and beat vigorously. Fold in the whipped cream.

Return the ice-cream to the container, cover and re-freeze for 45 minutes.

Turn the ice-cream into a bowl and beat again. Return it to the container, cover and re-freeze until firm.

To prepare the syrup, put the sugar and water in a pan over low heat, stirring constantly, until the sugar has dissolved. Bring the mixture to the boil, then cover and simmer for 15 minutes. Remove from the heat.

Dissolve the instant coffee in the boiling water. Stir into the syrup and set aside to cool.

Remove the ice-cream from the freezer 20 minutes before serving to let it soften slightly.

Put 2 scoops of ice-cream into 6 serving dishes and pour a little syrup over each. Top with a whirl of cream and sprinkle over the orange rind. Serve immediately with sponge fingers if you like.

*Use a special citrus fruit zester to remove the orange rind to give long pieces for decoration.

Fudge Ripple Moulds

Serves 6
225 g (8 oz) plain cooking chocolate, broken into small pieces
6 disposable, plastic yoghurt or mousse cartons
50 g (2 oz) vanilla fudge
15 ml (1 tablespoon) double cream
425 ml (15 fl oz) rich vanilla ice-cream (*see page 10*)
extra melted chocolate (*see recipe below*)

Melt the chocolate in a heatproof bowl set over a pan of hot water over low heat. Spoon about 60 ml (4 table-spoons) of the melted chocolate into one of the cartons. Swirl it about so that the base and sides are evenly coated. Tip any surplus back into the bowl. Coat the remaining moulds in the same way. Cover and freeze for 10 minutes. Reserve any remaining chocolate.

Put the fudge and cream in a saucepan over low heat until the fudge has melted. Remove the pan from the heat.

Beat the ice-cream to soften it slightly. Stir in the fudge mixture to give a ripple effect.

Divide the ice-cream between the individual moulds. Level the tops and cover with foil. Freeze for 45 minutes, or until firm.

Uncover the moulds and slice the cartons and ice-cream in half with a sharp knife. Remove the carton halves. Smooth the ice-cream halves together with a palette knife and add a little extra melted chocolate over the join to 'weld' the moulds back together. Refrigerate for 10 minutes before serving so this chocolate sets hard.

Café Liegeoise

Mousses, Creams & Jellies

Mousses and moulds, simple creams and jellies have a universal appeal for adults and children alike. They can be as simple or as sophisticated as you like. For the artistic, they offer a wonderful opportunity to show off skills by creating spectacular and colourful centrepieces. Even the less creative can produce pretty and appetizing displays simply by making full use of the many differently shaped moulds available, and practising a few techniques with piping whipped cream.

Creams, mousses and moulds, and jellies are 'all-occasion' puddings. At their simplest, they are quick and easy enough to make for every day, while in their more extravagant forms, they are quite stunning as a party pudding. Always impressive in appearance and perennially popular, they really come into their own when you want to get ahead with mealtime preparations, as they can be made well in advance. Indeed, many people feel that the flavour of most mousses will improve if left to develop overnight in the refrigerator.

Fruit Creams and Fools

Together with the various creams, we have included fools, an old-fashioned tansy, and blancmange, as well as a classic zabaglione and a creamier version of this delicious dessert. The basic method for making a cream or fool is simply to combine puréed or crushed, and generally sweetened, fruit with cream or a homemade egg custard. More modern day alternatives to these last ingredients are yoghurt—either plain, or flavoured to complement the fruit of the purée—or, for the less figure-conscious, evaporated milk or cream cheese. Nearly every kind of fruit lends itself to these puddings, and the taste is rich, yet fresh.

Mousses and Moulds

The preparation of mousses takes a little more time and effort, and the ingredients—a luscious combination of eggs, cream, chocolate, liqueurs or fruit —do cost rather more. However, the finished puddings look so mouth-wateringly splendid and taste so utterly delicious, that they are well worth a little more trouble and expense, particularly for special occasions. We have included a few 'cheating' mousses in this chapter; they leave out the egg mixture, so expect the finished dish to have a rather less rich texture.

Similar to mousses in preparation are Charlottes and Bavarian Creams or Bavarois, both recognized as being among the most glorious of desserts. Both generally have an egg yolk and sugar mousse-type base (although simpler 'cheating' versions can again be made) and thereafter may be flavoured with a variety of fruit,

liqueurs, vanilla, coffee or chocolate or perhaps chopped glacé fruits. Charlottes are generally made in a round mould, the sides of which are lined with sponge fingers. These then form a circle round the mousse-like mixture when it is unmoulded. Piped cream rosettes, decorations appropriate to the fillings, such as sugar violets or chocolate caraque, and perhaps a coloured ribbon tied round the sponge fingers turn the pudding into a real party delight.

Bavarois are more usually made in a shaped mould so they look spectacular when unmoulded. Flavourings are similar to those used for Charlottes, but the sponge fingers are omitted. For a special occasion, try dividing the basic custard mixture into three and flavouring each one with complementary flavours, such as vanilla, coffee and chocolate, or vanilla and two delicate tasting fruits. Layer these in the mould, letting each one set before adding a different flavour. The finished pudding should be chilled for at least 12 hours if it is to be turned out of the mould. If you decide to make and serve a Bavarois mixture in individual dessert glasses, it will need about 4 hours' chilling time.

Moulds, as their name suggests, are made in a shaped container and turned out just before serving. They can be made by adding flavouring—fruit or various others such as coffee or vanilla —to an ordinary egg custard base, before adding dissolved gelatine and cream. A simpler version can be made by combining fruit purée and whipped cream with the dissolved gelatine. In the Chestnut and Chocolate Mould on page 32, the softened butter and melted chocolate will provide a setting agent, thus eliminating the need for any gelatine in the mixture.

Jellies

Jellies have always been particular favourites with children, many of whom carry the liking with them into adulthood! Unfortunately the introduction of rubbery commercial jellies has caused these puddings as a whole to lose favour with the more discerning palates of some adults. Now you can revive this neglected culinary art to win applause from children and grown-ups alike as they discover the superb taste

and texture of 'real' homemade jellies.

Technique

The step-by-step instructions on the next page comprise the basic stages in making a custard-based fruit mould. For a mousse, the procedure differs, in that generally the base is made just from egg yolks and sugar whisked until thick, pale and creamy. Flavourings and dissolved gelatine are added to this, and whipped cream and whisked egg whites folded into the mixture when it is on the point of setting.

Step 4 gives instructions for dissolving gelatine, and this is the correct procedure for whenever you are using this setting agent. Always sprinkle the gelatine powder over the liquid, not the other way around. It is important to leave it for 5 minutes, before dissolving it, as the grains will swell and soften in this time. Never overheat it or it will not set properly and make sure it is evenly distributed throughout the base mixture.

Step-by-step instructions on page 29 are for making a jelly. Chill a serving plate while the jelly is setting, and then just before unmoulding, rinse the plate under cold water. Centre this on top of the mould and unmould it following the instruction in step 6. You can centre the jelly on the plate by tipping it gently; it will slide easily on the wet surface. Mop up any excess liquid with kitchen paper.

If you are using a shaped mould to make any of these puddings, make sure it is scrupulously clean and free from any chips, cracks or other imperfections. Always use the size recommended in the recipe; if it is too large, the shape may be disproportionate, and the pudding may well collapse as you turn it out. For jellies, chill the mould for 30 minutes, then rinse it out with cold water just before pouring in the jelly (it is easiest to do this using a jug, resting the lip on the edge of the mould). For a mousse, lightly brush the inside of the mould with flavourless vegetable oil to facilitate unmoulding. Cover a mousse with cling film or foil while it is setting in the refrigerator, but remove it and turn it out 30 minutes before serving. This allows the flavour to develop and takes off the chill.

Making a Custard-based Fruit Mould

225 g (8 oz) fruit (*see step 1*)
3 egg yolks
50 g (2 oz) sugar (*more if the fruit is very tart*)
275 ml (½ pint) milk
15 g (½ oz) gelatine
150 ml (5 fl oz) double cream

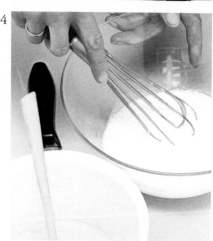

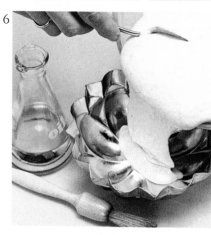

1 *Wash and hull soft fruit (raspberries, strawberries etc), and rub through a fairly fine wire sieve to make a smooth purée. If using plums, gooseberries, blackcurrants etc, stew first with a little sugar and water. Rub through a sieve and cool.*

2 *Fill a large container, with ice cubes and leave in a cool place. Prepare a double boiler, making sure that the water in the bottom does not touch the top. Put the egg yolks and sugar in the top and whisk, off the heat, until the mixture is light, thick and creamy.*

3 *Put the milk in a pan and bring almost to boiling point. Pour on to the egg mixture, stirring. Set over the bottom pan and cook, stirring, on a low heat for 15 minutes, or until the custard will coat the back of the spoon. Take off the heat, strain and place on the ice to cool.*

4 *Put 45 ml (3 tablespoons) cold water in a small saucepan and sprinkle over 15 g (½ oz) gelatine. Set aside for 5 minutes, then put over low heat for 3 minutes to dissolve completely. Remove from the heat and cool. Lightly whip the cream.*

5 *Pour the gelatine mixture into the cold custard in a thin stream, stirring constantly. Fold in the fruit purée. Put the mixture in the refrigerator for 20 minutes or so, stirring it frequently*

6 *When the mixture is on the point of setting, fold in the lightly whipped cream using a figure-of-eight movement. Lightly brush an 850-ml (1½-pint) mould with oil and pour in the mixture. Cover and leave for 1½–2 hours to set. Turn out on to a plate 30 minutes before serving.*

Making a Fruit Jelly

about 450 g (1 lb) fruit of your choice, such as apples,
strawberries, raspberries, gooseberries, blackberries etc.
15 g (½ oz) gelatine
about 75 g (3 oz) cube sugar (*adjust according to tartness of fruit*)
flavourings, such as pinch of cinnamon, dried ginger, vanilla essence etc.
2–3 drops food colouring (optional)

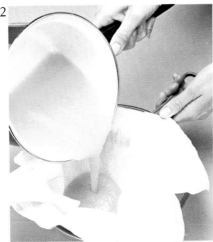

1 *Prepare the main flavouring, by squeezing the fruit to extract the juice, or chopping or puréeing it. Put this in a saucepan with sufficient water to make the quantity up to 575 ml (1 pint). Add the sugar and any other flavourings. Heat, stirring to dissolve the sugar.*

2 *Remove the pan from the heat, cover and set aside for 20 minutes to infuse. Prepare a jelly bag or line a sieve with a double thickness of muslin. Strain the liquid through it into a bowl. Add 2–3 drops of colouring for a deeper colour.*

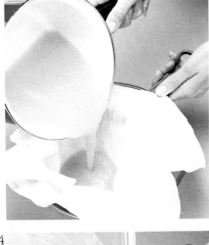

3 *Put 60 ml (4 tablespoons) of the cooled liquid in a small saucepan and sprinkle over 15 g (½ oz) gelatine. Set aside for 5 minutes, then put over low heat for 3 minutes to dissolve completely. Carefully pour the dissolved gelatine into the strained fruit syrup, stirring constantly.*

4 *To safeguard against any threads of gelatine which may have formed and to clarify the jelly further, pour it through a jelly bag or a sieve lined with a double layer of muslin into a clean jug. Leave until almost set. Pour the jelly into a chilled, rinsed mould.*

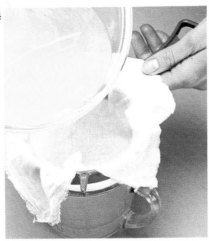

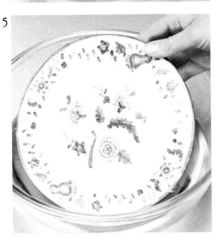

5 *Cover the mould and set aside in a cool place or in the refrigerator until the jelly has set. Before serving, put a plate in the refrigerator to chill thoroughly. Just before turning the jelly out of the mould, rinse the plate in cold water and shake off any excess.*

6 *Fill a sink or bowl with hot water. Hold the mould up to the rim in the water for a few seconds. Cover with the prepared plate, centring it, and invert. Holding the plate and mould firmly together, give a sharp shake. The jelly should slide out easily.*

Raspberry Cream

Serves 6
450 g (1 lb) raspberries, washed
60 ml (4 tablespoons) caster sugar
275 ml (½ pint) double cream, thickly whipped
DECORATION:
24 raspberries

Rub the raspberries through a sieve to form a smooth purée. Stir in sugar to taste. Carefully fold in the cream using a metal spoon.

Turn the raspberry cream into 6 individual serving bowls and chill in the refrigerator for 1 hour. Just before serving, decorate with the whole raspberries, frosted if you like, by placing in the freezer for 1 hour.

Blackcurrant Cream

Serves 6
450 g (1 lb) blackcurrants, washed
75 ml (5 tablespoons) caster sugar
150 ml (5 fl oz) double cream
150 ml (5 fl oz) soured cream

Stew the blackcurrants with a little water until soft. Rub them through a sieve to form a smooth purée and stir in sugar to taste.

Whisk together the double and soured cream until they form soft peaks. Fold the cream into the fruit purée, using a metal spoon.

Turn the blackcurrant cream into 6 individual serving dishes and chill in the refrigerator for 1 hour.

Loganberry Cream Surprise

Serves 4
225 g (8 oz) loganberries, washed
30 ml (2 tablespoons) caster sugar
225 g (8 oz) cream cheese
50 g (2 oz) candied peel, chopped

Rub the loganberries through a sieve to make a smooth purée. Stir in sugar to taste. Rub the cream cheese through the sieve into the purée. Beat the mixture until smooth and thoroughly blended. Chill in the refrigerator for 1 hour.

Pour the mixture into 4 serving dishes and decorate with the candied peel, dividing it evenly.

Economic Apricot Cream

Serves 6
225 g (8 oz) dried apricots
275 ml (½ pint) evaporated milk
50 g (2 oz) flaked almonds

Put the apricots in a bowl and pour over just enough tepid water to cover. Leave overnight.

At the same time, boil the unopened can of evaporated milk in a saucepan of water for 15 minutes. Set aside to cool and then chill in the refrigerator overnight.

Drain the apricots and rub them through a sieve to make a smooth purée.

Whisk the evaporated milk until it is thick. Fold it into the fruit purée. Turn the mixture into a serving dish and chill in the refrigerator for 1 hour.

Just before serving, sprinkle over the almonds.

Blancmange

Serves 6
5 ml (1 teaspoon) almond oil
450 g (1 lb) almonds, blanched
575 ml (1 pint) plus 10–15 ml (2–3 teaspoons) water
175 g (6 oz) caster sugar
45 ml (3 tablespoons) orange-flavoured liqueur
20 g (¾ oz) gelatine

Lightly brush a decorative mould with the almond oil.

Pound the almonds in a mortar, in batches, moistening with a few drops of water. When the almonds have been reduced to a smooth paste mix with 575 ml (1 pint) of water. Line a strainer with muslin. Turn the mixture into the muslin and twist the cloth to squeeze the juice into a bowl. Continue squeezing until you have 575 ml (1 pint) of juice.

Put the almond juice in a saucepan and add the sugar. Set over low heat and stir until the sugar has dissolved. Remove the pan from the heat and stir in the liqueur.

Put 30 ml (2 tablespoons) of the liquid in a small saucepan and sprinkle over the gelatine. Set aside for 5 minutes to soften. Set over low heat for 3 minutes, without stirring, until the gelatine has dissolved completely. Set aside to cool slightly.

Pour the gelatine into the remaining almond mixture in a thin stream, stirring constantly.

Pour the mixture into the prepared mould and leave in the refrigerator for at least 2½ hours to set. Turn out the blancmange just before serving.

Gooseberry Fool

Apricot Wine Fool

Serves 4
225 g (8 oz) dried apricots
5 ml (1 teaspoon) lemon juice
45 ml (3 tablespoons) icing sugar, sifted
275 ml (½ pint) double cream
150 ml (5 fl oz) sweet white wine
75 g (3 oz) caster sugar
few drops yellow food colouring
8 angelica leaves

Put the apricots in a bowl and pour over just enough tepid water to cover. Leave overnight in a cool place, but not the refrigerator.

Rub the apricots through a sieve to form a smooth purée. Stir in the lemon juice and the icing sugar, mixing together evenly.

Whip the cream until it is thick, but not stiff. Gradually whisk in the wine and the caster sugar.

Fold in the apricot purée and a few drops of food colouring. Pile the mixture into 4 glasses and chill in the refrigerator for 2 hours.

Top each glass with 2 angelica leaves and serve, with extra cream if liked.

Gooseberry Fool

Serves 6
900 g (2 lb) gooseberries, trimmed and washed
275 g (10 oz) sugar
45–60 ml (3–4 tablespoons) water
275 ml (½ pint) double cream

Put the gooseberries, sugar and water in a saucepan over a low heat and cook, shaking the pan occasionally, until the fruit is tender. Rub the berries through a sieve to form a purée and set aside to cool.

Whisk the cream until it just flops from the whisk. Fold it into the purée, but without blending it in completely in order to give a marble appearance.

Turn the mixture into individual glasses or dishes.

Apple Tansy

Serves 6
450 g (1 lb) tart apples, peeled, cored and sliced
100 g (4 oz) sugar
275 ml (½ pint) milk
1 vanilla pod
4 egg yolks
15 ml (1 tablespoon) caster sugar
5 ml (1 teaspoon) cornflour
150 ml (5 fl oz) double cream
30 ml (2 tablespoons) chopped walnuts

Put the apples and sugar in a saucepan over low heat and cook, shaking the pan occasionally, for 10–12 minutes. Crush the fruit with a fork to break it down, if necessary, and set aside to cool.

Put the milk and vanilla pod in a saucepan over medium heat and bring to just below boiling point. Remove from the heat, cover and set aside for 15 minutes to infuse.

Remove the vanilla pod. (You can wash it and use it again.) Beat the egg yolks together, then beat in the caster sugar and the cornflour. Pour the milk over this mixture in a thin stream, stirring constantly. Strain the mixture into the top of a double boiler and set over the bottom on a low heat. Cook, stirring constantly, for 15 minutes, or until the custard is thick and will coat the back of a spoon. Strain, cover and set aside to cool. Stir into the apple.

Whip the cream until it forms soft peaks. Fold this into the apple custard mixture, using a metal spoon. Turn the tansy into 6 individual serving bowls and chill in the refrigerator for 1 hour. Decorate with the chopped walnuts just before serving.

Apple Chartreuse

Serves 4–6
125 ml (4 fl oz) water
350 g (12 oz) sugar
juice of 1 lemon
2.5 ml (½ teaspoon) grated nutmeg
900 g (2 lb) tart apples, peeled, cored and sliced
50 g (2 oz) blanched slivered almonds
30 ml (2 tablespoons) redcurrant jelly
30 ml (2 tablespoons) boiling water
15 ml (1 tablespoon) brandy.

Oil a 575-ml (1-pint) mould and set aside.

Put the water and sugar in a saucepan over a low heat and stir to dissolve. Add the lemon juice, raise the heat a little and bring to the boil. Boil for 5 minutes, stirring occasionally. Add the nutmeg and apple slices to the

syrup and cook, stirring from time to time for 5–10 minutes. The syrup should boil briskly and the apples will pull away from the sides of the pan when they are ready.

Remove the pan from the heat and fold in the almonds. Pour the mixture into the prepared mould and set aside to cool. Then chill in the refrigerator for 1 hour.

Stir the redcurrant jelly and boiling water together to melt the jelly. Add the brandy. Set aside to cool.

Turn the chartreuse out on to a serving dish and spoon over the redcurrant sauce.

Chestnut and Chocolate Mould

Serves 8
225 g (8 oz) plain dessert chocolate, broken into small pieces
175 g (6 oz) unsalted butter, softened
175 g (6 oz) icing sugar, sifted
425 g (15 oz) can unsweetened chestnut purée
grated rind and juice of 1 orange
30 ml (2 tablespoons) orange-flavoured liqueur
275 ml (½ pint) double cream
2 marrons glacés, chopped

Lightly grease a 900-g (2-lb) loaf tin and set aside.

Melt the chocolate in a bowl over a pan of simmering water, stirring occasionally.

Beat the butter until smooth and creamy. Beat in the icing sugar and continue beating until the mixture is light and fluffy. Stir in the melted chocolate. Add the chestnut purée, the orange rind and juice and the liqueur. Beat the mixture until it is smooth.

Pour the mixture into the prepared tin. Cover with oiled greaseproof paper and chill in the refrigerator for 6 hours or overnight.

Run a knife around the edge of the mould and invert it on to a serving plate. Whisk the cream until it forms soft peaks and pipe rosettes around the base and on top of the mould. Decorate the top with the chopped marrons glacés. Cut in thin slices—it is very rich.

Chestnut and Chocolate Mould

Mousseline Creole

Serves 4–6
1 small pineapple
100 g (4 oz) caster sugar
3 large egg yolks
75 ml (5 tablespoons) dark rum
30 ml (2 tablespoons) double cream
25 g (1 oz) Demerara sugar

Fill a large mixing bowl with ice cubes and set aside.

Cut the pineapple into slices. Peel and remove the 'eyes'. Stamp out the core and cut the slices into chunks. Sprinkle half the sugar over them and toss the chunks well to distribute the sugar. Arrange them in the base of serving glasses. Set aside.

Put the egg yolks and remaining sugar in the top of a double boiler and whisk until frothy. Add the rum.

Set the top of the boiler over the bottom over low heat. Cook, whisking constantly, until the sauce will hold its shape.

Remove the top of the boiler from the heat and set in the bowl of ice. Whisk the mixture until it is cold.

Whisk in the cream, 5 ml (1 teaspoon) at a time. Pour the sauce over the pineapple chunks and chill in the refrigerator for 1 hour.

Sprinkle the Demerara sugar on top before serving.

Brown Bread Cream Mould

Serves 6–8
275 ml (½ pint) milk
1 vanilla pod
3 large egg yolks
40 g (1½ oz) caster sugar
5 ml (1 teaspoon) cornflour
4 thick slices brown bread, crusts removed
45 ml (3 tablespoons) water
15 g (½ oz) gelatine
275 ml (½ pint) double cream, lightly whipped
DECORATION:
45 ml (3 tablespoons) double cream, stiffly whipped
chocolate flake, broken into pieces

Oil an 850-ml (1½-pint) mould and set aside. Fill a washing-up bowl with ice cubes and set aside.

Put the milk and vanilla pod in a saucepan over low heat and bring to just below boiling point. Remove the pan from the heat, cover and set aside for 20 minutes.

Put the egg yolks, sugar and cornflour in the top of a double boiler and whisk until light and creamy. Remove and discard the vanilla pod from the milk. Pour the milk into the egg mixture, stirring constantly. Set the top of the boiler over the bottom and put on a low heat. Cook, stirring constantly, until the custard thickens and will coat the back of the spoon. Remove from the heat and place the bowl in the bowl of ice. Make the bread into crumbs and stir into the custard.

Put the water in a small saucepan and dissolve the gelatine in it (*see page 28*). Set aside to cool.

Pour the gelatine into the custard in a thin stream, stirring constantly. Put in a cool place and stir from time to time until the mixture is on the point of setting. Fold the custard into the whipped cream then turn the mixture into the prepared mould. Cover and chill in the refrigerator for at least 1½ hours.

Turn the cream out of the mould 30 minutes before serving. Pipe a border of cream rosettes around the base and decorate with the flaked chocolate.

Orange Mousse

Serves 6–8
4 oranges
5 large eggs
75 g (3 oz) caster sugar
15 g (½ oz) gelatine
150 ml (5 fl oz) double cream, thickly whipped

Oil an 850-ml (1½-pint) mould. Set aside.

Grate the rind of 3 oranges and squeeze the juice from all of them. Put in a small saucepan and sprinkle the gelatine on top. Set aside.

Separate 2 of the eggs. Reserve the whites and put the yolks, the remaining whole eggs and the sugar in the top of a double boiler. Set the top over the bottom and put on a low heat. Whisk the mixture until it is light and creamy and leaves a trail. Remove from the heat and set aside.

Put the gelatine over a very low heat until it has dissolved. Set aside to cool slightly.

Pour the gelatine into the egg mixture in a thin stream, stirring constantly, then stir in the grated orange rind. Fold the mixture into the cream, a little at a time. Leave in a cool place, stirring occasionally, until on the point of setting.

Whisk the egg whites until they form soft peaks and fold them into the mousse mixture. Turn the mixture into the prepared mould, cover and chill in the refrigerator for 1½–2 hours.

Turn out the mousse 30 minutes before serving.

Mousse Chinois (left) and Apple and Apricot Mousse

Apple and Apricot Mousse

Serves 6

225 g (8 oz) dried apricots, soaked overnight
450 g (1 lb) dessert apples
finely grated zest and juice of ½ lemon
15 g (½ oz) gelatine
45 ml (3 tablespoons) water
2 large eggs, separated
75 g (3 oz) sugar (see recipe)
150 ml (5 fl oz) double cream, softly whipped
1–2 drops almond essence

DECORATION:
60 ml (4 tablespoons) double cream, stiffly whipped
almond slivers

Drain the soaked apricots, reserving the liquid. Measure 275 ml (½ pint) of this and put in a medium-sized pan with the apricots.

Peel, core and roughly chop the apples. Add to the pan with the apricots and the lemon zest and juice. Put the pan over a medium heat and bring to the boil. Lower the heat and simmer the fruit gently for about 20 minutes, until the apricots are tender and the apples turning mushy.

Sprinkle the gelatine over the 45 ml (3 tablespoons) water and leave for 5 minutes to soften.

Purée the cooked fruits and their cooking juices in an electric blender or by rubbing through a sieve. Cool, then stir in the beaten egg yolks and sweeten with sugar to taste.

Dissolve the gelatine and stir into the purée. Measure the purée and make it up to 850 ml (1½ pints) with cold water if necessary. Put in a cool place and stir from time to time until on the point of setting.

Fold in the whipped cream. Then whisk the egg whites until they form soft peaks. Pour the apricot mixture on to the egg whites and fold together using a metal spoon. Add the almond essence to taste.

Pour the mousse into a rinsed 1.4-litre (2½-pint) mould and put in the refrigerator to set.

Unmould the mousse on to a serving plate and decorate with piped cream and the almond slivers.

Mousse Chinois

Serves 6
4 large egg yolks
15 ml (1 tablespoon) caster sugar
75 g (3 oz) preserved ginger, chopped
22 ml (1½ tablespoons) ginger syrup
45 ml (3 tablespoons) water
15 g (½ oz) gelatine
150 ml (5 fl oz) double cream, softly whipped
DECORATION:
4 kiwi fruit

Put the egg yolks and sugar in the top of a double boiler. Set over the bottom and put on a low heat. Whisk the mixture until it is light and creamy and will leave a trail. Remove from the heat and stir in the ginger and the syrup. Set aside.

Put the water in a small saucepan, sprinkle over the gelatine and leave for 5 minutes. Dissolve the gelatine over a low heat. Set aside to cool.

Pour the gelatine into the egg yolk mixture in a thin stream, stirring constantly. Fold the mixture into the whipped cream, a little at a time. Leave in a cool place, stirring occasionally, until on the point of setting.

Turn the mousse into 6 individual glass bowls and chill in the refrigerator for 1½ hours.

Remove from the refrigerator 30 minutes before serving and decorate with the kiwi fruit.

English Gooseberry Mousse

Serves 8
450 g (1 lb) tart, green gooseberries, trimmed and washed
275 ml (½ pint) plus 60 ml (4 tablespoons) water
45 ml (3 tablespoons) caster sugar
25 g (1 oz) gelatine
25 g (1 oz) hazelnuts, finely chopped
275 ml (½ pint) double cream, thickly whipped
2–3 drops green food colouring
DECORATION:
50 ml (2 fl oz) double cream, stiffly whipped
angelica

Oil an 850-ml (1½-pint) mould and set aside.

Put the gooseberries, the 250 ml (½ pint) water and the sugar in a saucepan over low heat and simmer for 10–15 minutes, or until tender. Rub the gooseberries through a sieve. Taste the purée and add more sugar if necessary.

Put the 60 ml (4 tablespoons) water in a small saucepan and dissolve the gelatine in it. Set aside to cool.

Fold the gooseberry purée and the hazelnuts into the whipped cream. Pour the gelatine into the mixture in a thin stream, stirring constantly. Stir in the colouring. Leave in a cool place, stirring occasionally, until on the point of setting.

Pour the mousse into the prepared mould. Cover and chill in the refrigerator for at least 1½ hours.

Turn out the mousse 30 minutes before serving. Decorate with the cream and angelica.

Blackcurrant Mousse

Serves 6
450 g (1 lb) blackcurrants, trimmed and washed
125 ml (4 fl oz) water
2 large egg yolks
3 large eggs
75 g (3 oz) sugar
15 g (½ oz) gelatine
150 ml (5 fl oz) double cream, thickly whipped
DECORATION:
150 ml (5 fl oz) double cream, stiffly whipped
citrus peel
15 ml (1 tablespoon) crème de cassis

Put the blackcurrants and water in a saucepan over low heat. Cover and simmer for 10 minutes, or until tender. Drain the blackcurrants and reserve the cooking liquid. Rub the fruit through a sieve to form a smooth purée. Stir the purée and reserved cooking liquid together and set aside.

Put the egg yolks, eggs and sugar in the top of a double boiler. Set the top over the bottom and put on a low heat. Whisk the mixture until it turns pale and creamy. Remove from the heat and set aside.

Put the 45 ml (3 tablespoons) of blackcurrant purée in a small saucepan. Sprinkle the gelatine on it. Let it soak for 5 minutes, then dissolve the gelatine over a low heat. Set aside to cool slightly.

Stir remaining blackcurrant purée into the egg mixture. Pour in the gelatine in a thin stream, stirring constantly. Stir the mixture into the whipped cream, a little at a time. Leave in a cool place, stirring occasionally, until on the point of setting.

Divide the mousse equally between 6 tall glasses. Cover and chill in the refrigerator for 1½ hours.

Remove from the refrigerator 30 minutes before serving. Top each glass with a whirl of cream and decorate with citrus rind. Spoon a little crème de cassis over each serving at the last minute.

Strawberry Jelly Mousse

Serves 4–6
450 g (1 lb) fresh strawberries
10 ml (2 teaspoons) lemon juice
50 g (2 oz) icing sugar
15 g (½ oz) gelatine
45 ml (3 tablespoons) water
150 ml (5 fl oz) double cream, lightly whipped
3 egg whites
DECORATION:
100 g (4 oz) blackberries

Pick out 100 g (4 oz) of the best strawberries and put on one side. Hull the remainder, then rub these through a sieve, or blend in an electric blender, to make a purée. Stir in the lemon juice and the icing sugar.

Sprinkle the gelatine over the 45 ml (3 tablespoons) water and leave for 5 minutes. Dissolve over a low heat (*see page 28*).

Pour the gelatine mixture into the strawberry purée in a thin stream, stirring all the time.

Rinse out a ring mould and spoon in enough of the purée to just cover the bottom. Put in the refrigerator. Leave the remainder in a cool place.

When the bulk of the purée is on the point of setting, fold in the lightly whipped cream.

Whisk the egg whites until stiff and fold these in. Pour the mixture into the ring mould and refrigerate until set.

When ready to serve, unmould the mousse on to a serving plate and fill the centre with the blackberries and reserved strawberries. Serve with extra pouring cream if you like.

Strawberry Jelly Mousse

Valencia Chocolate Mousse

Serves 4
4 eggs, separated
60 ml (4 tablespoons) milk
50 g (2 oz) caster sugar
15 g (½ oz) ground almonds
15 g (½ oz) flour
50 g (2 oz) butter, cut into small pieces
juice and grated rind of 1 orange
2.5 ml (½ teaspoon) gelatine
200 g (7 oz) bitter chocolate, broken into pieces
150 ml (5 fl oz) double cream, thickly whipped
50 g (2 oz) flaked almonds, lightly toasted

Beat together the egg yolks and milk in a bowl over a pan of hot water. Stir in the sugar, ground almonds and flour. Set the pan over very low heat and cook the mixture, stirring constantly, until it thickens. Do not let it boil.

Stir in the butter, one piece at a time. Then stir in the orange juice and rind and sprinkle over the gelatine. Stir in the chocolate, one piece at a time and continue stirring all the time until the chocolate has melted, the mixture is smooth and all the ingredients are thoroughly blended. Remove the bowl from the heat.

Whisk the egg whites until they form stiff peaks, then fold into the chocolate mixture. Turn the mousse into 4 individual dishes and chill in the refrigerator for 3–4 hours. Cover with the whipped cream and toasted almonds before serving.

Honey Mousse

Serves 4
4 large eggs, separated
450 g (1 lb) clear honey

Put the egg yolks and honey in the top of a double boiler. Set over the bottom and put on a low heat. Beat gently, using an electric whisk if possible, until the mixture thickens and is pale. Remove from the heat, whisk for a few minutes more, then set aside to cool.

Whisk the egg whites until they form stiff peaks. Fold the whites into the cold honey mixture. Turn the mixture into 4 individual bowls and chill in the refrigerator for 3 hours. Do not be perturbed if the mixture separates.

Quick Coffee Mousse

(Illustrated on page 26)
Serves 4–6
30 ml (2 tablespoons) instant coffee
50 g (2 oz) caster sugar
45 ml (3 tablespoons) boiling water
15 g (½ oz) gelatine
45 ml (3 tablespoons) cold water
275 ml (½ pint) double cream, softly whipped
2 egg whites
DECORATION:
150 ml (5 fl oz) double cream, stiffly whipped
coffee beans

Dissolve the coffee and caster sugar in the boiling water.

Sprinkle the gelatine over the cold water in a small pan. Leave to stand for 5 minutes, then dissolve over a low heat (*see page 28*).

Mix the coffee syrup and gelatine together, stirring well. Leave to go cold.

Fold the cold coffee mixture into the whipped cream. Whisk the egg whites until they form stiff peaks, and fold these into the coffee cream.

Pour into a glass serving dish and refrigerate until set.

When ready to serve, decorate the mousse with piped whipped cream and coffee beans.

Caramel Bavarois

Serves 4–6
265 g (9½ oz) caster sugar
150 ml (5 fl oz) water
275 ml (½ pint) milk
3 medium egg yolks
15 g (½ oz) gelatine
90 ml (6 tablespoons) water
150 ml (5 fl oz) double cream, softly whipped

Grease a 575-ml (1-pint) decorative mould with flavourless oil.

Put 100 g (4 oz) sugar into a medium saucepan with half the 150 ml (5 fl oz) water. Put over a low heat and stir until the sugar has dissolved. Raise the heat and boil the syrup until it turns a deep caramel brown. Pour the remainder of the water into the pan and stir with a wooden spoon until the caramel has dissolved. Add the milk, bring back to the boil and remove from the heat.

Beat the egg yolks with 40 g (1½ oz) caster sugar until pale and creamy. Pour the caramel-flavoured milk on to this, stir and return to the rinsed-out saucepan.

Put the pan over a low heat, and stir the custard until it is thick and will coat the back of the spoon. Do not let it boil. Strain into a clean bowl and leave to cool.

Sprinkle the gelatine over 45 ml (3 tablespoons) water in a small pan and leave for 5 minutes to soften. Dissolve over a low heat.

Add the gelatine in a thin stream to the custard. Put in a cool place and stir from time to time until the custard has thickened and is on the point of setting. Fold in 30 ml (2 tablespoons) of the whipped cream. Pour into the mould and chill in the refrigerator.

Put the remainder of the sugar in a heavy-based saucepan with the remaining 45 ml (3 tablespoons)

Caramel Bavarois

water. Set over a low heat and stir the syrup until the sugar has dissolved. Raise the heat and boil until the mixture is a rich golden brown.

Line a baking tray with foil and grease it. Quickly tip the caramel on to this and leave it to go hard. Remove the foil and caramel from the tray, break the caramel so that you can fold the foil over it, then break it up with a rolling pin.

30 minutes before serving, unmould the Bavarois on to a serving plate and decorate with the remainder of the whipped cream and the small pieces of caramel.

Orange Genoise Bavarois

Serves 8
275 g (10 oz) caster sugar
275 ml (½ pint) water
3 large oranges
sponge cake baked in a 16 cm (6½ in) square cake tin
BAVAROIS:
3 large egg yolks
175 g (6 oz) caster sugar
3 oranges.
1 lemon
150 g (5 oz) butter
15 g (½ oz) gelatine
30 ml (2 tablespoons) water
275 ml (½ pint) double cream, softly whipped
DECORATION:
150 ml (5 fl oz) double cream, stiffly whipped
1 extra orange

Put the sugar and water in a saucepan and set over a low heat. Stir until the sugar has dissolved, then bring to the boil. Turn down the heat and simmer for 5 minutes.

Peel the 3 large oranges in a spiral using a potato peeler. Remove all the pith and cut the flesh into thin slices. Poach these very gently in the syrup for about 30 minutes. They should be tender, but not broken up. Remove them with a slotted spoon and place on a wire rack to drain.

Line a 1.4-litre (2½-pint) ring mould with the orange slices, overlapping them slightly.

Make the bavarois. Put the egg yolks and sugar in the top of a double saucepan. Squeeze the 3 oranges and measure out 175 ml (6 fl oz) of the juice. Add this to the egg yolks with the squeezed juice of the lemon.

Orange Genoise Bavarois

Set the top of the boiler over the bottom filled with hot water and put on a low heat. Whisk the egg yolks until they leaves a trail when you lift the whisk.

Remove the pan from the heat and whisk in the butter, a small piece at a time, to melt it.

Sprinkle the gelatine over the 30 ml (2 tablespoons) water in a small saucepan. Leave for 5 minutes then dissolve over a very low heat.

Add the dissolved gelatine to the egg yolk mixture and put in a cool place, stirring from time to time, until on the point of setting.

Fold in the whipped cream and pour into the prepared ring mould taking care not to disarrange the orange segments.

Cut the sponge into 3 horizontally. Then cut these pieces to fit on top of the Bavarois mixture. When the mould is full, put in the refrigerator to set.

30 minutes before serving, unmould the Bavarois on to a serving plate. Peel the remaining orange and cut out the segments, discarding all the pith and dividing membranes. Mix with the remaining double cream and use to fill the centre of the mould.

Very Special Wine Jelly

Serves 6
½ bottle Muscat de Beaumes de Venise (serve the
remainder with the jelly)
90 g (3½ oz) caster sugar
150 ml (5 fl oz) fresh lemon juice
grated zest of 1 lemon
350 ml (12 fl oz) water
25 g (1 oz) gelatine
45 ml (3 tablespoons) water
DECORATION:
15 ml (1 tablespoon) icing sugar
150 ml (5 fl oz) double cream, stiffly whipped
seedless white grapes

Put the sugar, lemon juice and lemon zest into a pan with the 350 ml (12 fl oz) water. Set over a low heat and stir until the sugar has dissolved. Raise the heat and bring to the boil. Lower the heat and simmer for 10 minutes. Cool slightly, then add the wine.

Sprinkle the gelatine over the 45 ml (3 tablespoons) water in a small saucepan. Leave for 5 minutes, then dissolve over a low heat.

Add the dissolved gelatine to the wine mixture and mix well. Pour into a wetted 1-litre (1¾-pint) mould and put in the refrigerator to set.

About 15 minutes before serving, unmould the jelly on to a serving plate. Fold the icing sugar into the whipped cream. Decorate the jelly with piped rosettes of this mixture and the seedless grapes.

Port Wine Jelly

Serves 4
575 ml (1 pint) port
100 g (4 oz) caster sugar
pinch nutmeg
stick cinnamon
45 ml (3 tablespoons) lemon juice
150 ml (5 fl oz) water
25 g (1 oz) gelatine
2 egg whites
150 ml (5 fl oz) double cream, lightly whipped

Reserve 90 ml (6 tablespoons) of the port and put the remainder in a saucepan with the sugar, nutmeg, cinnamon, lemon juice and water. Set over low heat, stirring occasionally until the sugar has dissolved. Remove from heat, cover and set aside for 10 minutes.

Put the remaining port in a small saucepan and dissolve the gelatine in it (*see page 28*). Gradually pour the gelatine mixture into the spiced port mixture, stirring constantly.

Lightly whisk the egg whites, leaving them still runny. Wash the shells inside and out and crush them.

Pour the jelly into a clean saucepan and add the egg whites and shells. Place over medium heat and whisk constantly to produce a head of foam. Just before boiling point is reached, remove the pan from the heat and set aside for 5 minutes. Strain the jelly through a jelly bag twice or more until it is clear.

Pour the jelly into chilled, rinsed individual moulds (or 1 large one) and leave in a cool place to set.

When ready to serve turn out the jellies and pipe the cream around each base.

Simple Sherry Jelly

Serves 4–6
25 g (1 oz) gelatine
25 ml (4 fl oz) cold water
225 ml (8 fl oz) boiling water
100 g (4 oz) sugar
125 ml (4 fl oz) orange juice
30 ml (2 tablespoons) lemon juice
350 ml (12 fl oz) medium-dry sherry

Sprinkle the gelatine over the cold water in a bowl. Leave for 5 minutes, then pour the boiling water on top and stir until the gelatine has dissolved. Add the sugar and stir until this, too, has dissolved. Set aside for 10 minutes.

Mix together the fruit juices and sherry. Add the gelatine mixture, stirring constantly. Pour into a rinsed 850-ml (1½-pint) mould and leave to set.

Raspberry Jelly Whip

Serves 6
900 g (2 lb) raspberries, washed
50 g (2 oz) caster sugar
15 g (½ oz) gelatine
150 ml (5 fl oz) double cream, thickly whipped

Put a ring mould in the refrigerator to chill.

Set aside 225 g (8 oz) of the raspberries and rub the remainder through a sieve to form a smooth purée. Stir in sugar to taste.

Put 60 ml (4 tablespoons) of the purée into a saucepan and sprinkle the gelatine over it. Leave for 5 minutes, then dissolve over a low heat. Pour the gelatine mixture into the remaining raspberry purée in a thin stream, stirring constantly. Set aside to cool.

When the jelly is on the point of setting, whisk it vigorously with a rotary or hand-held electric whisk, until a thick foam is produced. Continue whisking until the whisk leaves a trail in the foam.

Rinse the chilled mould and shake off the excess water. Pour the jelly into the mould, cover and set aside in the refrigerator until set.

Turn the jelly out on to a serving plate (*see page 29*) and pipe cream around the base. Fill the centre with the reserved raspberries and serve as soon as possible.

Lemon Jelly

Serves 4
grated rind and juice of 3 lemons
100 g (4 oz) caster sugar
stick cinnamon
575 ml (1 pint) water
75 ml (3 fl oz) sherry
25 g (1 oz) gelatine

Put the lemon rind and juice, sugar, cinnamon and

Raspberry Jelly Whip

water in a saucepan over low heat, stirring occasionally, to dissolve the sugar. When the sugar has dissolved, remove the pan from the heat, cover and set aside for 20 minutes.

Strain the mixture through a jelly bag and stir in the sherry. When the liquid is cool, transfer 90 ml (6 tablespoons) to a small saucepan and dissolve the gelatine in it (*see page 28*). Pour the gelatine into the flavoured liquid and strain again through a jelly bag. Leave in a cool place until almost set.

Pour 575 ml (1 pint) of the jelly into a chilled, rinsed 575-ml (1-pint) mould. Rinse a shallow tin and pour in the remaining jelly. Put both jellies in the refrigerator until set.

Turn the jelly out of the ring mould on to a serving plate. Chop the remaining jelly into small pieces and arrange around the moulded jelly. Serve.

Gingered Grapefruit Jelly

Serves 4
275 ml (½ pint) ginger ale
40 g (1½ oz) loaf sugar
30 ml (2 tablespoons) lime juice cordial
15 g (½ oz) gelatine
2 small grapefruit, peeled, pith removed, seeded and segmented
20 ml (4 teaspoons) finely chopped crystallized ginger

Make the jelly using the first four ingredients following the step-by-step instructions on page 29.

Spoon a little jelly into the base of a chilled and rinsed 1.15-litre (2-pint) mould to make a layer 3–6 mm (⅛–¼ in). Leave to set in the refrigerator.

Dry the grapefruit segments on paper towels and chop them, if large. Arrange a layer of crystallized ginger and grapefruit on top of the set jelly. Spoon over sufficient jelly to cover and leave to set again.

Spoon over sufficient jelly to make another base layer and leave to set.

Continue making layers in this way until all the ingredients are used up, ending with a layer of jelly about 6–12 mm (¼–½ in) thick. Refrigerate until completely set.

Zabaglione

Serves 2
2 large egg yolks
30 ml (2 tablespoons) caster sugar
45 ml (3 tablespoons) Marsala

Beat together the egg yolks and sugar for 1 minute in the top of a double boiler set over the bottom on a low heat. Whisk with a balloon or electric whisk for 2 minutes, or until just beginning to thicken. Add the Marsala and continue whisking for about 5 minutes, until the mixture is pale and has doubled in bulk.

Rinse out 2 glasses in hot water and dry them thoroughly. Pour in the zabaglione and serve immediately.

Zabaglione Cream

Serves 4
4 large egg yolks
40 g (1½ oz) caster sugar
75 ml (5 tablespoons) Marsala
30 ml (2 tablespoons) water
5 ml (1 teaspoon) gelatine
150 ml (5 fl oz) double cream
30 ml (2 tablespoons) flaked almonds

Fill a large mixing bowl with ice cubes and set aside.

Whisk together the egg yolks and the sugar in the top of a double boiler. Whisk in the Marsala. Set the top of the boiler over the bottom on a low heat. Cook, whisking constantly, until the mixture is very thick and leaves a ribbon trail, which will hold for a count of four. Remove from the heat.

Put the water in a small saucepan and sprinkle over the gelatine. Set aside for 5 minutes to soften. Set the pan over low heat for 3 minutes, without stirring, until the gelatine has dissolved completely. Set aside to cool slightly.

Whisk the gelatine into the egg yolk mixture. Place the bowl on the ice cubes. Stir gently until the mixture is beginning to set.

Whip the cream until it will just hold its shape. Fold it into the zabaglione mixture. Pour into 4 chilled glasses and set aside in a cool place for 1–2 hours.

Sprinkle over the almonds before serving.

Charlotte Russe

Serves 6
sponge fingers (see recipe)
4 medium eggs, separated
100 g (4 oz) caster sugar
250 ml (9 fl oz) milk
vanilla pod
15 g (½ oz) gelatine
45 ml (3 tablespoons) water
275 ml (½ pint) double cream, softly whipped
225 g (8 oz) fresh or frozen raspberries
1 tablespoon Kirsch
icing sugar (see recipe)
DECORATION:
150 ml (5 fl oz) double cream, stiffly whipped

Estimate how many sponge fingers, split in half length-ways, you will need to line the sides of a 1-litre (1¾-pint) charlotte mould. Allow a few extra, and cut them all in half lengthways.

Cut a circle of greaseproof paper to fit the bottom of the mould and arrange the split sponge fingers, uncut side down on the paper like spokes coming out of the centre of a wheel. Trim them as necessary. Line the sides of the mould with the split sponge fingers, uncut side outwards and overlapping them slightly.

Put the egg yolks in a bowl and whisk with the sugar until the mixture is pale and frothy. Put the milk in a saucepan with the vanilla pod split open. Heat until bubbles appear round the edges of the pan.

Sprinkle the gelatine over the 45 ml (3 tablespoons) water in a small pan and leave for 5 minutes to soften.

Remove the vanilla pod and pour the milk over the egg yolk mixture. Rinse out the saucepan and pour the custard into it, then heat over a gentle heat until the custard thickens and just coats the back of the spoon.

Dissolve the softened gelatine (*see page 28*) and stir it into the custard. Strain the custard into a clean bowl and set aside to cool, stirring from time to time.

When the custard is beginning to set, fold in the softly whipped double cream. Whisk two of the egg whites (use the other two for meringues, or freeze them until you want them) until they form soft peaks.

Pour the custard on top of the egg whites and fold them in with a metal spoon. Very carefully pour this mixture into the lined charlotte mould, smooth the surface over and cover with foil or cling film. Refrigerate until set.

Purée the raspberries in an electric blender or by rubbing them through a sieve. Stir in the Kirsch and add icing sugar to taste.

When ready to serve, unmould the charlotte on to a serving plate. Decorate with piped rosettes of whipped cream and serve the raspberry purée separately.

Simple Charlotte Mexicaine

Serves 6
50 g (2 oz) ground coffee or 40 g (1½ oz) instant coffee
575 ml (1 pint) milk
100 g (4 oz) plain cooking chocolate, grated
4 egg yolks
50 g (2 oz) caster sugar
60 ml (4 tablespoons) water
15 g (½ oz) gelatine
275 ml (½ pint) double cream, lightly whipped
DECORATION:
225 ml (8 fl oz) double cream
24 sponge fingers
75 g (3 oz) plain cooking chocolate, grated
25 g (1 oz) flaked, toasted almonds

Put the coffee and milk in a saucepan over medium heat and bring to just below boiling point. Remove the pan from the heat and set aside for 15 minutes.

Strain the milk if using ground coffee (this is not necessary with instant coffee), then stir in the chocolate. Set over low heat, stirring constantly, until the chocolate is melted. Remove from the heat and set aside.

Whisk together the egg yolks and sugar in the top of a double boiler, until the mixture is thick and creamy. Add the flavoured milk and set the top of the boiler over the bottom on a low heat. Cook, stirring constantly, for 20 minutes. Remove from the heat and set aside to cool, stirring occasionally.

Put the water in a small saucepan and sprinkle the gelatine on top. Leave for 5 minutes, then dissolve over a low heat. Set aside and allow to cool slightly.

Pour the gelatine into the custard in a thin stream, stirring constantly. Set aside, stirring occasionally, until the mixture is on the point of setting.

Meanwhile, oil the sides of an 850-ml (1½-pint) charlotte mould or cake tin. Line the base with grease-proof paper and brush with oil.

Fold the whipped cream into the custard. Pour the mixture into the prepared mould and set aside for 2 hours, or until set.

Invert the mould on to a serving plate. Whisk the cream used for decoration until it forms soft peaks. Using a palette knife, spread it over the top and sides of the mould. Arrange the sponge fingers around the sides, with their rounded sides facing outwards. Sprinkle the chocolate and almonds over the top and serve, tied around with a ribbon if you like.

Simple Charlotte Mexicaine

Charlotte Turinoise

Serves 6
about 24 sponge fingers
about 30 ml (2 tablespoons) dark rum
50 g (2 oz) caster sugar
575 ml (1 pint) double cream, lightly whipped
275 ml (½ pint) can unsweetened chestnut purée
30 ml (2 tablespoons) water
6 g (¼ oz) gelatine
DECORATION:
150 ml (5 fl oz) double cream, stiffly whipped
100 g (4 oz) marrons glacés, halved

Oil an 850-ml (1½-pint) charlotte mould. Line the base with greaseproof paper and oil again.

Cut the sponge finges to size to line the base and calculate how many you will need to line the sides. Dip them, one by one, into the rum and drain on a rack over a plate for 5 minutes. Line the base and sides of the mould with these fingers.

Fold the sugar into the cream. Fold in any rum remaining in the saucer together with the chestnut purée.

Put the water in a small saucepan and sprinkle the gelatine on top. Leave for 5 minutes, then dissolve over a low heat. Allow to cool slightly.

Pour the gelatine mixture into the chestnut cream mixture in a thin stream, stirring lightly. Set aside in a cool place, stirring occasionally, or until the mixture is just on the point of setting.

Put the cream mixture into the sponge finger-lined mould. Cover with cling film or foil and chill in the refrigerator for 4 hours.

Trim away any protruding sponge fingers. Turn the charlotte out on to a serving plate. Decorate with piped cream and the halved marrons glacés.

Soufflés & Meringues

The ever-versatile and oh-so-useful egg is the basis of these delicious and spectacular desserts. Soufflés, both cold and hot, and meringues are elegant in appearance and so light and airy that they tempt even the most jaded palate. They are superb dinner party desserts and are real evidence of how much you esteem your guests. Often quite time-consuming to make, they are not, however, at all difficult, and the bulk of the preparation —even for hot soufflés—can be done well in advance.

We are using the term soufflé here to include the cold mousse-like mixtures made to look as if they have risen above their dish, as well as the deliciously fluffy, melt-in-the-mouth hot concoctions. Hot soufflés are all too often neglected by busy cooks under the mistaken impression that making, baking and getting them to the table is a path lined with pitfalls. In fact, they are an easy dessert to make and one that never fails to bring gasps of admiration.

Meringues are the simplest of puddings to make, yet they always look gorgeous and most people love them. Very versatile, they can be made as containers for fruit or other flavourings or the basic mixture can be flavoured with coffee, nuts or crushed ratafias.

Soufflés and meringues have their principal ingredient in common—egg whites—and it is the preparation of these that has much to do with the secret of success in both instances.

Always use egg whites at room temperature; they will not whisk as well if chilled. When separating them, make sure no spot of yolk gets into the white; even the tiniest speck will prevent them whisking to full volume. Ideally use a copper bowl for whisking, the next best thing being one of aluminium or stainless steel. Egg whites do not cling to glass or pottery, so it is impossible to get the same volume of air incorporated. Whatever the bowl, it must be scrupulously clean and dry.

For the best results, whisk the whites with a balloon whisk. It is more arm-breaking than an electric whisk, admittedly, but far more air can be incorporated. Start slowly using a circular motion, and lift the whisk higher, moving it more quickly as the whites begin to stiffen. For meringues and hot soufflés, the whites should be stiff and dry; whisk in a tablespoon or so of sugar towards the end to help with this. For cold soufflés, they should just form soft peaks and not look too dry.

Cold Soufflés

These are made in traditional soufflé dishes prepared with collars of grease-proof paper (see instructions overleaf). Once set and ready to serve, the paper collar is removed and the 'risen' soufflé decorated according to its flavour. It is

very important to use the correct size of dish. If you use one bigger than recommended, there will not be enough mixture to rise over the top. As with a mousse, remove the cold soufflé from the refrigerator at least 30 minutes before serving.

Hot Soufflés

There are four basic rules to ensure your hot soufflés are perfect. First, measure the ingredients accurately; any imbalance will destroy the delicate texture. Second, whisk the egg whites to their maximum volume and dryness. Third, make sure the oven has reached the correct temperature before cooking the soufflé. Fourth, serve it immediately it is ready; from the moment you take it from the oven, it is on its way down!

A hot soufflé is generally made from a white flour-based sauce to which such flavourings as vanilla, coffee, nuts, chopped fruits and liqueurs are added. Fruit purée can also be used as a base but it should not be combined with a white sauce. The base of a chocolate soufflé is generally melted chocolate to which a liqueur is added.

Egg yolks are beaten into the sauce when it has been cooked, and then the mixture is cooled slightly before the whites are folded in. As a general rule, add the sauce to the egg whites. Use a figure-of-eight motion to fold in the egg whites and turn the mixture over from the bottom of the dish.

Prepare the soufflé dish by brushing it with melted butter and then coating it with caster sugar, desiccated coconut or finely milled nuts. Tip the mixture into the dish. It should come to 2.5 cm (1 in) from the top in order for it to rise at least this height above the dish.

Once in the oven, the soufflé is not nearly as temperamental as it is generally credited with being. It will stand the oven door being opened, provided a cold draught is not allowed in. This means you can turn it during cooking so that it cooks evenly.

Check just before the recommended cooking time; when you shake the dish it should 'quake' all over. If the centre wobbles, it means the middle is still runny. Many people, the French in particular, consider this perfection.

Meringues

There are four basic types of meringue. *Meringue suisse* is the simplest to make consisting of stiffly whisked egg whites into which sugar is folded. When baked it is crisp and dry on the outside and very slightly softer on the inside.

Meringue cuite is made by beating egg whites and sugar together in a bowl over a pan of hot water set on a gentle heat. When baked, it is hard, dry and powdery. Use for baskets and nests.

Meringue italienne is made by whisking a sugar syrup into the egg whites. The cooked meringue is soft and smooth, suitable for cake fillings and sometimes used for Baked Alaskas.

American meringue has a marsh-mallow-like consistency. It is usually used for spectacular cakes, the famous Pavlova for example, piled high with cream and fruit. The method for making these meringues is given on page 56.

Most meringues are baked on baking sheets lined with greaseproof or non-stick paper. Brush this with a little vegetable oil before piping the meringue into the required shape using a plain or starred nozzle. Cake-type meringues can be cooked in a shallow, loose-bottomed tin, but never use one with a fixed base; it will be impossible to remove the meringue. Brush the sides of the tin with a little melted butter or margarine and dust with cornflour. Line the base with non-stick paper.

Meringues are usually cooked in a very slow oven, in which they 'dry out' rather than really cook. They should be left until they are crisp to the touch. Lift individual ones off the paper to ensure they are similarly crisp underneath. (This does not apply to American meringue which is supposed to be soft in the middle.) The most notable exception to cooking in a slow oven is when making a Baked Alaska, in which the meringue is used to encase ice-cream often combined with fruit and placed on a sponge base. The meringue is then cooked very fast in an extremely hot oven, so it hardens quickly before the ice-cream has a chance to melt. Similarly, when meringue is used to top a pudding, such as a pie or stewed fruit, it is generally cooked in a hotter oven.

Making a Cold Orange Soufflé

grated rind from 1 orange and 45 ml (3 tablespoons) juice*
75 g (3 oz) caster sugar
3 large eggs, separated
15 g (½ oz) gelatine
150 ml (5 fl oz) double or whipping cream
*flavourings will obviously vary; the amount of sugar varies accordingly.
Fruit flavourings are generally added just before the dissolved gelatine.

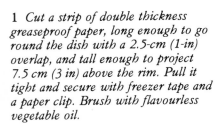

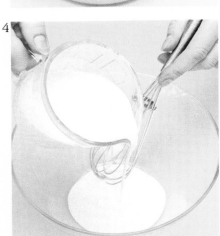

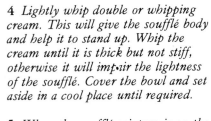

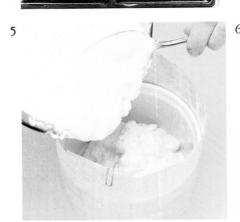

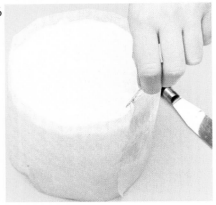

1 *Cut a strip of double thickness greaseproof paper, long enough to go round the dish with a 2.5-cm (1-in) overlap, and tall enough to project 7.5 cm (3 in) above the rim. Pull it tight and secure with freezer tape and a paper clip. Brush with flavourless vegetable oil.*

2 *Put the flavouring, egg yolks and sugar in the top of a double boiler. Set over the bottom, half-filled with warm water, and put on a low heat. Whisk until the mixture is thick and creamy. Cool, stirring occasionally.*

3 *Sprinkle the gelatine over 45 ml (3 tablespoons) cold water. Set aside for 5 minutes to soften. Place over very low heat for 3 minutes, without stirring, to dissolve completely. Pour the gelatine into the egg mixture in a thin continuous stream, stirring constantly to prevent threads forming.*

4 *Lightly whip double or whipping cream. This will give the soufflé body and help it to stand up. Whip the cream until it is thick but not stiff, otherwise it will impair the lightness of the soufflé. Cover the bowl and set aside in a cool place until required.*

5 *When the soufflé mixture is on the point of setting, fold in the cream. Then fold in the stiffly whisked (but not dry) egg whites. Do this gently or the soufflé will not be light and airy.*

6 *Put in the refrigerator to set. About 30 minutes before serving, remove the tape and clip. Gently insert a round-bladed knife between the soufflé and the paper. Press gently against the soufflé and peel off the paper. Decorate according to the flavourings.*

Meringue Techniques

meringue cuite (*see page 56*), quantity
according to size of pudding being made
double or whipping cream, flavoured with
sugar and liqueur, if liked, stiffly whipped
fruit, such as seedless grapes, strawberries (halved),
raspberries, peaches (sliced) etc.

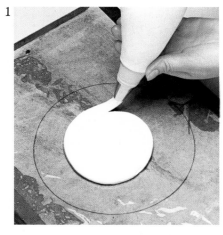

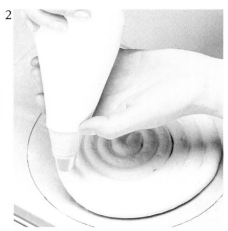

1 *Line a baking sheet with grease-proof or non-stick paper and brush with oil. Draw a circle around a 20-cm (8-in) plate. Spoon the meringue into the piping bag carefully so as not to crush the air out of it. Start piping in the centre of the circle.*

2 *Keep piping in a spiral so that each new 'ring' joins the previous one. Cook for 2–3 hours at 110°C, 225°F, Gas ¼, until dry. To make a layer cake, make 3 circles, the second and third 2.5 cm (1 in) and 5 cm (2 in) smaller than the first.*

3 *When cooked, remove the circles from the oven and gently peel the paper away from the bases. Set aside on wire racks to cool. When cold, spread the largest circle with stiffly whipped double cream. Arrange fruit on top and pipe cream around the edge.*

4 *Spread the second meringue circle with cream and place on top. Arrange the fruit and pipe swirls of cream around the edge as before. Place the smallest circle on top and decorate with cream and fruit. Serve within an hour or it will become soggy.*

1 *To make a meringue topping, spread meringue over the top of a prepared pudding with the back of a spoon. Make sure that it meets the rim of the dish or pastry. Roughen the surface of the meringue.*

2 *Alternatively, pipe the meringue on to the pudding using a star nozzle. Start by making a circle at the rim, then fill it in. For a soft topping, bake for 5 minutes at 220°C, 425°F, Gas 7. For crisper topping, bake for 30 minutes at 180°C, 350°F, Gas 4.*

Chocolate Soufflé

Serves 4–6
15 g (½ oz) butter
45 ml (3 tablespoons) caster sugar
100 g (4 oz) plain dessert chocolate, broken into pieces
45 ml (3 tablespoons) brandy
4 large eggs, separated
pinch of salt or cream of tartar
icing sugar

Preheat the oven to 200°C, 400°F, Gas 6. Place a baking sheet in the centre of the oven.

Grease a 1.4-litre (2½-pint) soufflé dish with the butter and coat with 15 ml (1 tablespoon) of the sugar. Shake out any excess.

Put the chocolate and the brandy in a heatproof bowl over a pan of hot water. Place over very low heat and stir until the chocolate has melted. Remove the pan from the heat. Lightly beat the remaining sugar into the egg yolks. Stir the mixture into the melted chocolate.

Whisk the egg whites for 30 seconds. Add the salt or cream of tartar and continue whisking until they form stiff peaks.

Add 2 spoonfuls of the egg whites to the chocolate base, then fold this into the remaining egg whites.

Transfer the mixture to the prepared dish and bake for 20–25 minutes.

Dust the soufflé with a little icing sugar and serve immediately.

Apricot Soufflé

Serves 6
175 g (6 oz) dried apricots
15 g (½ oz) butter
60 ml (4 tablespoons) caster sugar
2 large eggs, separated
15 ml (1 tablespoon) apricot brandy
1 large extra egg white
30 ml (2 tablespoons) double cream
pinch of salt or cream of tartar

Put the apricots in a saucepan and add just enough water to cover. Bring to the boil over low heat. Cover and simmer for 40 minutes, or until the fruit is plump and tender.

Preheat the oven to 190°C, 375°F, Gas 5. Place a baking sheet in the centre of the oven.

Grease a 1.4-litre (2½-pint) soufflé dish with the butter and coat with 15 ml (1 tablespoon) of the sugar. Shake out any excess.

Drain the apricots. Purée the fruit in an electric blender or by rubbing it through a sieve, then cool until just warm.

Lightly beat the remaining sugar into the egg yolks. Stir the mixture into the warm fruit purée and add the brandy. Stir in the cream and set aside.

Whisk the egg whites for 30 seconds. Add the salt or cream of tartar and continue whisking until they form stiff peaks. Add 2 spoonfuls of the egg whites to the purée base. Then fold the base into the remaining egg whites.

Turn the mixture into the prepared soufflé dish and bake for 25–30 minutes. Serve immediately.

Grand Marnier Soufflé

Serves 4
2 large oranges
275 ml (½ pint) plus 30 ml (2 tablespoons) milk
25 g (1 oz) cornflour
50g (2 oz) plus 15 ml (1 tablespoon) caster sugar
4 large eggs, separated
4 tablespoons Grand Marnier
icing sugar, for dusting

Thinly pare the zest from the oranges using a potato peeler and making sure you do not remove any of the pith. Put in a saucepan with the 275 ml (½ pint) milk and bring to the boil. Cover and leave on one side for 30 minutes.

Preheat the oven to 220°C, 425°F, Gas 7. Butter a 1.4-litre (2½-pint) soufflé dish and coat with the 15 ml (1 tablespoon) sugar, tipping out any excess.

Strain the milk, discarding the orange zest. Blend 30 ml (2 tablespoons) with the cornflour and add 25 g (1 oz) sugar. Stir this into the egg yolks, then stir in the remainder of the milk, gradually.

Put this custard into a clean pan and bring to the boil over a medium heat, stirring all the time. Turn the heat down and simmer for 5 minutes, stirring all the time as the custard thickens. If it shows signs of going lumpy, beat it quickly with a wire whisk. Remove from the heat and beat in the Grand Marnier.

Whisk the egg whites until they are stiff. Whisk in the remaining sugar, 15 ml (1 tablespoon) at a time. Add a little of this to the custard and stir together. Pour the custard on to the remainder of the egg whites, and fold in using a metal spoon.

Tip the mixture into the prepared soufflé dish and cook for 20–25 minutes until the soufflé is puffed up and golden. Take from the oven and dust quickly with the icing sugar, sifting it on to the surfaces. Serve at once, with Apricot Sauce (see opposite page).

Apricot Sauce

Serves 4
400 g (14 oz) canned apricots
15–30 ml (1–2 tablespoons) caster sugar
30 ml (2 tablespoons) fresh orange juice
5 ml (1 teaspoon) arrowroot
10 ml (2 teaspoons) Grand Marnier

Drain the apricots, reserving 45 ml (3 tablespoons) of the syrup. Purée the apricots in an electric blender or by rubbing them through a sieve and tip this into a small heavy-bottomed saucepan.

Grand Marnier Soufflé

Stir in 15 ml (1 tablespoon) caster sugar and strain in the orange juice.

Blend the arrowroot with the reserved syrup to a smooth paste and stir into the purée.

Place the pan on a medium heat and bring the sauce slowly to the boil, stirring all the time. Simmer very gently for 5 minutes. Cool slightly, stir in the Grand Marnier and taste for sweetness. Add a little more sugar if you feel it needs it. Serve the sauce warm with Grand Marnier Soufflé (see opposite page).

Raspberry Soufflé

Serves 4
225 g (8 oz) raspberries, fresh or frozen
30 ml (2 tablespoons) lemon juice
2 large egg whites
pinch of salt
20 g (2 oz) caster sugar

Preheat the oven to 180°C, 350°F, Gas 4. Grease four individual ramekin dishes.

Purée the raspberries in an electric blender and sieve. (Alternatively just rub them through a sieve.) Stir in the lemon juice.

Whisk the egg whites and salt until they form soft peaks. Whisk in the sugar 15 ml (1 tablespoon) at a time, until the mixture is stiff and glossy.

Tip the raspberry purée into the egg whites and fold together using a metal spoon. Divide between the ramekin dishes.

Put the dishes on a baking tray and bake in the oven for 10 minutes. Serve immediately.

Soufflé Rothschild

Serves 6
30 ml (2 tablespoons) Kirsch
175 g (6 oz) glacé fruit, finely chopped
50 g (2 oz) butter
75 g (3 oz) caster sugar
225 ml (8 fl oz) milk
25 g (1 oz) plain flour
4 large eggs, separated
1 large egg white
pinch of salt or cream of tartar
icing sugar

Sprinkle the Kirsch over the glacé fruit and set aside for 30 minutes.

Preheat the oven to 190°C, 375°F, Gas 5. Place a baking sheet in the centre of the oven.

Grease six individual ramekins with 15 g (½ oz) of the butter and coat them with 25 g (1 oz) of the sugar. Shake out any excess.

Put the milk and the remaining sugar in a small saucepan over a low heat and bring to just below boiling point. Remove the pan from the heat and set aside.

Melt the remaining butter over a low heat. Stir in the flour and cook, stirring constantly, for 30 seconds. Remove the pan from the heat and gradually stir in the milk. Return to the heat and, still stirring, bring the mixture to the boil. Simmer for 5 minutes, stirring occasionally. Remove from the heat and cool slightly.

Lightly beat the egg yolks and stir into the cooled sauce together with the glacé fruit and kirsch.

Whisk the egg whites briskly for 30 seconds. Add the salt or cream of tartar and continue whisking until they form stiff peaks. Add 2 spoonfuls of the egg whites to the sauce. Then fold the sauce into the remaining egg whites.

Divide the mixture between the prepared ramekins and place them on the baking sheet. Bake for 15–20 minutes.

Dust the soufflés with a little icing sugar and serve immediately.

Soufflé Omelette with Blackcurrants

Serves 2
225 g (8 oz) blackcurrants, washed
45 ml (3 tablespoons) caster sugar
3 eggs, separated
15 ml (1 tablespoon) water
pinch of salt
icing sugar

Put the blackcurrants in a pan and sprinkle over 30 ml (2 tablespoons) of the sugar. Break up the fruit with a fork and set aside for 2 hours to let the juices run. Place the pan over medium heat and cook the blackcurrants, shaking occasionally, for 8 minutes. Remove from the heat.

Preheat the oven to 190°C, 375°F, Gas 5. Grease a round gratin dish, 20 cm (8 in) in diameter, with butter.

Lightly beat together the egg yolks, water and the remaining sugar until the mixture is light and creamy. Whisk the egg whites for about 30 seconds. Add the salt and continue whisking until the egg whites form soft peaks.

Fold the yolk mixture into the egg whites. Pour the mixture into the prepared gratin dish and spread it quickly with a wet palette knife, making a depression in the centre.

Cook in the top of the oven for 7 minutes, or until the omelette is golden and puffy.

Meanwhile, preheat the grill to high.

Remove the omelette from the oven. Spoon the blackcurrants into the depression. Flip the omelette over and sprinkle generously with icing sugar, sifting it on to the surfaces.

Grill for 40 seconds, or until the sugar has caramelized. Serve immediately.

Lemon Soufflé

Serves 6
grated rind of 1 lemon
juice of 3 lemons
4 large eggs, separated
100 g (4 oz) caster sugar
15 ml (1 tablespoon) gelatine
45 ml (3 tablespoons) water
175 ml (6 fl oz) double cream, thickly whipped
DECORATION:
150 ml (5 fl oz) double cream, softly whipped
thinly pared rind of ½ lemon, blanched

Prepare a paper collar (*see page 48*) for an 850-ml (1½-pint) soufflé dish and brush the inside with vegetable oil.

Put the lemon rind, juice, egg yolks and sugar in the top of the double boiler and set over the bottom on a low heat. Beat the egg yolk mixture until it is thick and creamy and will coat the whisk. Remove from the heat and set aside to cool, stirring occasionally.

Dissolve the gelatine in the water (*see page 28*). Pour it into the soufflé mixture in a thin stream, stirring constantly. Put in a cool place and stir occasionally until the mixture is just setting. Fold it into the whipped cream.

Whisk the egg whites until they form soft peaks. Fold the cream and soufflé mixture into the egg whites.

Turn the mixture into the prepared soufflé dish. Cover loosely with cling film or foil and chill in the refrigerator for 3 hours, or until set.

Remove the paper collar (*see page 48*). Pipe rosettes of cream around the edge of the soufflé and decorate with lemon rind. Set aside in a cool place for 30 minutes before serving.

Lemon Soufflé

Strawberry Soufflé Omelette

Serves 2
225 g (8 oz) strawberries, washed and hulled
30 ml (2 tablespoons) Kirsch
45 ml (3 tablespoons) caster sugar
3 eggs, separated
15 ml (1 tablespoon) water
pinch of salt
20 g (¾ oz) butter

Set aside 5 strawberries for decoration and chop the remainder. Sprinkle the Kirsch and 30 ml (2 tablespoons) of the sugar over them. Cover with foil and set aside in the refrigerator for 2 hours.

Lightly beat together the egg yolks, water and the remaining sugar until the mixture is light and creamy.

Whisk the egg whites for 30 seconds. Add the salt and continue whisking until they form soft peaks. Fold the yolk mixture into the egg whites and set aside.

Preheat the grill to high.

Cut the reserved strawberries in half and set aside. Melt the butter in an omelette pan over medium heat. When the foam has subsided, pour in the egg mixture. Cook for 90 seconds, or until the bottom of the omelette is firm and golden but the top is still runny. Place under the grill and cook for 30 seconds, or until the omelette has risen and is golden.

Make a depression in the centre of the omelette. Using a slotted spoon, transfer the chopped strawberries into the omelette. Flip it over and transfer to a warm serving plate. Arrange the reserved strawberry halves along the edge and serve immediately.

Gooseberry Soufflé

Serves 6
450 g (1 lb) gooseberries, washed, topped and tailed
1 elderflower head (optional)
90 ml (6 tablespoons) water
4 large eggs, separated
100 g (4 oz) caster sugar
green food colouring
15 g (½ oz) gelatine
175 ml (6 fl oz) double cream, thickly whipped
DECORATION:
150 ml (5 fl oz) double cream, stiffly whipped
angelica

Put the gooseberries, elderflower head and 45 ml (3 tablespoons) of the water in a medium-sized saucepan over low heat. Cover and cook for 15 minutes, or until tender. Remove and discard the elderflower head. Purée the gooseberries in an electric blender and sieve to remove the pips. Alternatively, rub the gooseberries through a sieve without puréeing them first.

Prepare a paper collar for an 850-ml (1½-pint) soufflé dish (*see page 48*) and brush the inside with vegetable oil.

Put the egg yolks and sugar in the top of the double boiler and set over the bottom on a low heat. Beat until the mixture is thick and creamy and will coat the whisk. Remove from the heat and stir in the gooseberry purée. Stir in one or two drops of food colouring until the mixture is an attractive pale green colour. Cool, stirring occasionally.

Dissolve the gelatine in the remaining water (*see page 28*). Pour it into the soufflé mixture in a thin stream, stirring constantly. Set aside, stirring occasionally, until the mixture is just setting, then fold the soufflé mixture into the cream.

Whisk the egg whites until they form soft peaks. Fold in the cream and soufflé mixture.

Turn the mixture into the prepared soufflé dish. Cover loosely with cling film or foil and chill in the refrigerator for 3 hours, or until set.

Remove the paper collar (*see page 48*). Pipe the cream around the edge and decorate with the angelica. Set aside in a cool place for 30 minutes before serving to allow the flavour to develop slightly.

Pineapple and Orange Soufflé

Serves 6
1 medium-sized pineapple, peeled, cored and cut into chunks
60 ml (4 tablespoons) orange juice
25 g (1 oz) gelatine
4 eggs, separated
75 g (3 oz) caster sugar
30 ml (2 tablespoons) Grand Marnier
275 ml (½ pint) double cream, softly whipped
DECORATION:
ratafia biscuits
thin strips of orange zest

Prepare a paper collar (*see page 48*) for an 850-ml (1½-pint) soufflé dish and brush the inside very lightly with flavourless vegetable oil.

Purée the pineapple in an electric blender or food processor, or put it through a food mill to form a fairly rough purée.

Pineapple and Orange Soufflé

Put the orange juice in a small pan and sprinkle the gelatine over it. Leave to stand for 5 minutes, then set over a very low heat to dissolve.

Put the egg yolks, caster sugar and Grand Marnier in the top of a double boiler, set over the bottom on a low heat. Whisk until the mixture turns pale and creamy and leaves a ribbon trail when you lift the whisk. Remove the bowl, and whisk until the mixture cools.

Add the pineapple purée and the dissolved gelatine, stirring them into the egg mixture to distribute evenly. Put in a cool place, stirring from time to time.

When the mixture is on the point of setting, fold in the whipped cream. Whisk the egg whites until they will stand in soft peaks and fold these in, too. Chill until set.

About 30 minutes before serving, remove the paper collar (*see page 48*) and decorate the sides and top with the ratafias and orange zest.

Little Coffee Soufflés

Serves 6
40 ml (8 teaspoons) coarsely ground coffee
45 ml (3 tablespoons) boiling water
4 large eggs, separated
100 g (4 oz) caster sugar
10 ml (2 teaspoons) Tia Maria
15 ml (1 tablespoon) gelatine
175 ml (6 fl oz) double cream, thickly whipped
DECORATION:
100 g (4 oz) hazelnuts, very finely chopped
150 ml (5 fl oz) double cream, stiffly whipped

Prepare paper collars for 6 individual ramekins (*see page 48*) and brush the insides with the vegetable oil.

Mix the coffee and boiling water. Cover and set aside.

Put the egg yolks and sugar in the top of the double boiler and set over the bottom on a low heat. Beat until the mixture is thick and creamy and will coat the whisk. Remove from the heat and stir in the Tia Maria. Cool, stirring occasionally.

Strain the coffee into a small saucepan and dissolve the gelatine in it (*see page 28*). Pour it into the soufflé mixture in a thin stream, stirring constantly. Set aside in a cool place, stirring occasionally, until the mixture is just setting. Fold the soufflé mixture into the cream.

Whisk the egg whites until they form soft peaks. Fold in the cream and soufflé mixture.

Divide the mixture between the six prepared dishes. Cover loosely with cling film or foil and chill in the refrigerator for at least 2 hours, or until set.

Remove the paper collars. Gently press the chopped nuts into the sides of the soufflés and pipe rosettes of cream around the top. Set aside in a cool place for 30 minutes before serving.

Meringue Suisse

3 egg whites
pinch of salt
175 g (6 oz) caster sugar

Whisk the egg whites and salt together until they form stiff peaks. Whisk in half the sugar and continue beating until the whites regain their stiffness. They should be very white and glossy and you should be able to turn the bowl upside down without the mixture moving. Fold in the remaining sugar with a metal spoon.

The meringue is now ready for use most usually to make individual shells. Alternatively, other flavourings can be folded into the mixture before baking.

Meringue Cuite

4 egg whites
pinch of salt
250 g (9 oz) icing sugar, sifted
3 drops vanilla essence

Lightly whisk the egg whites and salt together until they are foamy, but not stiff.

Whisk in the icing sugar 5 ml (1 teaspoon) at a time, making sure that each spoonful has dissolved before adding the next one. Whisk in the vanilla essence.

Place the bowl with the egg whites over a pan of tepid water set on a low heat. Whisk the mixture for about 8 minutes until it thickens and will leave a thick trail.

The meringue is now ready to use for piping baskets and nests.

Meringue Italienne

175 g (6 oz) sugar
75 ml (3 fl oz) water
2 egg whites

Put the sugar and water in a saucepan over a low heat. Cook, stirring constantly, until the sugar has dissolved. Increase the heat to moderate and bring the mixture to the boil. Continue boiling until the temperature registers 138°C (290°F) on a sugar thermometer, or until a small amount of syrup dropped into cold water forms a hard ball.

Meanwhile, whisk the egg whites until they form stiff peaks.

Pour the syrup in a slow, steady stream on to the egg whites, whisking constantly. Continue whisking until they form stiff, glossy peaks. The meringue is now ready to use.

American Meringue

4 egg whites
250 g (9 oz) caster sugar
3–4 drops vanilla essence
5 ml (1 teaspoon) malt vinegar
20 ml (4 teaspoons) cornflour

Line a 20-cm (8-in) loose-bottomed cake tin with non-stick baking paper and brush with a little vegetable oil.

Whisk the egg whites until they form stiff peaks. Whisk in the sugar, 15 ml (1 tablespoon) at a time, making sure that each spoonful has dissolved before adding the next one. Whisk in the vanilla essence, vinegar and cornflour.

Pile the mixture into the prepared tin. Level the top and make a slight indentation in the middle.

The meringue is now ready for baking. It requires a considerably hotter oven than the other types of meringue, taking about 40 minutes to cook at 180°C, 350°F, Gas 4. Peel away the paper when it is cooked and cool on a wire rack. Serve it filled with cream and fresh fruit, ice-cream or a flavoured cream mixture of your choice.

Meringue Cake with Chestnuts

Serves 6
6 egg whites
pinch of salt
375 g (13 oz) caster sugar
10 ml (2 teaspoons) malt vinegar
22.5 ml (1½ tablespoons) cornflour
2–3 drops vanilla essence
225 g (8 oz) canned sweetened chestnut purée
425 ml (15 fl oz) double cream, stiffly whipped
4 marrons glacés, sliced

Preheat the oven to 180°C, 350°F, Gas 4. Line two loose-bottomed cake tins, 20 cm (8 in) in diameter, with non-stick baking paper and brush with a little vegetable oil.

Whisk together the egg whites and salt until they form stiff peaks. Whisk in the sugar, 15 ml (1 tablespoon) at a time. Whisk in the vinegar, cornflour and vanilla essence.

Using a piping bag with a 2.5-cm (1-in) star nozzle, pipe six meringue shells on to the baking sheet. This will require about one-third of the mixture. Divide the remaining mixture equally between the two prepared tins.

Bake the shells and the cakes for 40 minutes, putting the shells at the bottom of the oven. Peel away the paper and cool the meringue on wire racks.

Mix together the chestnut purée and two-thirds of the cream and use most of it to sandwich the cakes together.

Arrange the shells on top of the cake, using the remainder of the cream to stick them in place. With the remaining cream, pipe rosettes between the shells and arrange the marrons glacés in the centre of the cake.

Meringue Basket with Flambéed Peaches

Serves 6
1 quantity meringue cuite (*see page 56*)
30 ml (2 tablespoons) double cream, stiffly whipped
FILLING:
3 large peaches, skinned, halved and stoned
350 ml (12 fl oz) white wine
1 × 22.5 cm (9 in) sponge cake
50 ml (2 fl oz) orange juice
350 ml (12 fl oz) rich vanilla ice-cream (*see page 10*), slightly softened
50 ml (2 fl oz) orange-flavoured liqueur

Preheat the oven to 110°C, 225°F, Gas ¼. Line three baking sheets with non-stick baking paper and draw three circles 25 cm (10 in) in diameter on the paper.

Fill a forcing bag, fitted with a 12-mm (½-in) plain nozzle, with the meringue. Pipe a 25-cm (10-in) circle on one baking sheet. Gradually fill in the centre. Pipe two 25-cm (10-in) rings on the other baking sheets.

Bake as close to the bottom of the oven as possible for 2–2½ hours, or until the meringue is crisp and dry.

Poach the peach halves in the white wine for 15 minutes. Drain and set aside to cool.

Remove the circles from the oven and gently peel away the baking paper. Transfer the circles to wire racks to cool.

Place the solid circle on a serving plate. Spread half the cream around the edge. Place one ring on this and spread its top with the remaining cream. Place the remaining ring on top.

Trim the sponge cake to fit inside the meringue basket, then put it on a plate and pour over the orange juice. Set aside for 30 minutes.

Carefully transfer the soaked sponge into the meringue basket. Spread over the ice-cream to make a smooth surface and arrange the peach halves on top.

Put the orange liqueur into a saucepan over low heat, until it is hot but not boiling. Pour over the peaches and ignite. Take to the table and serve immediately the flames have died down.

Chestnut Meringue Basket

Serves 6–8
4 large egg whites
pinch of cream of tartar or salt
250 g (9 oz) icing sugar, sifted
3 drops of vanilla essence
FILLING:
100 g (4 oz) plain chocolate
50 g (2 oz) unsalted butter, softened
100 g (4 oz) caster sugar
grated zest of 1 orange
450 g (1 lb) canned unsweetened chestnut purée
30 ml (2 tablespoons) brandy
DECORATION:
75 ml (5 tablespoons) double cream, softly whipped
chocolate caraque (*see page 116*)

Chestnut Meringue Basket

Preheat the oven to 140°C, 275°F, Gas 1. Line two baking sheets with non-stick baking paper.

Whisk the egg whites with the cream of tartar or salt until stiff, then whisk in the icing sugar 15 ml (1 tablespoon) at a time. Whisk in the vanilla essence at the same time.

Place the bowl over a saucepan of simmering water making sure the bowl does not touch the water. Continue whisking until the meringue is very thick and stiff; it should hold its shape when you lift up the whisk. Keep the whisk moving round the sides and bottom of the bowl or else the meringue will cook.

Fill a piping bag fitted with a plain nozzle with the meringue and pipe a solid 23-cm (9-in) circle on one of the baking sheets. Mark out a circle the same size on the other sheet, and put the remainder of the meringue into a piping bag fitted with a 25-mm (1-in) star nozzle. Pipe a 23-cm (9-in) decorative ring with this.

Make the filling: break the chocolate into small pieces and melt in the top of a double boiler. Beat the butter in a bowl until it is pale and creamy, then beat in the sugar and orange zest. Pour in the melted chocolate and add the chestnut purée and brandy. Beat everything together well.

Bake the meringue in the oven for about 1½ hours. Peel off the paper and cool on a wire rack.

Use the whipped cream to stick the decorative ring to the circle. Then spoon the filling into the centre and chill for about 1 hour before serving. Decorate with the chocolate caraque.

Almond and Apricot Meringue Cake

Serves 6
100 g (4 oz) dried apricots
425 ml (15 fl oz) lukewarm strained tea
4 egg whites
pinch of salt
250 g (9 oz) caster sugar
5 ml (1 teaspoon) malt vinegar
2–3 drops vanilla essence
75 g (3 oz) ground almonds
50 g (2 oz) extra caster sugar
150 ml (5 fl oz) water
10 ml (2 teaspoons) lemon juice
425 ml (15 fl oz) double cream, softly whipped
25 g (1 oz) plain dark chocolate, grated

Soak the apricots in the tea for 8 hours, or overnight.

Preheat the oven to 180°C, 350°F, Gas 4. Line two loose-bottomed cake tins, 20 cm (8 in) in diameter with non-stick baking paper and brush with a little vegetable oil.

Whisk together the egg whites and the salt until they form stiff peaks. Whisk in the caster sugar, 15 ml (1 tablespoon) at a time. Whisk in the vinegar and the vanilla essence, then fold in the almonds.

Divide the mixture equally between the two prepared tins. Bake for 40 minutes.

Meanwhile, transfer the apricots and soaking liquid to a medium-sized saucepan over low heat and stew for 15 minutes. Put the sugar, water and lemon juice in a small saucepan over low heat. Bring to the boil, stirring constantly, and boil for 2 minutes. Remove from the heat and cool.

When the apricots are tender, purée them in an electric blender or by rubbing them through a sieve. Stir one-third of the purée into two-thirds of the whipped cream and set aside.

Gently peel the paper away from the meringue cakes. Cool them on wire racks.

Sandwich the cakes together with the apricot cream. Pipe rosettes of cream around the edge and sprinkle over a little grated chocolate.

Stir the remaining apricot purée into the cold lemon syrup to make a sauce and serve this separately.

Hazelnut Meringue Cake with Raspberry Sauce

Serves 6
4 egg whites
pinch of salt
250 g (9 oz) caster sugar
5 ml (1 teaspoon) malt vinegar
2–3 drops vanilla essence
100 g (4 oz) ground hazelnuts
275 ml (½ pint) double cream, softly whipped
450 g (1 lb) fresh or frozen raspberries
60 ml (4 tablespoons) icing sugar, sifted

Preheat the oven to 180°C, 350°F, Gas 4. Line two loose-bottomed cake tins, 20 cm (8 in) in diameter with non-stick baking paper and brush with a little vegetable oil.

Whisk together the egg whites and salt until they form stiff peaks. Whisk in the sugar, 15 ml (1 tablespoon) at a time. Whisk in the vinegar and the vanilla essence, and fold in the hazelnuts.

Divide the mixture equally between the two prepared tins and bake for 40 minutes. Peel away the paper and cool the cakes on wire racks.

Reserve a little cream for the decoration. Spread the remainder over one of the cakes. Top with half the raspberries and place the other cake on top.

Reserve 10 raspberries for decoration. Rub the remainder through a sieve, and stir the icing sugar into the purée.

Pipe rosettes of cream around the top of the cake and decorate with the reserved raspberries. Serve with the sauce separately.

Strawberry Meringue Basket

(Illustrated on page 46)
Serves 6
1 quantity meringue cuite (*see page 56*)
275 ml (½ pint) double cream
30 ml (2 tablespoons) caster sugar
450 g (1 lb) strawberries, hulled and halved

Preheat the oven to 140°C, 275°F, Gas 1. Line baking sheets with non-stick baking paper and brush with vegetable oil. Mark two 20-cm (8-in) diameter circles.

Fill a piping bag with a star nozzle and pipe 2 solid circles on the baking sheets. Bake the meringue in the oven for about 1½ hours, until dry and crisp. Peel off the paper and cool on a wire rack.

When ready to serve, whip the double cream and sweeten it with the sugar. Use a little to sandwich the circles together. Pipe a decorative border round the top circle, then pipe any remaining cream into the centre and smooth it with a palette knife. Arrange the strawberries over this, and serve.

Raspberry and Meringue Delight

Serves 6–8
1 quantity meringue cuite (*see page 56*)
275 ml (½ pint) double cream
175 ml (6 fl oz) single cream
30 ml (2 tablespoons) Tia Maria
350 g (12 oz) raspberries, hulled and washed
50 g (2 oz) grated chocolate

Preheat the oven to 110°C, 225°F, Gas ¼. Line a baking sheet with non-stick baking paper and brush with a little vegetable oil.

Fill a piping bag, fitted with a 12-mm (½-in) plain nozzle, with the meringue. Pipe a solid circle 25 cm (10 in) in diameter (mark this out on the paper first). Pipe a ring of meringue on top of the circle round the edge, and then another ring on top of this, to form the sides of the basket. Bake in the bottom of the oven for 2–2½ hours. Peel off the paper and cool on a wire rack.

Put the meringue basket on a serving dish. Whisk together the creams and the Tia Maria until the mixture forms stiff peaks. Spread the flavoured cream over the bottom of the basket. Arrange the raspberries on top and sprinkle over the chocolate.

Raspberry Meringue Tower

Serves 10–12
8 egg whites
2 pinches of salt or cream of tartar
450 g (1 lb) caster sugar
575 ml (1 pint) double cream, stiffly whipped
350 g (12 oz) raspberries, hulled and washed
angelica

Preheat the oven to 110°C, 225°F, Gas ¼. Line two baking sheets with non-stick baking paper and brush with a little vegetable oil.

Prepare the meringue in two batches. Whisk together 4 egg whites and 1 pinch of salt or cream of tartar until they form stiff peaks. Whisk in 100 g (4 oz) of the sugar. Fold in a further 100 g (4 oz).

Using a piping bag with a large, plain nozzle, pipe three solid circles on the prepared baking sheets; one 23 cm (9 in) in diameter, the second 12 cm (5 in) in diameter and the third 7.5 cm (3 in) in diameter. Bake for 2½–3 hours. Peel away the paper and set the meringue circles aside on wire racks to cool.

Reline the baking sheets and make a second batch of meringue, in exactly the same way as the first, using the remaining egg whites and sugar.

Using a piping bag with a large, plain nozzle, pipe one solid circle, 18 cm (7 in) in diameter, on one of the prepared baking sheets. Then using a piping bag with a star nozzle, pipe 24 shells with the remaining meringue mixture on the second prepared sheet. Bake for 2½–3 hours. Peel away the paper and cool the meringue circle and shells on wire racks.

Mix together half the cream and half the raspberries.

Put the largest meringue circle on a serving plate. Arrange 10 meringue shells around the edge, 2.5 cm (1 in) away from the rim. Spread a little raspberry cream in the centre.

Place the 18-cm (7-in) meringue circle on top. Spread a little raspberry cream in the centre and arrange 8 meringue shells around the edge. Cover with the 12-cm (5-in) circle. Spread the remaining raspberry cream in the centre and arrange the remaining meringue shells around the edge. Top with the smallest circle.

Using the remaining cream, pipe a shell on the top circle and one rosette of cream between the meringue shells on each layer. Place one raspberry and two angelica 'leaves' on each rosette of cream.

Fruit Nests

Serves 8
1 quantity meringue cuite (*see page 56*)
425 ml (15 fl oz) double cream, stiffly whipped
4 peaches, skinned, halved and stoned
100 g (4 oz) strawberries, washed and hulled
45 ml (3 tablespoons) redcurrant jelly

Preheat the oven to 110°C, 225°F, Gas ¼. Line two baking sheets with non-stick baking paper and brush with a little vegetable oil.

Using a piping bag with a 12-mm (½-in) plain nozzle, pipe eight solid circles, 10 cm (4 in) in diameter. Then, using a 12-mm (½-in) star nozzle, pipe a thick ring of meringue around the edges of the circles to make sides.

Bake on the bottom shelf of the oven for about 2 hours, until the nests are dry and crisp. Peel away the paper and cool meringues on a wire tray.

Spread a generous amount of the cream over the base of each meringue nest.

Cut each peach half into four slices. Arrange four slices in each nest, so that a space is left in the middle. Fill this with a strawberry or two.

Put the redcurrant jelly in a small saucepan over low heat to melt. Brush a little over the fruit to glaze.

Coffee Meringues with Hazelnut Cream

Serves 8
15 ml (1 tablespoon) coffee essence
1 quantity meringue suisse (*see page 56*)
100 g (4 oz) hazelnuts, very finely chopped
275 ml (½ pint) whipping cream, stiffly whipped

Preheat the oven to 110°C, 225°F, Gas ¼. Line two baking sheets with non-stick baking paper and brush with a little vegetable oil.

Lightly stir the coffee essence into the meringue mixture, then arrange it in 16 mounds on the prepared baking sheets, smoothing each one into a good rounded shape with a wet palette knife.

Put in the bottom of the oven and bake for 2½ hours, or until the meringues are firm, dry and pale coffee-coloured. If they seem to be getting too dark, turn off the heat and leave the oven door ajar. Peel off the paper and cool the shells on a wire rack.

Fold two-thirds of the chopped nuts into the cream and use to sandwich the meringues together in pairs. Press the remaining nuts into the sides of the filling.

Meringues with Rum and Chocolate

Serves 8
1 quantity meringue suisse (*see page 56*)
275 ml (½ pint) double cream
45 ml (3 tablespoons) rum
100 g (4 oz) plain dark chocolate, broken into pieces
15 ml (1 tablespoon) butter, cut into small pieces

Preheat the oven to 110°C, 225°F, Gas ¼. Line two baking sheets with non-stick baking paper and brush with a little vegetable oil. Arrange the meringue mixture in 16 mounds on the prepared sheets, smoothing each one into a good rounded shape with a wet palette knife.

Put in the bottom of the oven and bake for 2½ hours, or until they are firm and dry. If they begin to colour too much, turn off the heat and leave the oven door ajar. Peel off the paper and cool on wire racks.

Whisk the cream until it is thick. Add 30 ml (2 tablespoons) of the rum and continue whisking until the mixture is stiff.

Sandwich the meringue halves together with the rum-flavoured cream. Arrange them on a serving plate.

Put the chocolate and the remaining rum in a small saucepan over low heat. As soon as the chocolate has melted, remove the pan from the heat and beat in the butter, one piece at a time, until it has all been absorbed. Trickle a little chocolate sauce over each meringue and serve immediately.

Chocolate Chinchilla

Serves 6
6 egg whites
pinch of salt
225 g (8 oz) caster sugar
50 g (2 oz) powdered drinking chocolate, sifted
5 ml (1 teaspoon) ground cinnamon, sifted

Preheat the oven to 180°C, 350°F, Gas 4. Grease a 1.1-litre (2-pint) oven dish with a little butter.

Whisk together the egg whites and the salt until they form stiff peaks, then beat in half the sugar. Fold in the remaining sugar in two batches. Fold in the chocolate powder and the cinnamon.

Pile the meringue mixture into the prepared dish and bake for 45 minutes, or until well risen.

Set the dish aside in a draught-free place to cool before serving.

Strawberry Baked Alaska

Serves 6
1 × 25-cm (10-in) diameter sponge cake
15 ml (1 tablespoon) sherry
350 g (12 oz) strawberries, washed, hulled and sliced
4 egg whites
pinch of salt
225 g (8 oz) caster sugar
575 ml (1 pint) strawberry ice-cream

Preheat the oven to 230°C, 450°F, Gas 8.

Put the sponge on an ovenproof serving dish and sprinkle it with the sherry. Pile the strawberries on top, keeping them about 1.25 cm (½ in) in from the edge.

Whisk together the egg whites and salt until they form soft peaks. Gradually whisk in one-quarter of the sugar, then fold in the remainder in two batches.

Working quickly, slice the ice-cream and arrange it in a dome-shape over the strawberries. Spread the meringue mixture over the top, making sure that all the ice-cream and the sides of the sponge are covered.

Bake in the centre of the oven for 4 minutes, or until the meringue is lightly browned. Serve immediately.

Meringue Ice-cream

Serves 6–8
2 ripe bananas, peeled
2 drops vanilla essence
275 ml (½ pint) double cream, chilled
125 ml (4 fl oz) single cream, chilled
75 g (3 oz) icing sugar, sifted
meringue suisse made with 2 egg whites (*see page 56*),
cooked, cooled and broken into walnut-sized pieces

If using the refrigerator rather than a freezer, turn it to its coldest setting. Grease a 1.1-litre (2-pint) bowl with a little butter.

Mash together the bananas and vanilla essence until smooth.

Whisk together the double and single cream until thick, but not stiff. Add the sugar and mashed bananas and whisk until smooth. Add the meringue pieces and any crumbs. Stir gently until the ingredients are evenly combined.

Transfer the mixture to the prepared bowl and smooth the top with the back of a spoon. Cover with foil and freeze for 2 hours or until firm.

Apple and Ginger Cloud

Serves 4
3 cooking apples, peeled, cored and chopped
15 ml (1 tablespoon) water
50 g (2 oz) sugar
50 g (2 oz) preserved ginger, sliced
2 egg whites
pinch of salt
30 ml (2 tablespoons) caster sugar

Put the apples, water and sugar in a saucepan over low heat and simmer for 10 minutes, or until soft. Remove from the heat and purée the apples by rubbing through a sieve.

Stir the sliced ginger into the purée and transfer the mixture to a flameproof serving dish. Set aside to cool.

Preheat the grill to high.

Whisk together the egg whites and salt until they form stiff peaks. Gradually whisk in the caster sugar.

Pile the meringue mixture in the centre of the apple purée and grill for 1 minute, or until the meringue turns very pale gold. Serve immediately.

Pavlova

Serves 6
4 egg whites
pinch of salt
225 g (8 oz) caster sugar
10 ml (2 teaspoons) malt vinegar
20 ml (4 teaspoons) cornflour
2–3 drops vanilla essence
275 ml (½ pint) whipping cream, stiffly whipped
100 g (4 oz) strawberries, washed and hulled
6 slices pineapple, chopped
2 passion fruit, peeled and chopped

Preheat the oven to 180°C, 350°F, Gas 4. Line a baking sheet with non-stick baking paper and brush with a little vegetable oil.

Whisk together the egg whites and salt until they form stiff peaks. Whisk in the sugar, 15 ml (1 tablespoon) at a time, then whisk in the vinegar, cornflour and the vanilla.

Pile the mixture on to the prepared baking sheet to form a solid circle, slightly hollowing the centre with a spatula. Bake in the bottom of the oven for 40 minutes or until the outside is lightly coloured. Peel away the paper and cool the cake on a wire rack.

Transfer the cake to a serving dish. Pile the cream into the centre and arrange the fruit on top.

Pavlova with Lemon Filling

Serves 6
Pavlova meringue case (*see recipe below left*)
FILLING:
4 egg yolks
50 g (2 oz) caster sugar
4 tablespoons lemon juice
1 tablespoon grated lemon zest
175 ml (6 fl oz) whipping cream
extra lemon zest for decoration

Make the Pavlova meringue case as described below left. Leave to cool.

To make the filling, put the egg yolks in a large bowl and whisk until foamy. Add the caster sugar, lemon juice and zest, and set the bowl over a pan of hot but not boiling water. Stir the mixture until it is thick and smooth. It should slide off the spoon, rather than trickle from it; this will probably take about 10 minutes. Leave to go cold.

When ready to serve, whip the cream until it will stand in soft peaks and fold in the lemon mixture. Spoon into the meringue case, decorate with a little extra lemon zest and serve.

Pavlova with Fruit and Lemon Filling

Australian Apple Meringue Tart

Serves 6
900 g (2 lb) cooking apples, peeled, cored and chopped
25 g (1 oz) butter
15 ml (1 tablespoon) water
100 g (4 oz) sugar
75 ml (3 tablespoons) mincemeat or apricot jam
2.5 ml (½ teaspoon) ground cinnamon
1 × 22-cm (8½-in) pastry case, baked blind (*see page 85*)
2 egg whites
pinch of salt
100 g (4 oz) caster sugar
10 ml (2 teaspoons) cornflour
2 drops vanilla essence
5 ml (1 teaspoon) malt vinegar
25 g (1 oz) almonds, blanched and split

Put the apples, butter, water and sugar in a saucepan over low heat and simmer for 10–15 minutes, or until soft. Remove from the heat and purée the apples in an electric blender or by rubbing them through a sieve. Preheat oven to 140°C, 275°F, Gas 1.

Put the purée, mincemeat or jam and cinnamon into a saucepan over a moderate heat. Cook, stirring constantly, until all the purée is thick and stiff. Spoon into the pastry case and smooth the top.

Whisk together the egg whites and salt until they form stiff peaks. Whisk in the caster sugar, 15 ml (1 tablespoon) at a time, then whisk in the cornflour, vanilla essence and vinegar.

Pile the meringue mixture on top of the apple, spreading it out to ensure that it joins the edge of the pastry. Fluff it into peaks with the handle of a spoon. Stick the almonds upright into the meringue spacing them evenly.

Bake for 1 hour, or until just coloured. Serve hot or cold with chilled pouring cream.

Floating Islands with Coffee-flavoured Custard

Floating Islands

Serves 4–6
425 ml (15 fl oz) milk
275 ml (½ pint) single cream
100 g (4 oz) plus 30 ml (2 tablespoons) caster sugar
1 vanilla pod, split lengthways
10 ml (2 teaspoons) cornflour
4 eggs, separated
575 ml (1 pint) water
pinch of salt

Put 275 ml (½ pint) of the milk in a medium-sized pan, with the cream, the 30 ml (2 tablespoons) of caster sugar and the vanilla pod. Put on a medium heat and bring to just below boiling point. Remove from the heat, cover and set aside for 10 minutes.

Remove the vanilla pod. Blend 15 ml (1 tablespoon) of the milk mixture with the cornflour and stir this into the remaining milk mixture, return the pan to the heat and bring the mixture to the boil, stirring constantly. Reduce the heat to low and simmer for 2–3 minutes still stirring.

Meanwhile, prepare a double boiler with hot, but not boiling, water. Put the egg yolks into the top and beat until just frothy. Add the milk mixture in a thin stream, beating constantly. Set over a low heat and cook the mixture, stirring constantly, until the sauce is thick and will coat the back of the spoon. Remove from the heat and cool, stirring occasionally to prevent a skin forming.

Put the water and the remaining milk in a wide, deep frying-pan. Whisk the egg whites with the salt until they form stiff peaks. Whisk in the remaining sugar, 15 ml (1 tablespoon) at a time.

Put the frying-pan over medium heat and bring the liquid to the boil. Reduce the heat to low, so that the liquid is just simmering. Shape 15 ml (1 tablespoon) of the meringue mixture into a mound with a knife and drop it into the milk and water mixture. Repeat three more times. Poach the 'islands' for 4 minutes, turning with a palette knife halfway through so that all sides are evenly cooked.

Remove the 'islands' with a slotted spoon and set aside on a wire rack or kitchen paper towels to drain. Cook the remaining meringue mixture in the same way draining each 'island' well.

Pour the sauce into a serving dish and arrange the meringue 'islands' on top. Chill in the refrigerator for 30 minutes before serving.

*To make a coffee-flavoured custard as shown in the picture, make the custard as described in the recipe, then dilute 15 ml (1 tablespoon) instant coffee in 5 ml (1 teaspoon) boiling water and stir this into the custard.

Fruit

You need never be at a loss for a fresh, nourishing and tasty dessert. You can do just about anything with fruit—bake, grill, fry, poach and purée. Serve it on its own or with other ingredients. Keep it simple or be ultra-sophisticated. Hot and sweet, it's comforting in the winter, or cold and juicy, it's refreshing in the summer.

Fresh fruit offers endless opportunities for delicious, nutritionally-balanced, economic and really stunning desserts. Low in calories, high in vitamins, fruit is the ideal way to end family meals or more elaborate feasts. With the immense range of tropical and exotic fruits available all year round, the clever cook will never be at loss to provide a tempting treat for even the most jaded palate.

Choosing Fruit

Whatever fruit you are buying, be sure it is fresh and unblemished. Apples and pears should have shiny, unwrinkled and unblemished skins. Oranges, tangerines, satsumas, mandarins and clementines (avoid Seville oranges which are best used for marmalade) should feel firm and have shiny, bright and slightly oily skins. Melons should be free from bruises and 'give' slightly when pressed on the end opposite the stalk. Avoid bunches of grapes with any brownish-looking or squashed berries. The best bananas for slicing have bright yellow skins, lightly flecked with brown, but over-ripe bananas with black spots or patches may be cheap and are excellent for mashing. The colour of a pineapple skin is no guide to the fruit's freshness, but dark patches usually indicate that the pineapple is over-ripe. Always avoid heavily bruised stone fruit; light bruising can be cut away, if you are going to purée the fruit, and may indicate a bargain price. Wrinkled skin is a bad sign when buying peaches and apricots. Soft berries are often sold in punnets; avoid plastic punnets and straw punnets with excessive staining. Do not buy hulled strawberries.

Stewing and Poaching

Stewing and poaching are both methods of cooking fruit in liquid until it is tender, but not disintegrating. In either case, it is important that the fruit should be cooked slowly over gentle heat so that it retains its shape while becoming tender and sweet.

Most fruits can be cooked, by either of these methods, citrus fruits, melons, pineapples and grapes being the exceptions. Fruits particularly suitable for stewing are cooking apples, rhubarb, gooseberries, blackberries, bilberries, currants, loganberries and raspberries. Good fruits for poaching are cherries, cooking pears, quinces, peaches, apricots, plums, damsons and greengages.

When fruit is stewed, the liquid (water, fruit juice, cider or wine) is added before the bulk of the sweetener (white sugar, brown sugar or honey). Use the minimum amount of liquid required to cover the bottom of the pan. About 60 ml (4 tablespoons) water is sufficient for 450 g (1 lb) fruit. Very juicy fruit, such as blackcurrants or raspberries, requires no liquid at all. The amount of sweetener required depends upon the tartness of the fruit and on personal taste.

To stew fruit, prepare it and put it in a heavy-based saucepan or ovenproof casserole. Add a third of the sweetener, the liquid and any flavourings. Cover and cook over low heat or in an oven preheated to 180°C, 350°F, Gas 4. Half-way through the cooking time, taste and add the remaining sweetener, if required. Test fruit towards the end of the cooking time with the point of a knife to see if it is tender.

When poaching fruit, the sweetener and liquid are made into a syrup before the fruit is added. Further sweetener cannot, therefore, be added during cooking, so it is important to get the degree of sweetness right from the start. For 450 g (1 lb) apricots or peaches, use 75 g (3 oz) sugar or 15 ml (1 tablespoon) honey in 275 ml (½ pint) liquid. For 450 g (1 lb) cherries, gooseberries, pears, plums, damsons or quinces, use 100 g (4 oz) sugar or 22 ml (1½ tablespoons) honey in 275 ml (½ pint) liquid.

Put the sweetener and water in a saucepan over low heat and stir until the sweetener has dissolved. Bring to the boil and continue boiling for 3 minutes. Remove the pan from the heat and add any flavourings, such as cinnamon or chopped crystallized ginger. Lower the prepared fruit into the syrup and return to a very low heat.

Grilling and Baking

Grilling is a very quick method of cooking fruit. The surface is cooked and the fruit is heated through without spoiling the flavour and freshness.

Suitable fruit for grilling includes cooking and dessert apples, apricots, peaches, bananas, oranges and pineapple. Use only ripe fruit. Peel, core and slice apples. Skin, halve and stone apricots and peaches. Peel bananas and cut in half lengthways. Peel and slice oranges. Cut pineapple in slices.

To prevent the fruit drying out under the grill, brush with melted butter, flavoured with spices such as cinnamon or ground ginger, if you like. Alternatively, soak the fruit for 1 hour in fruit juice, wine, brandy or syrup from a jar of preserved ginger.

Adding sweetener is a matter of taste, but the addition of brown sugar or honey gives the fruit a most attractive appearance. Fruit slices can be tossed in a bag of brown sugar. To coat slices with honey, dip a knife in boiling water and use it to spread clear honey on both sides of the fruit.

Cook the fruit in a heatproof dish under a preheated moderate grill for a maximum of 5 minutes, turning once. Serve immediately.

Baking in an uncovered dish in the oven is a much slower process, but once the fruit is in the oven it requires no attention until serving time. It is an economical method of cooking fruit, too, if something else, such as a joint, is being cooked in the oven at the same time.

Most fruit, even when hard and unripe, can be baked. Particularly suitable fruits include cooking apples, apricots, peaches, bananas, cooking pears, plums, damsons and greengages.

Apples and pears require some liquid (water, syrup, wine, cider or fruit juice) to prevent them from sticking during cooking. Apricots, peaches and peeled bananas should be baked in a well buttered dish.

Apples and the stone cavities of apricots can be stuffed and this may provide adequate sweetness. Sliced pears are best cooked in a syrup. Bananas can be lightly sprinkled with brown sugar or spread with honey.

Preheat the oven to 180°C, 350°F, Gas 4 and bake the fruit on the centre shelf for the times shown below. If other things in the oven require a higher temperature, place the fruit dish right at the bottom of the oven.

Preparing Pineapple

1 *To prepare fresh pineapple slices, cut away the leafy foliage from the top and take a small slice from the bottom of the pineapple. Cut into 1.25-cm (½-in) thick slices, using a sharp, serrated knife with a long blade. Using the point of the knife, carefully remove all the woody 'eyes' from the edge of the flesh of each pineapple slice.*

2 *Cut away the skin, keeping as close to the flesh as possible. Stamp out the central core, using an apple corer.*

3 *To make a pineapple 'container', cut away the leafy foliage and take a small slice from the bottom. Insert a long, serrated knife blade between the skin and the flesh. Gently move the knife around the fruit to free the flesh. Remove from the 'shell'.*

4 *For pineapple 'halves', leaving the spiky top attached, cut the pineapple in half lengthways. Insert a sharp knife between the shell and the flesh of one half. Move the knife carefully round the half to loosen the flesh. Repeat with the other half. Dice the flesh and mix with other fruit. Serve in the shells.*

Cooking Fresh Fruit

Stewing Times

Fruit	Open heat	Oven
Apples (sliced)	10–12 mins	20 mins
Blackberries	10 mins	15–20 mins
Currants	10 mins	15–20 mins
Bilberries	10 mins	15 mins
Loganberries	10 mins	12–15 mins
Raspberries	10 mins	12–15 mins
Rhubarb*	10–15 mins	20–25 mins

*When stewing rhubarb, put it in the pan and sprinkle over the sugar. Set it aside for 1 hour for the juice to be drawn out and there is then no need to add any liquid.

Poaching Times

Fruit	Open heat	Oven
Apples (quartered)	15 mins	25 mins
Apricots	10–20 mins	25–30 mins
Cherries	20–30 mins	25–40 mins
Damsons	15–20 mins	25–30 mins
Gooseberries	20–30 mins	25–40 mins
Greengages	15–20 mins	25–30 mins
Peaches	15–20 mins	25–30 mins
Pears		
(whole)	40 mins	50–70 mins
(halved)	30 mins	40–45 mins
(quartered)	25 mins	35 mins
Plums		
(whole)	15–20 mins	25–30 mins
(halved)	10–15 mins	20–25 mins

Baking Times

Fruit	Oven
Apple	
(whole)	1 hour
(whole and stuffed)	45 minutes
(halved)	40 minutes
(quartered)	35 minutes
Apricots	30 minutes
Bananas	
(in skins)	30 minutes
(peeled)	20 minutes
Peaches	15 minutes
Pears	
(whole)	45–50 mins
(halved)	40–50 mins
(quartered)	35–45 mins

Sautéeing and Flambéeing Fruit

fruit (*see step 1*)
60 ml (4 tablespoons) brandy, rum or a liqueur to
225 g (8 oz) prepared fruit
50 g (2 oz butter) to 225 g (8 oz) prepared fruit
sweetener (*see step 4*) to taste
nuts, dried or candied fruit and cream, to decorate

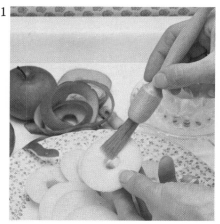

1 *First prepare the fruit. Peel, core and slice dessert apples; peel bananas and halve lengthways; prepare and slice pineapple (see opposite); halve and stone plums; skin, halve, stone and slice peaches. Put brandy, rum or liqueur into a small frying pan.*

2 *Melt the butter in a large frying pan over moderate heat. Put in as many slices as the pan will take in a single layer. Brown the fruit on both sides, turning it carefully with a fish slice and small palette knife. Drain on kitchen paper and keep warm.*

3 *Add more butter to the pan, if necessary, and cook the remaining fruit in the same way. Drain off excess fat. Set the pan of brandy, rum or liqueur over very low heat to warm. Do not allow it to boil or the alcohol will be lost and it will not set alight.*

4 *Return all the fruit to the pan. Sprinkle or spoon over the sweetener and any flavourings. You can use granulated, caster, vanilla or cinnamon sugar to give a light brown glaze or soft brown sugar for a darker glaze. Honey goes well with most fruit; use carefully—it is very sweet.*

5 *Remove the small frying-pan from the heat and ignite the spirit by holding the flame of a lighted match just above the liquid at the side of the pan. Standing well back, pour the burning spirit over the fruit. Do not hold the handle of the fruit pan.*

6 *Let the flames die down completely. Transfer the fruit and all the rich, sticky sauce to a warmed serving dish. Sprinkle over chopped nuts, dried or candied fruit and decorate with stiffly whipped cream. Alternatively, serve the cream separately.*

Flaming Fruit Kebabs with Cinnamon Orange Cream

Serves 8
90 ml (6 tablespoons) soured cream
15 ml (1 tablespoon) icing sugar, sifted
grated rind of 1 orange
15 ml (1 tablespoon) ground cinnamon
200 ml (7 fl oz) double cream, lightly whipped
16 large, stoneless prunes or 8 dessert plums, stoned
juice of 1 orange
juice of 1 lemon
60 ml (4 tablespoons) soft brown sugar
8 apricots or small peaches
2 small dessert pears
4 large, firm bananas
45 ml (3 tablespoons) brandy

Fold the soured cream, icing sugar, orange rind and 5 ml (1 teaspoon) of the cinnamon into the lightly whipped cream. Tip into a sauceboat, cover and chill.

If using prunes, put them in a small saucepan and cover with boiling water. Simmer for 10 minutes. Remove the pan from the heat and set aside for 40 minutes.

Mix together the orange juice, lemon juice, brown sugar and remaining cinnamon in a large mixing bowl.

If using peaches, blanch, skin, halve and stone them. Halve and stone apricots and plums (if using). Peel, quarter and core pears. Peel bananas and cut each into four. Put all the fruit into the mixing bowl as you prepare it.

Lightly toss the fruit to coat thoroughly with the juice mixture. Chill for 1 hour.

Drain prunes and macerated fruit. Thread pieces of fruit onto metal skewers, alternating them.

Preheat the oven to 200°C, 400°F, Gas 6.

Arrange the kebabs in a single layer in the centre of a very large, double thickness sheet of foil. Fold the sides and ends of the foil over the top and crimp to seal. Lay the parcel in a large ovenproof dish and bake for 10–15 minutes.

Remove the dish from the oven. Unwrap the parcel and transfer the kebabs to a serving dish.

Heat the brandy in a small saucepan. Pour over the fruit and ignite. Serve as soon as the flames die down, with the chilled sauce.

Party Oranges

Serves 6
12 small seedless oranges
150 g (5 oz) sugar
30 ml (2 tablespoons) brandy
12 cocktail sticks

Thinly pare the rind from 1 orange and reserve for julienne strips. Reserve 1 strip from another orange for flavouring the syrup.

Remove the rind and pith from all the oranges. Catch the juice in a plate and reserve.

Cut an orange into 4 slices across the fruit. Catch the juice in a plate and reserve. Using the tip of the knife remove the core of pith from the centre of each slice. Thread the slices on to a cocktail stick to re-form the orange shape.

Cut and re-form the remaining oranges in the same way. Arrange them in a single layer in a large, shallow dish.

Measure the reserved orange juice and make it up to 150 ml (5 fl oz) with water. Put the orange and water mixture in a small saucepan. Add the sugar and the reserved single strip of rind. Stir over low heat until the sugar has dissolved, then boil for 2 minutes. Remove from the heat and set aside to cool.

Cut the remaining orange rind into thin julienne strips. Put them in a small saucepan and cover with cold water. Bring to the boil. Turn off the heat and allow to stand for 30 seconds. Strain and refresh under cold running water. Transfer to a covered container and chill in the refrigerator.

Remove the strip of peel from the cool syrup and stir in the brandy. Pour the syrup over the oranges, cover and chill in the refrigerator for 2 hours.

Transfer the oranges to a serving dish, piling them into a pyramid. Pour over a little syrup and scatter over the julienne strips. Serve the remaining syrup separately.

Caramelized Grapes

Serves 6–8
450 g (1 lb) large, sweet, white grapes, skinned and seeded
125 ml (4 fl oz) maraschino
275 ml (½ pint) double cream
175 g (6 oz) brown sugar

Put the grapes in a shallow flameproof dish. Sprinkle over the maraschino and turn over with a spoon.

Beat the cream until it is thick and spread it over the grapes. Chill overnight in the refrigerator.

Preheat the grill to high.

Remove the dish from the refrigerator. Cover the cream with an even layer of sugar. Grill for 5–8 minutes, until the sugar melts. Serve immediately.

Caramelized Grapes

Quince Cream

Serves 4–6
4 quinces, peeled, cored and chopped
60 ml (4 tablespoons) water
2 eggs, separated
100 g (4 oz) icing sugar, sifted
200 ml (7 fl oz) double cream, lightly whipped
25 g (1 oz) almonds, blanched and split
25 g (1 oz) glacé cherries, halved
15 g (½ oz) candied angelica, thinly sliced

Put the quinces and water in a saucepan. Cover and cook over low heat for 15 minutes, until soft. Remove from heat.

Beat the quinces to a thick purée and then rub through a sieve. Return the purée to a clean saucepan and beat in the egg yolks, one at a time.

Set over a low heat and stir until the mixture thickens. Do not allow it to boil. Remove the pan from the heat and beat in the icing sugar. Set aside to cool completely.

Fold the lightly whipped cream into the purée. Stiffly whisk the egg whites and fold them into the purée. Pile the cream into a serving bowl and chill in the refrigerator for 1 hour.

Decorate the cream with the almonds, cherries and angelica and serve immediately.

Summer Fruit Salad

(Illustrated on page 66)
Serves 6–8
1 Cantaloupe or Galia melon
juice of 1 lemon
1 red-skinned apple
1 pear
1 orange
1 peach
50 g (2 oz) cherries, stoned
50 g (2 oz) strawberries, hulled and washed
8 sprigs of mint
DRESSING:
90 ml (6 tablespoons) pineapple juice
60 ml (4 tablespoons) lemon juice
1 egg, well beaten
75 g (3 oz) sugar
4 ml (¾ teaspoon) paprika

With a sharp, serrated knife, cut a horizontal sliver from the top of the melon. Then cut lengthwise into 6 or 8 sections to two-thirds of the melon's depth. Cut a very thin slice from the base, if necessary, so that the melon stands upright firmly. Carefully remove the seeds and membrane with a spoon.

Brush the melon sections with the lemon juice and reserve any remaining juice. Wrap the melon tightly in foil and chill until required.

Make the dressing. Put the pineapple juice, lemon juice, egg, sugar and paprika in the top of a double boiler and set over boiling water. Cook, whisking constantly, for 5 minutes, until the dressing is thick. Pour the dressing into a serving jug, cool and then chill.

Core and dice the apple. Place in a bowl with half the reserved lemon juice. Core and dice the pear and add to the apple. Mix well, cover with foil and chill in the refrigerator.

Peel the orange and remove the pith. Cut into slices and remove the pips and the pithy white core. Halve the slices and transfer to a bowl.

Blanch, peel, halve and stone the peach. Slice and add to the orange slices. Add the remaining lemon juice and toss the fruit lightly. Cover with foil and chill in the refrigerator. Chill the cherries and strawberries separately.

To serve, place the melon on a serving dish. Drain the apple and pear and mix all the fruit together. Pile the fruit into the centre of the melon, using any surplus to surround the base. Garnish with the mint sprigs and serve with the jug of dressing.

Exotic Fruit and Berry Salad

Serves 6
4 passion fruits
2 mangoes, peeled and sliced
225 g (8 oz) blueberries, washed
225 g (8 oz) loganberries, hulled and washed
225 g (8 oz) raspberries, hulled and washed
30 ml (2 tablespoons) sugar
juice and finely grated rind of 1 lime
5 ml (1 teaspoon) angostura bitters
5–7 mint sprigs

Halve the passion fruits and scoop out the flesh. Push through a sieve.

Combine the sieved passion fruit flesh with the mangoes, blueberries, loganberries and raspberries. Sprinkle over the sugar and the lime juice and rind and the angostura bitters. Lightly toss the fruit.

Reserve a few mint sprigs for garnish. Snip the remaining leaves from their stalks and cut into thin strips. Scatter over the fruit and toss the mixture.

Transfer the fruit mixture to a serving bowl and chill in the refrigerator for 2 hours.

Remove the bowl from the refrigerator, garnish with the reserved mint leaves and serve.

Fruit Salad à la Russe

Serves 8
2 ripe pears, peeled and cored
4 peaches, skinned, halved and stoned
juice of 2 oranges
½ pineapple, peeled, cored and cut into chunks
100 g (4 oz) grapes, seeded, or
4 kiwi fruit, peeled and cut into chunks
225 g (8 oz) raspberries or strawberries, hulled and washed
225 g (8 oz) red plums, halved and stoned
100 g (4 oz) sugar*
¼ bottle medium-dry Champagne or
sweet sparkling wine
DECORATION:
1 kiwi fruit

Cut the pears and peaches into chunks and put into a large shallow dish. Pour over the orange juice and toss the fruit to mix it and coat with the juice.

Add the pineapple, grapes or kiwi fruit chunks, half the raspberries or strawberries and the plums to the dish. Gently spoon it over to mix. Sprinkle over the sugar and set aside to macerate for 1–2 hours.

Rub the remaining raspberries or strawberries through a sieve to purée. Divide the purée between 8 large coupe glasses or individual serving dishes. Top with the fruit and the juice.

Top up the glasses with the Champagne or sparkling wine and chill in the refrigerator for 1 hour.

Remove the fruit salad from the refrigerator, garnish with the kiwi fruit slices and serve.

*Preferably vanilla sugar. Crush together 1 vanilla pod and 225 g (8 oz) sugar and then mix with a further 225 g (8 oz) sugar; store in an airtight container.

Fruit Salad a la Russe

Apricot Toasts

Serves 4
30 ml (2 tablespoons) apricot brandy
15 ml (1 tablespoon) orange juice
150 ml (5 fl oz) double cream, lightly whipped
8 ripe apricots
175 ml (6 fl oz) dry white wine
275 ml (½ pint) water
75 g (3 oz) caster sugar
100 g (4 oz) butter
8 slices white bread, crusts removed

Fold the brandy and orange juice into the whipped cream and set aside to chill in the refrigerator.

Peel, halve and stone the apricots, reserving the stones. Crack the stones to obtain the kernels.

Put the wine, water and sugar in a saucepan over low heat and stir to dissolve the sugar. Bring to simmering point and add the apricot halves and the kernels. Simmer for 3–4 minutes. Remove from the heat and set aside.

Melt half the butter in a frying-pan and fry half the bread until golden brown on both sides. Keep warm while you fry the remaining bread in the rest of the butter.

Divide the fried bread between 4 individual serving plates. Top each slice with apricot halves, half with the cavity side up and the other half with the cavity side down. Put a kernel in the exposed cavities. Spoon over a little syrup. Top with the chilled cream and serve immediately.

Apricot Toasts

Fig and Almond Roll

Serves 4–6
225 g (8 oz) dried figs
75 g (3 oz) blanched almonds
50 g (2 oz) icing sugar, sifted

Remove the stalks from the figs and cut into small pieces. Finely chop the almonds.

Pound them together in a mortar into a well-blended paste. Shape the mixture into a fat sausage and roll it in half the icing sugar.

Wrap the roll in foil and chill overnight.

Slice the roll thinly and dust the slices with the remaining icing sugar.

Bramble and Apple Dumplings

Serves 4
5 ml (1 teaspoon) butter
225 g (8 oz) shortcrust pastry (*see page 84*) or 350 g (12 oz) commercial frozen shortcrust pastry
4 small cooking apples, peeled and cored
20 ml (4 teaspoons) caster sugar
100 g (4 oz) blackberries, washed
1 small egg, beaten
4 cloves

Preheat the oven to 220°C, 425°F, Gas 7. Grease a baking sheet with the butter and set aside.

Divide the pastry into 4. Roll each piece out on a lightly floured board to 20-cm (8-in) squares.

Cut two opposite corners off each pastry square and set aside.

Stand each apple on a square of pastry and fill each core cavity with 5 ml (1 teaspoon) caster sugar and as many blackberries as you can fit in.

Dampen the edges of 1 pastry square with cold water. Then gather up the edges neatly to the top of the apple, moulding the pastry around the fruit. Press edges together firmly to seal. Repeat with the remaining dumplings.

Turn the dumplings, sealed edge down, on to the baking sheet. Pierce a hole in the top of each one.

Make 'leaves' from the reserved pastry trimmings and seal them on the dumplings with a little beaten egg. Pierce a clove in the centre as a stalk. Brush the dumplings with the remaining beaten egg, to glaze.

Bake for 15 minutes. Reduce the oven temperature to 180°C, 350°F, Gas 4 and continue baking for a further 30 minutes, until cooked. Serve hot or cold.

Raspberry and Oatmeal Cream

Serves 2
60 ml (4 tablespoons) medium oatmeal
275 ml (½ pint) double cream, chilled
1.5 ml (¼ teaspoon) vanilla essence
30 ml (2 tablespoons) caster sugar
225 g (8 oz) fresh raspberries, washed and hulled or canned raspberries, drained
2 mint sprigs

Preheat the grill to medium-low.

Spread the oatmeal over a baking tray and grill lightly. Remove from the heat and set aside.

Whip together the cream and the vanilla essence. Add the sugar 5 ml (1 teaspoon) at a time until the cream forms soft peaks.

Fold the oatmeal into the cream mixture.

Remove 8 raspberries for decoration and fold the remainder into the cream mixture.

Spoon into 2 individual serving dishes and decorate with the reserved raspberries and the mint sprigs. Serve immediately.

Bananas Foster

Serves 4
50 g (2 oz) unsalted butter
75 g (3 oz) soft brown sugar
1.5 ml (¼ teaspoon) ground cinnamon
large pinch freshly grated nutmeg
125 ml (4 fl oz) dark rum
4 firm, ripe bananas, peeled and sliced lengthways
vanilla ice-cream (optional)

Melt butter in a large shallow frying-pan set over a low heat. Stir in the sugar, cinnamon, nutmeg and half the rum. Add the bananas and cook until golden. Simmer for a further 2 minutes. Remove from the heat and transfer bananas to a warmed serving dish with a perforated spoon.

Heat the remaining rum in a small saucepan. Remove from the heat and ignite. Stir the flaming rum into the sugar mixture and then pour slowly over the bananas.

Serve warm with ice-cream, if wished.

Wheatmeal Plum and Sultana Cobbler

Serves 6–8
2 × 550-g (1¼-lb) cans red plums in syrup
TOPPING:
250 g (9 oz) wheatmeal self-raising flour
5 ml (1 teaspoon) salt
1.5 ml (¼ teaspoon) grated nutmeg
50 g (2 oz) lard
50 g (2 oz) Demerara sugar
75 g (3 oz) sultanas
200 ml (7 fl oz) plain yoghurt

Preheat the oven to 200°C, 400°F, Gas 6.

Drain the plums and reserve the syrup. Stone the plums and put them in a 1.4-litre (2½-pint) pie dish. Pour over enough syrup just to cover and set aside.

Put the flour, salt and nutmeg in a mixing bowl. Add the lard and rub in with the fingertips. Stir in the sugar and sultanas.

Make a well in the centre and pour in the yoghurt. Gradually incorporate the dry ingredients to form a soft dough.

Divide the dough into 8 and form them into 25-mm (1-in) thick rounds. Arrange them on top of the plums.

Bake for 35 minutes, until the scones are golden brown on top. Serve immediately.

Stuffed Baked Apples

Serves 6
6 large Bramley apples
25 g (1 oz) butter, cut into 6 pieces plus 10 ml (2 teaspoons) butter
125 ml (4 fl oz) dry cider
STUFFING:
100 g (4 oz) seedless raisins
150 g (5 oz) light brown sugar
2.5 ml (½ teaspoon) ground cinnamon
finely grated rind of ½ lemon
15 ml (1 tablespoon) lemon juice

Preheat the oven to 180°C, 350°F, Gas 4. Grease a large ovenproof dish with the 10 ml (2 teaspoons) butter and set aside.

Core each apple to within 1 cm (½ in) of the base. Score the skin horizontally around the middle of each one, then arrange them in the prepared dish.

To make the stuffing, mix together the raisins, sugar, cinnamon, lemon rind and juice. Divide the mixture evenly between the apples, pressing it down well into the cavities. Put a piece of butter on top of each apple and pour the cider around them carefully.

Bake, basting occasionally, for 45 minutes, until the apples are soft. Remove from the oven and serve immediately.

Rhubarb Roulade

Serves 6
700 g (1½ lb) rhubarb, wiped clean, trimmed and chopped
100 g (4 oz) sugar
45 ml (3 tablespoons) water
10 ml (2 teaspoons) butter
4 eggs, separated
50 g (2 oz) self-raising flour, sifted
50 g (2 oz) caster sugar
few drops red food colouring
30 ml (2 tablespoons) icing sugar, sifted
FILLING:
1 dessert apple, cored
finely grated rind and juice of ½ lemon
225 g (8 oz) cottage cheese, sieved
25 g (1 oz) caster sugar

Put the rhubarb, sugar and water in a saucepan over low heat. Cover and simmer until tender. Remove from the heat and set aside to cool completely.

Preheat the oven to 190°C, 375°F, Gas 5. Grease a 33 × 23-cm (13 × 9-in) Swiss roll tin with the butter and line with non-stick vegetable parchment.

Drain the rhubarb and mix with the egg yolks until blended. Stir in the flour, caster sugar and colouring. Stiffly whisk the egg whites and fold into the rhubarb mixture. Pour the mixture into the prepared tin and bake for 20–25 minutes, until springy to the touch.

Meanwhile, begin making the filling. Grate the apple and stir together with the lemon rind and juice. Set aside.

Lay a large sheet of greaseproof paper on top of a clean, damp tea-towel. Evenly sprinkle over the icing sugar. Remove the sponge from the oven and allow to cool in the tin for 10 minutes. Run a round-bladed knife around the sides to loosen it. Turn out on to the prepared paper.

Drain the apple and mix with the cheese and sugar. Spread the mixture over the sponge.

Roll up the sponge, from one short end with the aid of the paper. Press the join. Transfer to a serving plate, seam-side down and serve immediately.

Summer Fruit Loaf

Serves 6

450 g (1 lb) mixed blackcurrants and redcurrants, stripped
from stalks
225 g (8 oz) caster sugar
30 ml (2 tablespoons) water
450 g (1 lb) raspberries, hulled and washed
6 large thin slices white bread, crusts removed

Put the blackcurrants, redcurrants, sugar and water in
a saucepan over low heat and bring to the boil. Cover
and simmer for 5 minutes, stirring occasionally, until
the fruit is tender and the juices are flowing.

Add the raspberries and cook over very low heat for
2–3 minutes. Remove the pan from the heat. Strain the
fruit and reserve the juice.

Use 2 slices of bread to line the base of a 500-g (1-lb)
loaf tin. Use trimmings to fill any gaps which would
prevent the pudding holding its shape.

Spoon half the fruits and 60 ml (4 tablespoons) of the
reserved juice over the bread. Cover with another layer
of bread. Then spoon in the remaining fruits and a
further 60 ml (4 tablespoons) juice. Place the remaining bread on top and press down firmly.

Place a double layer of greaseproof paper on top of the
pudding. Weight it down and chill in the refrigerator
for 8 hours. Chill the remaining fruit juice separately.

To serve, uncover the pudding and run a rounded
knife blade around the sides to loosen it. Turn out on to
serving dish and spoon reserved juice over any uncovered areas. Serve the juice separately.

Summer Fruit Loaf

Poached Pears with Butterscotch Sauce

Poached Pears with Butterscotch Sauce

Serves 4
275 ml (½ pint) water
30 ml (2 tablespoons) golden syrup
7.5-cm (3-in) cinnamon stick
strip of lemon rind
4 firm dessert pears, peeled and cored
25 g (1 oz) walnuts, finely chopped
SAUCE:
60 ml (4 tablespoons) Demerara sugar
30 ml (2 tablespoons) golden syrup
25 g (1 oz) butter
15 ml (1 tablespoon) lemon juice
275 ml (½ pint) double cream
2 egg yolks, lightly beaten

Stir together the water, syrup, cinnamon and lemon rind in a saucepan over low heat until the syrup has melted. Bring to simmering point and add the pears.

Cook gently for 30 minutes until tender and transparent, but still firm. Remove from the heat and set aside to cool.

To make the syrup, put the sugar, syrup, butter and lemon juice in a saucepan over low heat until the mixture has melted. Set aside.

Put the cream in a saucepan and bring to just below boiling point. Stir the cream into the sugar mixture.

Beat 90 ml (6 tablespoons) of the cream mixture into the egg yolks. Stir this into the rest of the cream mixture in the saucepan and set over low heat. Cook, stirring constantly, until the mixture begins to thicken. Set aside to cool completely.

Transfer the pears, with a perforated spoon, to a serving dish. Spoon over the sauce and garnish with the walnuts. Serve immediately.

Rum Savarin with Cream and Fruit

Serves 10–12
225 g (8 oz) strong white plain flour
large pinch salt
30 ml (2 tablespoons) caster sugar
15 g (½ oz) fresh yeast
10 ml (2 teaspoons) lukewarm water
2 eggs, beaten
50 g (2 oz) unsalted butter, melted
10 ml (2 teaspoons) butter
RUM SYRUP:
225 g (8 oz) sugar
425 ml (15 fl oz) water
125–150 ml (4–5 fl oz) rum
GLAZE AND FILLING:
30 ml (2 tablespoons) rum
45 ml (3 tablespoons) apricot jam, sieved and dissolved in
15 ml (1 tablespoon) boiling water
275 ml (½ pint) double cream, lightly whipped
225 g (8 oz) mixed fruit or drained canned fruit, diced

Sieve the flour and salt into a large, warmed mixing bowl. Stir in the sugar.

Blend together the yeast and water and pour on to the flour. Add the eggs and melted butter and mix to a soft, slightly sticky dough.

Turn the dough on to a lightly floured surface and knead vigorously for 5 minutes, until it is smooth, elastic and no longer sticky. Shape into a ball and place in a lightly floured bowl. Cover with cling film or a clean damp cloth and set aside in a warm place for 1½–2 hours, until the dough has doubled in bulk.

Knock back the risen dough and form it into a long sausage.

Grease a 1.1-litre (2-pint) metal savarin or ring tin with the butter. Lightly press the dough evenly into the tin, pressing together firmly at the join. Cover loosely with cling film or a clean cloth and set aside in a warm place for 1½–2 hours, until the dough has risen almost to the top of the tin.

Preheat the oven to 190°C, 375°F, Gas 5.

Bake the savarin for 20 minutes, until well browned. Remove the tin from the oven and cover with foil. Return the tin to the oven and continue cooking for 10 minutes, until the savarin is just shrinking from the sides of the tin.

Meanwhile, make the rum syrup. Put the sugar and water in a saucepan over low heat and stir until the sugar has dissolved. Bring to the boil and continue boiling for 5 minutes. Set aside to cool slightly. Stir in the rum and set aside.

Remove the savarin from the oven and allow to cool in the tin for 5 minutes. Turn the savarin out on to a wire rack and prick it all over with a fine skewer.

Transfer the savarin to a deep dish, rounded side up. Slowly pour over the warm rum syrup. Set aside to soak, basting frequently, for 30 minutes, until the syrup is absorbed.

Transfer the savarin to a serving plate and sprinkle over the 30 ml (2 tablespoons) rum. Bring the apricot jam mixture to the boil and brush it over the entire surface of the savarin to glaze. Pile the cream into the centre of the savarin and arrange the fruit on top. Serve immediately.

Compôte of Cherries

Serves 4–6
1 kg (2¼ lb) fresh cherries
25 g (1 oz) caster sugar
5-cm (2-in) cinnamon stick
thinly pared rind of 1 orange
juice of ½ orange
150 ml (5 fl oz) dry red wine
30 ml (2 tablespoons) redcurrant jelly
10 ml (2 teaspoons) arrowroot
30 ml (2 tablespoons) water
60 ml (4 tablespoons) cherry brandy or Kirsch (optional)

Put the fresh cherries, sugar, cinnamon and a small piece of the orange rind in a saucepan. Cover and set over low heat until the juices begin to run. Remove from the heat and pour into a bowl. Reserve the cinnamon and discard the orange rind.

Cut the remaining orange rind into thin slices to make julienne strips. Put the julienne strips into a small saucepan and cover with cold water. Bring to the boil, turn off the heat and allow to stand for 30 seconds. Strain the julienne strips and refresh with cold running water. Set aside.

Put the reserved cinnamon and red wine into a saucepan and bring to the boil. Cook until the wine is reduced by about one quarter. Remove from the heat.

Beat the redcurrant jelly with a fork and stir it into the wine. When it has melted, stir in the orange juice. Drain the cherries and stir the syrup into the mixture.

Blend together the arrowroot and water and stir into the wine mixture. Bring to the boil, stirring constantly. Simmer, stirring constantly, for 1 minute.

Remove the pan from the heat and stir in the cherries, cherry brandy or Kirsch, if using, and the orange strips. Serve immediately, if serving hot. Otherwise, allow to cool, cover and chill for 1 hour. Serve with lightly whipped cream or Crème Chantilly (*see page 175*).

Peach Melba

Serves 4
225 g (8 oz) raspberries, washed
45–60 ml (3–4 tablespoons) icing sugar, sifted
2 peaches, skinned, halved and stoned
425 ml (15 fl oz) vanilla ice-cream
30 ml (2 tablespoons) toasted, slivered almonds

Rub the raspberries through a sieve into a heatproof bowl. Set the bowl over very low heat until the purée is just warm. Remove from the heat and beat in the sugar to taste.

Transfer the sauce to a covered container and chill for 1 to 2 hours.

Divide the ice-cream between 4 individual serving dishes and top with a peach half. Spoon one quarter of the sauce over each portion and decorate with the almonds.

Rhubarb Amber

Serves 4–6
175 g (6 oz) plain flour
pinch of salt
7.5 ml (1½ teaspoons) caster sugar
115 g (4½ oz) butter
1 egg yolk
2.5 ml (½ teaspoon) iced water
TOPPING:
450 g (1 lb) rhubarb, stewed with sugar, drained and puréed
5 ml (1 teaspoon) finely grated lemon rind
25 g (1 oz) butter, melted
2 eggs, separated
pinch of salt
50 g (2 oz) caster sugar

To make the pastry, sift together the flour and salt into a large mixing bowl and stir in the sugar. Add the butter and cut it into the flour with a palette knife, until mixture resembles fine breadcrumbs. Make a well in the centre. Beat together the egg yolk and water and pour into the well. Draw the dry ingredients into the egg mixture and mix to form a soft dough. Turn on to a lightly floured surface and knead briefly until smooth. Wrap in foil and chill in the refrigerator for at least 30 minutes.

Preheat the oven to 200°C, 400°F, Gas 6.

Remove the dough from the refrigerator and let it soften slightly. Roll out and line a 20-cm (8-in) fluted flan tin. Chill in the refrigerator for 10 minutes.

Line the pastry case with foil and dried beans and bake blind for 10 minutes. Remove the foil and beans and continue baking for a further 5 minutes.

Reduce the oven temperature to 180°C, 350°F, Gas 4.

Meanwhile, make the filling. Beat together the rhubarb, lemon rind, butter and egg yolks until smoothly blended.

Pour the rhubarb filling into the pastry case and bake for 15 minutes, until just set.

Meanwhile, whisk together the egg whites and the salt until stiff. Whisk in half the caster sugar. Reserve 5 ml (1 teaspoon) of the sugar and fold the remainder into the egg whites.

Pile the meringue over the rhubarb filling taking care to spread it to the edges so that it meets the pastry rim. Sprinkle over the reserved sugar. Bake for a further 10 minutes until the meringue is lightly browned. Serve warm.

Apricot Sudeoise

Serves 4–6
175 g (6 oz) caster sugar
425 ml (15 fl oz) plus 60 ml (4 tablespoons) water
strip of lemon peel
900 g (2 lb) fresh apricots, skinned, halved and stoned
15 g (½ oz) butter
7 blanched almonds, split in half
juice of ½ lemon
25 g (1 oz) powdered gelatine

Dissolve the sugar in the 425 ml (15 fl oz) water in a saucepan over low heat, stirring constantly. Bring to the boil and boil for 5 minutes. Remove from the heat. Add the lemon peel and set aside to cool slightly.

Put the apricots in the syrup and cook over moderate heat for 8 minutes, until tender. Reserve 14 apricot halves. Push the remaining apricots through a sieve or purée in a blender. Set aside.

Thoroughly grease an 850-ml (1½-pint) soufflé dish, cake tin or charlotte mould with the butter.

Put 1 almond half in the cavity of each reserved apricot half. Arrange the apricot halves, almond side down, in the bottom of the prepared dish. Set aside.

Put the remaining water and the lemon juice in a small saucepan and sprinkle over the gelatine. Set aside for 5 minutes to soften, then dissolve over a low heat (*see page 28*). Pour the gelatine into the apricot purée in a thin stream, stirring constantly. Set aside to cool.

When the purée is almost set, pour it into the prepared dish. Leave to set.

To set, dip the dish into hot water for 3 seconds and then invert on to a serving plate.

Italian Apricots

Serves 4
4 large apricots
15 g (½ oz) butter
50 g (2 oz) icing sugar
25 g (1 oz) ground almonds
75 g (3 oz) Ricotta cheese
5 ml (1 teaspoon) ground ginger

Skin, stone and halve the apricots. Reserve the stones.

Grease a flameproof dish with the butter and arrange the apricot halves, cavity sides up, in it. Set aside.

Mash together the sugar, almonds and cheese with a fork.

Preheat the grill to medium.

Crack the apricot stones with a hammer or nutcrackers. Skin the kernels and crush them with a rolling pin.

Stir the crushed kernels and ginger into the cheese mixture.

Pile the cheese mixure into the apricot cavities. Grill for 5 minutes and serve immediately.

Tudor Pears

Serves 4
4 large cooking pears
175 g (6 oz) caster sugar or
30 ml (2 tablespoons) honey
75 ml (3 fl oz) water
5 ml (1 teaspoon) lemon juice
200 ml (7 fl oz) medium red wine
4 cloves
5-cm (2-in) piece cinnamon stick

Peel the pears, leaving the cores and stalks intact. Arrange them, on their sides, top to tail in a shallow saucepan or casserole. Set aside.

Put the sugar or honey, the water and the lemon juice in a small saucepan. Bring to the boil over low heat, stirring constantly. Boil for two minutes.

Remove the pan from the heat and stir in the wine, cloves and cinnamon. Cover and cook over low heat for 40 minutes or bake in an oven, preheated to 180°C, 350°F, Gas 4, for about 50 minutes or until tender. Turn the pears halfway through the cooking time.

Remove the pears from the heat and transfer to individual serving dishes. Strain the syrup over the fruit. Cool, cover and chill in the refrigerator for 1 hour before serving.

Blackcurrant Creams

Serves 4
150 ml (5 fl oz) double cream
150 ml (5 fl oz) plain yoghurt
30 ml (2 tablespoons) caster sugar
100 g (4 oz) shortbread biscuits
5 ml (1 teaspoon) lemon juice
5 ml (1 teaspoon) cassis (optional)
75 g (3 oz) blackcurrant jam

Whip the cream until it will just hold its shape. Stir together the yoghurt and sugar until smooth. Lightly stir the yoghurt mixture into the cream and whip again.

Pound the shortbread biscuits to crumbs with a rolling pin or in a blender. Set aside.

Blend together the lemon juice, cassis (if using), and jam. Reserve 10 ml (2 teaspoons) of the mixture.

Put a layer of jam mixture in the bottom of 4 stemmed glasses. Cover with a layer of cream mixture and then a layer of crumbs. Repeat the layers until all the ingredients are used, ending with cream mixture.

Decorate the centre of each glass with 2.5 ml (½ teaspoon) of the reserved jam mixture. Chill for 1 hour before serving.

Pineapple flamed with Kirsch

Serves 4
1 medium to large pineapple
40 g (1½ oz) butter (see recipe)
60 ml (4 tablespoons) sugar
60 ml (4 tablespoons) Kirsch
15 ml (1 tablespoon) chopped, candied angelica

Cut the skin from the pineapple (*see page 68*). Cut the flesh into 1-cm (½-in) slices and stamp out the cores.

Melt 25 g (1 oz) of the butter in a large frying-pan over a high heat. Put as many pineapple slices as the pan will take in a single layer and brown them on both sides. Remove and keep warm, while you cook the remaining slices, adding more butter, if necessary.

Warm the Kirsch.

Return the pineapple slices to the pan and sprinkle over the sugar. Ignite the Kirsch and pour it over the pineapple.

As soon as the flames die down, transfer the contents of the pan to a warmed serving dish. Scatter over the angelica and serve immediately.

Pies, Flans & Tarts

Crisp and light pastry is the perfect dessert, whether made into a filling pie, an open tart or a crumbly double crust. It is quick and easy to make and the filling can be as simple or as elaborate as you like. Served hot or cold, it looks marvellous and tastes wonderful. A light touch is all you need to have an inexhaustible repertoire of mouthwatering desserts at your fingertips.

With a repertoire of pies and tarts, the imaginative cook has endless scope for mouthwatering desserts. As you will see on the following pages, the range and variation is immense.

Types of Pastry

Shortcrust Pastry (*basic recipe, see page 84*) is the easiest, quickest, cheapest and most adaptable type. It can be used for single crust and double crust pies, tarts, flans and tartlets.

Sweet Shortcrust Pastry (*page 86*) is a slight variation used mainly for flan cases to be filled by a variety of fruits. The very sweet-toothed can substitute this where basic shortcrust is specified in flan and tart recipes.

All-in-one Shortcrust Pastry (*page 86*) provides an easy introduction to pastry-making for the timid or an alternative method for those who have never mastered the rubbing-in method and have given up in despair. The resulting pastry is not quite as crisp and melt-in-the-mouth as traditional shortcrust, but it is a very fair substitute.

Puff Pastry (*page 86*) is probably the lightest and finest of all pastries and, hardly surprisingly, is quite the most time-consuming to make. It is not, however, difficult, although it has a reputation for being so. What is important is that you follow the method precisely and do not try to cut corners.

The methods for making other types of pastry are included in specific recipes.

Handling Pastry

The secret of success is to handle pastry, whatever the type, as lightly and as little as possible. Keep your hands cool by rinsing them in cold water and work in the coolest part of the kitchen. When rubbing-in use only the fingertips (that is, the coolest part of the hand), and for mixing and stirring use metal, rather than plastic, implements.

If, in spite of your efforts, the dough begins to turn oily, wrap it in greaseproof paper and chill in the refrigerator for a minimum of 30 minutes. In any case, always follow the instructions for resting the dough, leaving it in a cool place or chilling it in the refrigerator.

Chilling the dough is especially important with flaky and puff pastry, which are made by different, but related, methods. In both cases, fat and air are trapped between layers of dough and, in order to obtain the required lightness and delicacy, it is essential that the fat does not even begin to melt until it is actually in the oven.

When rolling dough out, always roll in the same direction and then turn the dough. Rolling backwards and forwards, from side to side or diagonally, results in uneven thicknesses.

Baking Blind

Some tart recipes require the pastry case to be partially or wholly cooked before the filling is added. This is necessary for a filling which does not require cooking at all, or for one which might sink into the uncooked pastry dough and make it soggy.

To bake blind, line the flan tin with the pastry (*see page 84*) and prick the base with a fork to prevent air bubbles forming. Cut a circle of foil (or greaseproof paper) 7.5 cm (3 in) larger than the diameter of the flan tin. Crumple it to soften and then place the foil circle in the pastry lined tin. Weigh the lining down with a layer of dried beans, making sure that there are plenty of these around the sides. Place the tin on a baking tray.

Bake on the shelf above the centre of the oven preheated to 200°C, 400°F, Gas 6, for 10 minutes. Remove the tin from the oven. Carefully lift out the foil and beans.

Return the tin to the oven and bake for a further 3–5 minutes until the pastry is just set, but not coloured, if partially baking; or for a further 5–10 minutes, until the pastry is dry and slightly brown if baking completely.

Remove the tin from the oven and allow the shell to cool completely inside the tin because it is very brittle when hot. Wait until it is cold before transferring to a serving plate.

To bake tartlets blind, follow the same procedure, cutting the foil or greaseproof paper 12 mm (½ in) larger than the hollows in the tartlet tins. Bake on the upper centre shelf of the oven preheated to 190°C, 375°F, Gas 5, for 10 minutes. Remove the foil and beans and bake for a further 3 minutes, if partially baking; or for a further 8 minutes, if baking fully.

Keep the beans for further baking blind in the future; they cannot, of course, be cooked and eaten. Special ceramic baking beans can be bought at kitchen shops and in department stores, if you prefer to use these.

Dishes, Plates and Tins

Single and double crust pies are baked in deep pie dishes. Traditionally, round dishes are used for sweet pies and oval dishes for savoury ones. More important than the shape of the dish, however, is the width of the rim. There must be plenty of room to seal the pastry, because it shrinks slightly during cooking and the pie will be spoiled if the crust and filling are all mixed up together. Pie dishes should be made of earthenware or ovenproof glass. (Metal dishes are only suitable for savoury pies.)

Double crust pies can also be baked individually in tartlet tins. These look like baking trays with a series of sloping-sided hollows—usually 6, 9 or 12. Note they are not the same as bun tins, which are unsuitable because of their shape.

Yorkshire Pudding tins are a perfectly good substitute. If the tins do not have a non-stick lining, they must be greased before use.

Open-plate tarts are baked on pie plates. Enamelled or plain metal is the most suitable material because it conducts the heat through to the underside of the pastry. Earthenware and ovenproof glass can be used, but are less satisfactory. Whatever the material, it is important that the rim of the plate is wide enough to provide a seal to prevent the pastry slipping back during cooking.

Pastry flans and tarts are always baked in flat-bottomed containers. The shaped flan tin used to make a sponge base is not suitable. A loose-bottomed tin is ideal because it facilitates removing the rather fragile pastry case without breaking it. Both French flan tins and English flan rings can be used, although the former are easier to handle and the fluted edge is extra decorative. Alternatively, you can cook and serve sweet tarts in the kind of porcelain or glass fluted dish often used for savoury quiches and flans.

Making Shortcrust Pastry

Makes 225 g (8 oz)
225 g (8 oz) plain flour
2.5 ml (½ teaspoon) salt
50 g (2 oz) butter
50 g (2 oz) lard
45–60 ml (3–4 tablespoons) iced water

1 Sift together the flour and salt into a cold glass or earthenware mixing bowl. Add the butter and lard. Using a round-bladed knife, 2 knives or a pastry blender, cut the fats into the flour until the mixture resembles coarse breadcrumbs.

2 Using your fingertips only, rub the fat into the flour until the mixture resembles fine breadcrumbs. Lift the mixture high each time and let it fall back into the bowl to aerate the mixture. Shake the bowl to bring the lumps to the surface and rub these in.

3 Sprinkle 15 ml (1 tablespoon) iced water over the surface of the mixture and stir this in with the round-bladed knife. Sprinkle another 15 ml (1 tablespoon) iced water over the surface and stir until the mixture clings together in small lumps.

4 Add another 15 ml (1 tablespoon) iced water and use the flat side of the blade to press the mixture into fairly large lumps. Finally, gather the dough together with your fingers, adding more water, if necessary. Knead lightly. Form the dough into a ball. Wrap in foil and chill for 30 minutes.

Lining a Flan Ring

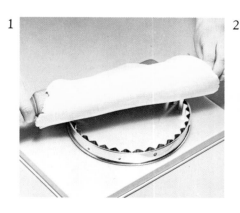

1 To line a flan ring, roll out the pastry to a circle 4 cm (1½ in) larger than the diameter of the ring. Place the ring on a metal baking sheet. Using the rolling pin, lift the pastry and centre it over the flan ring. Carefully unroll the pastry over the ring.

2 Gently press the pastry into the ring. Roll the pin over the surface to remove surplus pastry and neaten the rolled edge with a skewer.

Making a Single Crust Pie

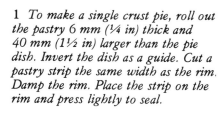

1 *To make a single crust pie, roll out the pastry 6 mm (¼ in) thick and 40 mm (1½ in) larger than the pie dish. Invert the dish as a guide. Cut a pastry strip the same width as the rim. Damp the rim. Place the strip on the rim and press lightly to seal.*

2 *If the pie filling is very soft and moist, stand an egg cup in the centre of the dish to prevent the pastry from becoming soggy. Place half the filling in the dish and sprinkle over sugar and any flavourings. Add the rest of the filling, piling it high in the centre.*

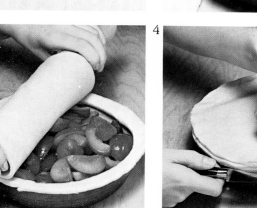

3 *Brush the pastry rim with water. Lift the pastry lid with the rolling pin and place it over the pie dish. Do not stretch the pastry. Press the lid and the pastry strip together and trim the edge by cutting with a sharp knife.*

4 *To seal the edge, hold the blunt side of a knife against the pastry edge. Press your forefinger against the inside of the rim of the dish. Gently tap the knife against the pastry edge, making 2 or 3 cuts in each place, all round the tin.*

5 *When the entire edge has been 'knocked up' and the pastry lid and rim are blended together, flute the edge with the blade of the knife. Hold the knife vertically and mark the edge by drawing up the blade lightly against it at intervals of 8 mm (⅓ in).*

6 *The steam produced while the filling is cooking must be allowed to escape, or the pastry will become soggy. Insert a knife under the pastry edge on one side of the dish and raise the pastry slightly. Repeat on the opposite side of the dish.*

Quantities

Home-made pastry dough is always measured by the quantity of flour. Thus, if a recipe calls for 225 g (8 oz) shortcrust pastry dough, this means dough made with 225 g (8 oz) flour. The actual dough will weigh 350 g (12 oz) because it will include 125 g (4 oz) fat.

However, if you are using frozen pastry this rule changes slightly. The recipe still refers to the dough in terms of the amount of flour. However, commercially made pastry dough, because of consumer legislation, is sold by total weight. Therefore, a recipe which requires 225 g (8 oz) shortcrust pastry dough will need 350 g (12 oz) commercially made frozen pastry.

All-in-One Shortcrust Pastry

Makes 225 g (8 oz)
100 g (4 oz) soft fat
2.5 ml (½ teaspoon) salt
45 ml (3 tablespoons) iced water
225 g (8 oz) plain flour, sifted

Put the fat, salt and water in a mixing bowl. Add about one-third of the flour and stir together for 30 seconds. Add the remaining flour and stir until the ingredients are thoroughly blended.

Gather the dough together with one hand and form it into a ball. Turn out and knead until smooth. Wrap in greaseproof paper and chill in the refrigerator for 30 minutes.

Sweet Shortcrust Pastry

Makes 225 g (8 oz)
225 g (8 oz) plain flour
30 ml (2 tablespoons) icing sugar
2.5 ml (½ teaspoon) salt
150 g (5 oz) butter, cut into small pieces
1 egg yolk
5 ml (1 teaspoon) lemon juice
15 ml (1 tablespoon) iced water

Sift together the flour, icing sugar and salt into a mixing bowl. Add the butter and cut it into the dry ingredients with 2 knives or a pastry blender until the mixture resembles coarse breadcrumbs. Rub the fat into the flour with the fingertips until the mixture resembles fine breadcrumbs.

Beat together the egg yolk, lemon juice and water. Sprinkle over the flour mixture and mix with a fork until the dough is beginning to hold together.

Lightly gather all the dough together into a ball, using one hand. Wrap the dough in greaseproof paper and a damp cloth and chill in the refrigerator for a minimum of 1 hour and up to 24 hours.

Puff Pastry

Makes 225 g (8 oz)
225 g (8 oz) plain flour
90–105 ml (6–7 tablespoons) iced water
5 ml (1 teaspoon) salt
15 ml (1 tablespoon) lemon juice
225 g (8 oz) unsalted butter, chilled

Sift the flour and salt into a mixing bowl and chill.

Make a well in the flour. Pour in half the water and all the lemon juice. Beat in some flour with the fingers until it resembles thick cream. Add the remaining water and beat in the rest of the flour.

Form the dough into a ball and turn out on to a highly floured surface. Knead lightly 3 or 4 times. Wrap in greaseproof paper and a damp cloth. Chill for 30 minutes.

With a spatula, work the butter until it is spreadable. Spread on to a sheet of greaseproof paper to make a rectangle 10 × 15 cm (4 × 6 in). Chill.

Unwrap the dough and lightly flour a cold working surface. Roll out the dough to a circle 30 cm (12 in) in diameter. Unwrap the butter and place it lengthwise in the centre of the circle.

Lift the dough at two sides of the circle over the butter so that they overlap. Press gently with the rolling pin to seal. Lift the dough at the other sides over the butter. Press gently with a rolling pin to seal.

Turn the dough so that the longer sides face you. Rolling in one direction, lightly roll out until the pastry is twice the size. Fold the bottom third of the pastry up and the lower third down on top. Seal all edges lightly. Wrap in greaseproof paper and chill in the refrigerator for 15 minutes. Note: the pastry has had one rolling.

Remove the pastry from the refrigerator and unwrap. Place it so that the fold is on your left and the longest sealed edge is on the right. Roll, fold and chill as before.

Repeat this operation, rolling, folding, chilling and turning until the pastry has been rolled 6 times in all. Wrap in greaseproof paper and a damp cloth. Chill in the refrigerator for at least 2 hours before use.

Grape Tart

Serves 4–5
225 g (8 oz) sweet shortcrust pastry (*see left*)
1 egg white, lightly beaten
350 g (12 oz) large green grapes, seeded
50 g (2 oz) caster sugar
45 ml (3 tablespoons) greengage, quince or crab-apple jelly

Preheat the oven to 190°C, 375°F, Gas 5.

Roll out the pastry and use it to line a 20-cm (8-in) flan tin. Brush the inside of the pastry case with some of the egg white. Arrange the grapes, cut side down, inside the pastry case. Sprinkle over the sugar.

Bake for 35–45 minutes. Remove the tin from the oven. Put the jelly in a saucepan over low heat until liquid. Brush it over the fruit.

Serve the tart warm or cold.

Glazed Fruit Tarts

Glazed Fruit Tarts

Makes 12
275 g (10 oz) shortcrust pastry (*see opposite*)
75 g (3 oz) full-fat soft cheese
90 ml (6 tablespoons) icing sugar, sifted
30 ml (2 tablespoons) white rum
300 g (11 oz) can mandarin orange segments, drained with
100 ml (3½ fl oz) syrup reserved
6 maraschino cherries, drained and halved
100 ml (3½ fl oz) water
35 g (1¼ oz) sachet orange-coloured, quick-setting jelly
glaze powder

Preheat the oven to 200°C, 400°F, Gas 6.

Roll out the pastry and use it to line a 12-hole tartlet tin.

Bake blind for 10 minutes. Remove the foil and beans and bake for a further 10 minutes, until the pastry is dry and lightly browned.

Remove the tin from the oven. Carefully remove the tartlets and put on a wire tray to cool.

Beat the cheese until softened. Beat in the icing sugar and rum.

Divide the cheese mixture between the pastry cases and smooth the surface of each. Top with mandarin segments and decorate each with half a cherry.

Put the reserved mandarin syrup and the water in a saucepan over low heat. Stir in the jelly glaze powder. Bring to the boil, stirring constantly. Remove the pan from heat and set aside, stirring occasionally, for 5 minutes.

Carefully spoon the glaze over the tarts and allow to set before serving, with whipped cream if you like.

French Pear Tart

Chilled Lemon Tartlets and French Pear Tart

Serves 4
175 g (6 oz) sweet shortcrust pastry (*see page 86*)
175 g (6 oz) sugar
850 ml (1½ pints) water
3 small ripe dessert pears, peeled, halved and cored
30 ml (2 tablespoons) brandy
200 ml (7 fl oz) double cream
15 ml (1 tablespoon) cornflour
15 ml (1 tablespoon) lemon juice
1 egg, separated

Preheat the oven to 200°C, 400°F, Gas 6.

Roll out the pastry and use to line an 18-cm (7-in) tart tin (*see page 84*). Partially bake blind for 10 minutes.

Remove the tin from the oven and set aside to cool. Reduce the oven temperature to 150°C, 300°F, Gas 2.

Put 100 g (4 oz) sugar and the water in a saucepan over low heat. Stir until the sugar has dissolved. Bring to the boil and boil for 3 minutes.

Remove the pan from the heat and add the pears. Return to low heat and poach for 5–10 minutes, until tender.

Remove the pan from the heat. With a perforated spoon, drain the pears thoroughly and transfer to a dish. Pour over the brandy and set aside.

Put the cream and half the remaining sugar in a saucepan over low heat.

Spoon 45 ml (3 tablespoons) of this warmed cream into a bowl. Stir in the cornflour. Tip this back into the rest of the cream. Bring to the boil, stirring constantly. Simmer, still stirring all the time, for 3 minutes, until thickened. Remove the pan from the heat.

Lightly beat the egg yolk. Stir into the cream mixture. Pour off the brandy syrup from the pears and stir this into the custard cream.

Drain the pears on kitchen paper towels. Cut them into thin slices.

Lightly beat the egg white and brush the inside of the pastry shell with it. Pour in the custard cream. Arrange the pears in a circle on top. Sprinkle over the remaining caster sugar.

Bake for 30 minutes, until the custard is set.

Remove the tin from the oven, then remove the tart from the tin and serve straight away.

Chilled Lemon Tartlets

Serves 4
225 g (8 oz) sweet shortcrust pastry (*see page 86*)
150 ml (5 fl oz) milk
50 g (2 oz) sugar
2 egg yolks
7.5 ml (1½ teaspoons) gelatine
30 ml (2 tablespoons) water
50 ml (2 fl oz) lemon juice
25 ml (1 fl oz) dry white wine
grated rind of ½ lemon
150 ml (5 fl oz) double cream
1 egg white, lightly beaten
DECORATION:
1 lime
1 egg white
50 ml (2 tablespoons) caster sugar

Preheat the oven to 190°C, 375°F, Gas 5.

Roll out the pastry and use it to line 4 individual tartlet tins, 7.5-cm (3½-in) in diameter and 2.5 cm (1 in) deep.

Bake for 10 minutes. Remove the foil and beans and bake for a further 8 minutes, until the pastry is dry and lightly browned.

Remove the tins from the oven and set aside to cool.

Prepare the decoration: thinly pare the rind from the lime and cut into fine julienne strips. Put it in a saucepan and cover with boiling water. Boil for 5 minutes, until soft and curled. Strain and drain on absorbent kitchen paper. When the julienne strips are dry, dip them in the egg white and coat in caster sugar. Set aside to dry.

Pour the milk into a saucepan. Add half the sugar. Set over low heat and stir until the sugar has dissolved. Bring to just below boiling point. Remove the pan from the heat.

Beat together the eggs and the remaining sugar until the mixture is thick and will leave a ribbon trail when the whisk is lifted. Gradually pour in the scalded milk, beating constantly.

Return the mixture to the saucepan. Heat slowly, stirring constantly, until the custard will coat the back of the spoon. Do not boil.

Remove the pan from the heat and set aside to cool completely.

Put the water in a small saucepan and sprinkle over the gelatine. Set aside for 5 minutes to soften, then dissolve (*see page 28*).

Remove from the heat and set aside to cool slightly.

Pour the gelatine mixture into the custard, stirring constantly. Stir in the lemon juice, wine and lemon rind. Set over a bowl of ice and stir until the mixture is thick and syrupy.

Whip the cream until it forms soft peaks. Fold the cream into the custard mixture.

Brush the inside of the pastry cases with egg white. Pour in the custard mixture. Chill in the refrigerator until set.

Remove the tarts from the tins. Decorate with the sugared lime strips and serve.

Cherry Sherry Tart

(Illustrated on page 82)
Serves 6
175 g (6 oz) shortcrust pastry (*see page 84*)
45 ml (3 tablespoons) custard powder
20 ml (4 teaspoons) sugar
200 ml (7 fl oz) milk
15 ml (1 tablespoon) sweet sherry
150 ml (5 fl oz) plain yoghurt
150 ml (5 fl oz) double cream, lightly whipped
75 ml (5 tablespoons) redcurrant jelly
20 ml (4 teaspoons) water
350 g (12 oz) cherries, stoned

Preheat the oven to 200°C, 400°F, Gas 6.

Roll out the pastry and use it to line a 20-cm (8-in) flan tin (*see page 84*).

Bake blind for 10 minutes. Remove the foil and beans and bake for a further 10–15 minutes, until the pastry is dry and lightly coloured.

Remove the tin from the oven and set aside to cool completely.

Mix together the custard powder, sugar and 15 ml (1 tablespoon) of the milk to a smooth paste. Put the remaining milk in a saucepan over the heat and bring to the boil. Slowly stir the milk into the custard mixture. Return the mixture to the pan and set over low heat. Bring to the boil, stirring constantly. Continue cooking and stirring for 1–2 minutes, until the custard is very thick and smooth.

Remove the pan from the heat and stir in the sherry. Pour into a bowl, cover with cling film and set aside to cool completely.

Whisk the cold custard with a fork. Gradually whisk in the yoghurt. Continue whisking until smooth. Fold the lightly whipped cream into the custard mixture and set aside.

Put the redcurrant jelly and water in a saucepan over low heat. Stir until the jelly has melted. Remove the pan from the heat.

Transfer the pastry shell to a serving dish. Brush the inside with a little of the glaze. Spread the custard mixture evenly over the base of the shell. Arrange the cherries on top. Brush with the remaining glaze. Put in a cool place to let it set before serving.

Frangipani Tart

Serves 6
100 g (4 oz) plus 5 ml (1 teaspoon) butter
225 g (8 oz) puff pastry dough (*see page 86*)
6 canned apricot halves, drained and finely chopped
½ teaspoon finely grated orange rind
100 g (4 oz) caster sugar
2 eggs, lightly beaten
100 g (4 oz) ground almonds
ICING:
50 g (2 oz) icing sugar, sifted
30 ml (2 tablespoons) orange juice, warmed

Preheat the oven to 190°C, 375°F, Gas 5. Grease a 20-cm (8-in) flan tin with the 5 ml (1 teaspoon) butter.

Roll out the pastry and use it to line the prepared tin.

Arrange the chopped apricots over the base of the pastry case. Sprinkle with the orange rind.

Beat together the remaining butter and the sugar until pale and fluffy. Beat in the eggs a little at a time. Stir in the almonds. Spoon this evenly over the apricots.

Bake for 40 minutes, until the filling is set and browned. Remove the tin from the oven and set aside for 15 minutes.

Meanwhile, make the icing. Blend the icing sugar and orange juice until smooth.

Remove the tart from the tin and transfer to a serving dish. Brush the icing over the top. Serve warm or cold.

Linzertorte

Serves 8
150 g (5 oz) plus 5 ml (1 teaspoon) plain flour
150 g (5 oz) caster sugar
150 g (5 oz) ground almonds
pinch of ground cloves
pinch of ground cinnamon
pinch of nutmeg
pinch of allspice
150 g (5 oz) butter, chilled and cut into small pieces plus
5 ml (1 teaspoon) butter
3 egg yolks
juice of ½ lemon
1.25 ml (¼ teaspoon) grated lemon rind
225 g (8 oz) raspberry jam
15 ml (1 tablespoon) icing sugar, sifted

Sift 150 g (5 oz) of the flour into a mixing bowl and stir in the sugar, almonds, cloves, cinnamon, nutmeg and allspice. Add the chilled, diced butter and rub in with the fingertips.

Add the egg yolks, lemon juice and rind and working with your fingertips, mix to form a dough.

Turn the dough on to a lightly floured surface and knead briefly. Form the dough into a ball. Wrap in greaseproof paper and chill in the refrigerator for 30 minutes.

Preheat the oven to 180°C, 350°F, Gas 4. Grease and flour a 23-cm (9-in) flan case with the remaining butter and flour.

Reserve one-third of the pastry. Flatten the remaining pastry with your hand and use it to line the bottom and sides, pressing it into place with the fingertips.

Spread the jam over the bottom of the pastry case.

Roll out the remaining pastry until it is 3 mm (⅛ in) thick. Cut into strips 12 mm (½ in) wide. Arrange the strips in a lattice pattern over the jam. Arrange one strip around the edge to neaten the top.

Bake for 40 minutes, until the pastry is dark golden. Remove from the oven and sprinkle over the icing sugar. Allow to cool completely before serving.

French Apple Tart

Serves 6
175 g (6 oz) shortcrust pastry (*see page 84*)
275 ml (½ pint) thick, sweet apple purée
450 g (1 lb) dessert apples
60 ml (4 tablespoons) golden syrup
grated rind of 1 lemon
juice of ½ lemon
60 ml (4 tablespoons) redcurrant or apple jelly
30 ml (2 tablespoons) Calvados or water

Preheat the oven to 200°C, 400°F, Gas 6.

Roll out the pastry and use to line a 20–30-cm (8–9-in) French flan tin. Partially bake blind for 10 minutes. Remove the foil and beans and bake for a further 3 minutes.

Remove the tin from the oven and set aside to cool.

When the flan is cold, spread the apple purée over the bottom. Set aside.

Put the syrup, lemon rind and lemon juice in a saucepan over a low heat. When the syrup has begun to melt, stir to mix the ingredients, then remove from the heat.

Peel and core the apples. Cut them into very thin slices and arrange these in concentric rings, overlapping slightly on top of the apple purée. Pour the lemon syrup evenly over the apple slices.

Bake for 20 minutes. Remove the tart from the oven and set aside to cool.

Put the jelly and Calvados or water in a small saucepan over low heat. Stir until the jelly has melted. Brush the glaze over the apple slices. Serve cold.

Treacle Tart

Serves 6
175 g (6 oz) golden syrup
50 g (2 oz) fresh white breadcrumbs
100 g (4 oz) shortcrust pastry dough (*see page 84*)

Preheat the oven to 200°C, 400°F, Gas 6.

Put the syrup in a small saucepan over low heat until liquid. Stir in the crumbs and remove from the heat. Set aside.

Roll out the pastry and line a 23-cm (9-in) pie plate.

Do not make a folded edge. Snip about 24 strips 2 cm (1 in) wide around the rim of the pastry.

Spoon the syrup and breadcrumb mixture over the centre of the pastry and spread it lightly over the base.

Fold alternate pastry strips over the filling, leaving others on the rim of the plate to make a castellated edge. Fold the extended edges under at the edge.

Bake the tart for 25 minutes. Serve hot or cold.

French Apple Tart

Flaky Chocolate Tart

Serves 6
50 g (2 oz) plain dessert chocolate, broken into small pieces
50 g (2 oz) butter
50 g (2 oz) caster sugar
2 eggs, separated
pinch of ground cinnamon
50 g (2 oz) ground almonds
50 g (2 oz) plain cake crumbs
pinch of salt
FLAKY PASTRY:
75 g (3 oz) lard, chilled
75 g (3 oz) butter, chilled
225 g (8 oz) plain flour
2.5 ml (½ teaspoon) salt
10 ml (2 teaspoons) lemon juice

First make the pastry. Divide the lard into 4 equal portions on 4 separate plates. Divide the butter into 4 equal portions and put with the lard. Put 3 of the plates in the refrigerator.

Sift together the flour and salt. Cut in the first plate of lard and butter and rub them into the flour. Add the lemon juice and enough chilled water to make a soft pliable dough.

Turn the dough out on to a lightly floured surface. Knead slightly and pat into a rectangular shape. Lightly flour a rolling pin.

Lightly roll out the dough into an oblong. With a round-bladed knife, lightly mark the dough into 3 sections.

Remove one plate of fats from the refrigerator and cut them into fairly small pieces. Dot them, alternating butter and lard, over 2 adjoining sections of the pastry.

Fold the fatless section of pastry over the centre section, keeping the edges straight. Lightly brush off surplus flour. Carefully fold the remaining section over the centre section, keeping the edges straight. Brush off surplus flour.

Lightly seal the raw edges with a rolling pin and gently press the dough at intervals to distribute the air. Cover and chill in the refrigerator for 15 minutes.

Repeat the rolling and folding process twice more, using the remaining 2 plates of butter and lard. Chill for 15 minutes in between. Finally, cover and chill for 30 minutes.

Roll out the pastry and use to line a 20-cm (8-in) flan tin. Chill for 15 minutes.

Meanwhile, preheat the oven to 200°C, 400°F, Gas 6.

Remove the flan tin from the refrigerator and partially bake blind for 10 minutes. Remove the foil and the beans and bake for a further 3–5 minutes, until the pastry is just dry. Remove the flan tin from the oven. Reduce the oven temperature to 180°C, 350°F, Gas 4.

Put the chocolate in a heatproof basin over a saucepan of hot water. Heat, stirring occasionally, until the chocolate has melted. Remove from heat.

Cream together the butter and sugar until light and fluffy.

Beat the egg yolks together and then add to the butter mixture, a little at a time, beating well after each addition. Beat in the melted chocolate. Stir in the cinnamon, almonds and cake crumbs.

Stiffly whisk together the egg whites and salt and fold into the chocolate mixture.

Using a spatula, scrape the mixture into the flan case. Bake for 20 minutes.

Remove the flan from the tin and serve immediately.

Apricot Bourdaloue Tarte

Serves 6
175 g (6 oz) sugar
275 ml (½ pint) water
450 g (1 lb) apricots, skinned, halved and stoned
BOURDALOUE:
275 ml (½ pint) milk
2 egg yolks
50 g (2 oz) sugar
15 g (½ oz) plain flour
15 g (½ oz) cornflour
grated rind of 1 orange
1 egg white
30 ml (2 tablespoons) double cream, lightly whipped
PÂTE SUCRÉE:
100 g (4 oz) plain flour
pinch of salt
50 g (2 oz) butter, chopped
50 g (2 oz) caster sugar
2 drops vanilla essence
2 egg yolks

First make the pastry. Sift together the flour and salt on to a marble slab or pastry board. Spread into a circle and make a well in the centre. Put the butter and sugar in the centre of the well. Mix together the vanilla essence and egg yolks and pour into the well.

Draw these ingredients together using the fingertips of one hand. Gradually draw the flour into the paste in the centre of the well. When all the flour has been incorporated, smooth the pastry by pressing down with the heel of the hand and then lifting it away smartly. Do this all over the pastry, but do not allow it to become sticky.

Wrap in greaseproof paper and chill for 1 hour.

Begin making the Bourdaloue cream. Put the milk in

a saucepan over low heat and bring to just below boiling point. Set aside.

Cream together the egg yolks, sugar, flour and cornflour until light. Gradually pour on the hot milk stirring constantly. Return the mixture to the pan and set over low heat, stirring constantly until boiling and thickened. Set aside to cool completely.

Meanwhile, prepare the fruit. Put the sugar and water in a saucepan over low heat and stir until the sugar has dissolved. Bring to the boil and continue boiling for 3 minutes.

Remove the pan from the heat and add the apricots. Return to low heat and poach for 10−15 minutes, until tender. Remove the pan from the heat and set aside.

Preheat the oven to 190°C, 375°F, Gas 5.

Roll out the pastry carefully on a lightly floured surface and use it to line an 18-cm (7-in) flan ring.

Bake blind for 5−6 minutes. Then remove the foil and beans and bake for a further 8−10 minutes.

Remove the flan from the ring and set aside to cool.

Meanwhile, finish the Bourdaloue cream. Stir the orange rind into the cold milk mixture.

Whisk the egg white and fold it into the mixture with the lightly whipped cream.

Pour the Bourdaloue cream into the pastry shell. Drain the apricots and reserve the syrup. Arrange the apricots on top of the cream.

Bring the apricot syrup to the boil and continue boiling until very thick and reduced by about two-thirds. Brush it over the apricots before serving.

Custard Tarts

Makes 12
150 g (5 oz) shortcrust pastry (*see page 84*)
150 ml (5 fl oz) milk
1 vanilla pod
1 egg
15 g (½ oz) caster sugar
1.25 ml (¼ teaspoon) grated nutmeg

Preheat the oven to 190°C, 375°F, Gas 5.

Roll out the pastry and use it to line a 12-hole tartlet tin. Partially bake blind for 3 minutes. Remove the tin from the oven. Remove the foil and beans. Set aside.

Reduce the oven temperature to 180°C, 350°F, Gas 4.

Put the milk and vanilla pod into a saucepan over a low heat and bring to just below boiling point. Remove from the heat and cover.

Whisk together the egg and sugar until the mixture

is light and frothy. Pour the hot milk into the egg mixture stirring constantly. Strain the custard into a jug.

Pour the custard into the pastry cases, taking care not to overfill. Dust the surface of the filling with nutmeg.

Bake for 30 minutes, until the custard has set. Remove the tin from the oven and set aside to cool completely before removing the tarts from the tin. Serve cold.

Tranche aux Fruits

Serves 8−10
225 g (8 oz) puff pastry (*see page 86*)
1 egg, beaten
275 ml (½ pint) double cream
1 banana
15 ml (1 tablespoon) lemon juice
100 g (4 oz) black grapes
100 g (4 oz) strawberries
1 large, ripe peach
30 ml (2 tablespoons) apricot jam

Preheat the oven to 200°C, 400°F, Gas 6. Dampen a baking tray.

Roll out the pastry to a rectangle 30×17.5 cm (12×7 in). Fold in half lengthwise. Cut away a 4-cm (1½-in) wide border and set aside.

Roll out the remaining pastry to the same size as the border. Lift on to the prepared baking tray and brush the edges with some of the egg. Lift the border on top and press lightly to seal. Brush the border with egg.

Bake for 30 minutes, until golden and puffy. Remove the baking tray from the oven and transfer the tranche to a wire rack to cool completely.

Whip the cream until it will just hold its shape. Fill the tranche with the cream and smooth the top.

Peel and slice the banana and brush with the lemon juice to prevent it discolouring. Skin and seed the grapes. Wash, hull and halve the strawberries. Peel, halve, stone and slice the peach.

Arrange the fruit decoratively over the cream to cover it completely.

Rub the jam through a sieve into a small saucepan. Set over low heat until it has melted. Pour the jam over the fruit. Set aside to cool and set before serving.

Rhubarb and Banana Pie

Rhubarb and Banana Pie

Serves 4
100 g (4 oz) shortcrust pastry (*see page 84*)
450 g (1 lb) rhubarb, wiped clean, trimmed and cut into
4-cm (1½-in) lengths
50–75 g (2–3 oz) Demerera sugar
1 large banana
5 ml (1 teaspoon) lemon juice
5 ml (1 teaspoon) ground mixed spice
1 egg white, lightly beaten
10 ml (2 teaspoons) caster sugar

Preheat the oven to 200°C, 400°F, Gas 6.

Roll out the pastry until 40 mm (1½ in) larger than the surface of a 700-ml (1¼-pint) pie dish.

Cut a strip of pastry the width of the rim. Dampen the rim of the dish and seal the strip on it.

Place half the rhubarb in the dish and sprinkle over the Demerera sugar in an even layer.

Peel and thinly slice the banana. Toss the slices in the lemon juice and then spread over the rhubarb. Sprinkle over the mixed spice. Pile the remaining rhubarb on top, heaping it in the centre.

Brush the pastry rim with some of the egg white. Lift the lid into position and press to seal. Knock up and flute the edge. Decorate with pastry trimmings, sealing them to the lid by brushing the undersides with egg white.

Brush the lid and decoration with egg white and sprinkle over the caster sugar. Prick the pie with the prongs of a fork.

Bake for 30 minutes, until the rhubarb is tender and the pastry is golden. Serve hot, warm or cold.

Traditional Plum Pie

Serves 4–6
900 g (2 lb) plums, halved and stoned
juice of 1 orange
225 g (8 oz) shortcrust pastry dough (*see page 84*)
150 g (5 oz) soft brown sugar
2.5 ml (½ teaspoon) ground cinnamon
10 ml (2 teaspoons) milk
10 ml (2 teaspoons) caster sugar

Preheat the oven to 200°C, 400°F, Gas 6.

Put the plums in a bowl and sprinkle over the orange juice. Set aside.

Roll out the pastry until 40 mm (1½ in) larger than the surface of the dish. Cut a strip 25 mm (1 in) wide and seal on to the dish with water.

Put half the plums in the dish. Sprinkle over the brown sugar and cinnamon. Add the remaining plums, piling them high in the centre of the dish.

Dampen the pastry rim. Lift the pastry lid into position and press to seal. Knock up and flute the edge.

Insert a knife under the pastry on either side of the pie and raise it slightly to make steam vents.

Brush the surface with a little milk and sprinkle over the caster sugar.

Bake for 20 minutes. Reduce the oven temperature to 180°C, 350°F, Gas 4 and cook for a further 20 minutes.

Remove from the oven and serve immediately.

Mince Pies

Makes 16
350 g (12 oz) shortcrust pastry (*see page 84*)
100 g (4 oz) mincemeat
45 ml (3 tablespoons) milk
30 ml (2 tablespoons) sugar

Preheat the oven to 200°C, 400°F, Gas 6.

Divide the dough into two pieces. Roll out the slightly larger piece and cut out 16 circles, 7.5 cm (3 in) in diameter. Use to line a 16-hole tartlet tin.

Place 5 ml (1 teaspoon) mincemeat in each pastry case. Dampen the edges.

Roll out the remaining dough and cut 16 circles, 6.5 cm (2½ in) to make lids. Lift the lids on to the cases and gently press to seal. Brush the tops with milk.

Bake for 20 minutes, until golden brown.

Remove the tin from the oven and set aside for 3 minutes to cool slightly. Transfer the mince pies to a serving dish, sprinkle over the sugar and serve immediately with softly whipped cream if you like.

Shoo-fly Pie

Serves 8
125 ml (4 fl oz) molasses
100 g (4 oz) light brown sugar
125 ml (4 fl oz) hot water
2.5 ml (½ teaspoon) bicarbonate of soda
2 eggs, lightly beaten
175 g (6 oz) plain flour
1.25 ml (¼ teaspoon) salt
1.25 ml (¼ teaspoon) ginger
1.25 ml (¼ teaspoon) nutmeg
2.5 ml (½ teaspoon) cinnamon
pinch of mixed spice
25 g (1 oz) butter, cut into small pieces
125 g (4 oz) seedless raisins
PASTRY:
150 g (5 oz) plain flour
2.5 ml (½ teaspoon) salt
125 g (4 oz) lard
45 ml (3 tablespoons) iced water

Preheat the oven to 230°C, 450°F, Gas 8.

To make the pastry, sift together the flour and salt into a mixing bowl. Add the lard and cut into the flour until the mixture resembles fine breadcrumbs. Sprinkle over the water, a little at a time, and stir with a fork until the dough forms a ball.

Turn the pastry out on to a lightly floured surface. Pat it flat and roll it out. Use to line a 25-cm (10-in) flan tin. Set aside.

Stir together the molasses, sugar and water. Stir in the bicarbonate of soda and the eggs. Set aside.

Sift together the flour, salt, ginger, nutmeg, cinnamon and mixed spice into a bowl. Add the butter and rub in with fingertips until the mixture resembles fine breadcrumbs.

Sprinkle the raisins over the pastry case. Add alternate layers of molasses mixture and flour mixture, finishing with a layer of flour mixture.

Bake for 10 minutes. Reduce the oven temperature to 180°C, 350°F, Gas 4 and bake for a further 20 minutes, until the top is firm to the touch.

Remove from the oven and serve warm or cool with softly whipped cream.

Old-fashioned Cheese and Apple Pie

Serves 6–8
275 g (10 oz) shortcrust pastry (*see page 84*)
900 g (2 lb) cooking apples
1 egg white
30 ml (2 tablespoons) Demerera sugar
175 g (6 oz) Cheshire cheese, grated
10 ml (2 teaspoons) caster sugar
275 ml (½ pint) double cream

Roll out slightly more than half the pastry and use it to line a 20-cm (8-in) pie dish. Set aside.

Preheat the oven to 200°C, 400°F, Gas 6. Peel, core and slice the apples.

Old-fashioned Cheese and Apple Pie

Brush the inside of the pastry shell and the rim of the dish with some of the egg white. Pack half the apple slices into the pastry shell. Sprinkle over half the Demerera sugar and half the cheese. Add the remaining apple slices and sprinkle over the remaining Demerera sugar and cheese.

Roll out the remaining pastry and use to cover the apples. Trim and knock up edges, then flute them. Brush the lid with egg white and sprinkle over the caster sugar. Cut 4 arrow-shaped slits in the lid. Open up the pointed end of each slit, but do not detach.

Bake for 25–30 minutes. Reduce the oven temperature to 180°C, 350°F, Gas 4 and bake for a further 20—25 minutes.

Remove the pie from the oven and set aside to cool slightly.

Meanwhile, put 75 ml (3 fl oz) of the cream in a saucepan over low heat. Bring to just below boiling point. Pour the scalded cream through the slits in the pie.

Whip the remaining cream and serve separately with the warm pie.

Pumpkin Pie

Serves 8
225 g (8 oz) shortcrust pastry (*see page 84*)
2 eggs
100 g (4 oz) sugar
15 ml (1 tablespoon) molasses
1.25 ml (¼ teaspoon) ground ginger
2.5 ml (½ teaspoon) grated nutmeg
5 ml (1 teaspoon) ground cinnamon
pinch of ground cloves
2.5 ml (½ teaspoon) salt
450 g (1 lb) canned or stewed pumpkin, puréed
375 ml (13 fl oz) milk

Roll out the pastry and use it to line a 25-cm (10-in) flan tin. Chill in the refrigerator until required.

Preheat the oven to 200°C, 400°F, Gas 6.

Beat together the eggs, sugar, molasses, ginger, nutmeg, cinnamon, cloves and salt. Stir in the pumpkin and milk.

Pour the filling into the pastry case and bake for 40 minutes, until set. Serve hot or cold.

Apple Strudel

Serves 6—8
225 g (8 oz) plain flour
2.5 ml (½ teaspoon) salt
1 egg, lightly beaten
30 ml (2 tablespoons) oil
60 ml (4 tablespoons) warm water
50 g (2 oz) butter, melted
FILLING:
50 g (2 oz) butter
75 g (3 oz) dry white breadcrumbs
100 g (4 oz) sugar
2.5 ml (½ teaspoon) ground cinnamon
2.5 ml (½ teaspoon) ground cloves
grated rind of ½ lemon
75 g (3 oz) blanched almonds, coarsely chopped
50 g (2 oz) sultanas
900 g (2 lb) cooking apples
60 ml (4 tablespoons) icing sugar, sifted

Sift the flour and salt into a mixing bowl and make a well in the centre. Beat together the egg, oil and water. Pour into the well and mix to a soft dough.

Turn the dough out on to a lightly floured surface and knead vigorously for 15 minutes, until smooth and elastic. Cover with a warmed, inverted bowl and set aside for 1 hour.

Meanwhile, make the filling. Put the butter in a small saucepan over low heat. When the butter has melted, add the breadcrumbs and fry gently until crisp and browned. Remove the pan from the heat and set aside.

Mix together the sugar, cinnamon, cloves, lemon rind, almonds and sultanas. Set aside.

Preheat the oven to 190°C, 375°F, Gas 5. With some of the melted butter, grease 1 or 2 large baking sheets (*see below*). Warm and lightly flour a rolling pin. Cover a large work-surface with a clean, patterned cloth, approximately 75 × 63 cm (30 × 25 in). Lightly flour the cloth.

Place the dough on the cloth and roll it out as thinly as possible. Flour your hands and ease them gently, palms down, under the dough. Gently stretch the dough, moving your hands apart and working from the centre. Do not tear the dough, although small holes are not important. Brush the dough with melted butter if it begins to dry out. Continue gently pulling and stretching the dough as evenly as possible, until it is sufficiently transparent for the pattern on the cloth to show through clearly.

Peel, core and quarter the apples. Cut into medium thick slices.

Trim the edges of the dough to make a rectangle 63 × 50 cm (25 × 20 in). With one long side facing you, brush the surface with melted butter and scatter over the prepared breadcrumbs. Spread the apple slices over half the dough, leaving a clear margin of 5 cm (2 in) on the edge nearest you and 2.5 cm (1 in) at the sides. Sprinkle over the sugar and sultana mixture. Fold the side edges over the apple filling. Fold the long edge nearest you over the apple filling.

Using the cloth to help, gradually roll the strudel up away from you. Keep patting the strudel into shape as you roll to keep the edges straight.

Form the rolled-up strudel into a horseshoe shape or cut it in half. Carefully transfer it to the prepared baking sheet/sheets, seamside down. Brush with melted butter and bake for 35—40 minutes, until crisp and golden. Cover with greaseproof paper during the cooking if the pastry browns too quickly.

Remove the strudel from the oven and set aside to cool slightly. Dredge with icing sugar, cut into slices and serve warm or cold.

Cheesecakes

Cheesecakes have an irrepressible air of festivity and sense of special occasion. They always seem exotic and yet they are quick and easy to make and needn't cost a small fortune. The irresistible combination of crunchy base and melt-in-the-mouth filling guarantees success at family meals, dinner parties and buffet suppers. Fruit toppings, which only take a moment to prepare, make sure the cheesecakes look as good as they taste; the combination of sweet fruit with a slightly tangy filling is wholly delicious.

Cheesecakes are astonishingly easy to make and yet they always look and taste as if you have lavished hours of care and attention on their preparation. Their rich, creamy texture might suggest that they can only be served as an extravagant and luxurious treat, but they are not necessarily expensive.

In essence, a cheesecake is simply a flan case filled with a sweetened creamy cheese. It may be cooked or uncooked and the variations in flavour are immense. Additions or toppings to the filling might include raw, poached, canned or dried fruits, fresh or soured cream, various spices or even a combination of some of these.

The most common type of flan case is made from crushed biscuits. Its popularity is no doubt derived from the pleasing contrast of textures between this and the filling. However, there are other possibilities, including sponge cake and pastry. Flavourings—spices, grated citrus rind, chopped nuts or chocolate—can be added to the base.

Even the shape of the case can be varied. An ordinary flan shape is the most common, but you can also make cheesecakes with a crust base that has no sides or with horizontal crust layers.

Biscuit Crumb Crust

This is made by mixing together crushed biscuits (various types are suitable—see below), sugar and melted butter. This mixture is pressed into the base only or into the base and sides of a flan tin and hardened, either by refrigeration or by cooking it briefly.

The best biscuits to use are plain, crumbly and slightly porous, as they make good crumbs and readily absorb the butter used to stick them together. Digestives are ideal and can be used with most flavourings. Other good choices are gingersnaps, shortbread and plain, fruited biscuits. A kind of rusk-like sweet bread from Germany, called Zwieback, is particularly suitable. It is available from large bakeries and delicatessens. Very closed textured biscuits are unsuitable as they tend to go into powder rather than crumbs. Cream sandwich and chocolate covered biscuits are too sticky to crush successfully into crumbs.

Melted butter is usually used to bind the crumbs together. Cut the butter into small pieces, put it into a heavy-based saucepan and stir gently over very low heat until it has melted. Remove it immediately from the heat and never allow it to burn.

Other binding agents can also be used; for example, a mixture of butter and syrup or black treacle is particularly good with gingersnaps. Put both ingredients in a heavy-based pan and cook gently over low heat, stirring constantly. As soon as they have melted and are thoroughly blended, remove the pan from the heat.

Sweet biscuit crusts and chocolate-flavoured cheesecakes are especially delicious when melted chocolate is used as the binding agent in the base. Melt plain dessert or cooking chocolate in a bowl over a saucepan of hot water, then combine it with the crumbs.

A little caster sugar is used to sweeten the flan case and is stirred into the melted butter before combining with the biscuit crumbs. Sugar is not required when syrup or chocolate are the binding agents.

It is important to use the ingredients in the correct proportions to obtain a really crisp and crunchy texture. As a general rule, use half as much binding agent as crumbs. In the case of very buttery biscuits, such as shortcake, reduce the amount of butter by one-third. The amount of sugar should be about one-sixth the amount of crumbs. In the case of sugar-coated biscuits, such as shortcake, again reduce the sugar by half.

Biscuit crumb crust made with butter is usually hardened by baking for 10 minutes. This makes it firm and crisp and prevents the filling soaking through. Allow the crust to cool before adding the filling. Flan cases made with chocolate or syrup cannot be baked and are hardened by refrigeration instead. Allow a minimum of 5 hours for the crust to set firm. Cases made with butter can also be set by chilling.

Fillings

Unsalted cottage, curd or cream cheeses provide the basis of the filling of a cheesecake, whatever additional flavourings are to be used. Cream cheese alone is the simplest filling, but a mixture of cottage cheese and full fat soft cream cheese gives the ideal combination of firmness and richness. Many Italian recipes specify Ricotta, a creamy, delicate tasting cheese made from ewe's milk. If this is unavailable, substitute cottage cheese.

Cottage cheese and Ricotta should be sieved before mixing to break down any lumps. All cheeses should be thoroughly beaten with a wooden spoon to make them as smooth, light and fluffy as possible.

Beating one or more eggs into the cheese filling gives it body, additional richness and helps it to set. A lightly beaten egg is often all that is necessary, but more elaborate, richly decorated cheesecakes can be made rather like cold soufflés. The egg yolk is beaten into the cheese and the white is stiffly whisked and folded in at the end.

Gelatine is not usually required for setting the filling, although it may be necessary for some cold cheesecakes.

When adding sugar or honey and other flavourings to the filling, beat thoroughly with a wooden spoon to ensure that they are dissolved and thoroughly dispersed throughout the other ingredients.

Toppings, such as fresh or canned fruit, especially if glazed, should be drained (if necessary) and added at the latest possible moment before serving. However, do allow sufficient time for cooling and/or chilling.

Little in the way of special equipment is required to make cheesecakes. Use a heavy duty plastic bag (or two thinner ones) to prevent the biscuit crumbs from flying everywhere when you are crushing them. A heavy rolling pin is the best instrument for crushing and a coarse sieve is essential to separate any over-large crumbs which may prevent the crust from sticking together.

The flan ring or cake tin is the most important piece of equipment. It must have a loose bottom, otherwise it will be impossible to get the crust or cheesecake out in one piece. Use a tin with plain sides unless you are particularly ambitious; generally speaking the crust is too brittle to mould into crinkled edges. A spring form pan is ideal and ensures success in removing the cheesecake from the tin.

99

Making a Biscuit Crumb Base

Diameter of Tin	Dry Ingredients (including flavourings)	Binding Ingredients (e.g. butter, butter and syrup)	Sugar (if necessary)	Servings
18 cm (7 in)	175 g (6 oz)	75 g (3 oz)	25 g (1 oz)	4–5
20 cm (8 in)	225 g (8 oz)	100 g (4 oz)	40 g (1½ oz)	5–6
23 cm (9 in)	350 g (12 oz)	175 g (6 oz)	50 g (2 oz)	6–7
25 cm (10 in)	450 g (1 lb)	225 g (8 oz)	65 g (2½ oz)	8–9

1 *Lightly grease the sides and base of a plain-sided, loose-bottomed flan tin. Put the biscuits in a heavy-duty plastic bag, squeeze out air and seal top. Crush the biscuits by pressing down firmly with a rolling pin.*

2 *Sieve the crushed biscuits through a coarse sieve over a mixing bowl. Melt the butter (see page 99) and add any sugar to it. Add any flavourings to the biscuit crumbs. Stir the butter and crumbs together.*

3 *Scatter a 6-mm (¼-in) layer of crumbs over the base of the tin. Press them into place with the back of a spoon. Tilt the tin towards you and put two spoonfuls of crumbs in the section nearest to you. Press into place up the sides. Continue adding crumbs and pressing them into place with a spoon until the tin is covered. To make sure that the case is really even, work a smooth-sided jar around the inside of the ring against the sides.*

4 *Bake for 10 minutes in an oven, preheated to 180°C, 350°F, Gas 4.*

5 *Check the case towards the end of the recommended cooking time in case it is beginning to burn. Let it cool. Gently run a round-bladed knife around the inside edge. Stand the tin on an inverted bowl and slide the ring down off the sides of the case.*

6 *Insert the round-bladed knife under the biscuit crumb crust and ease it gently off the base. Tilt the biscuit crust case and gently push it off the base on to a flat serving plate. It is now ready for filling and decoration.*

Decorations, Toppings and Glazes

FRUIT DECORATION: choose from fresh grapes, strawberries,
raspberries, blackberries etc, or canned fruit, such
as mandarin oranges or black cherries
SOURED CREAM TOPPING:
150 ml (5 fl oz) soured cream mixed with
15 ml (1 tablespoon) sugar and flavourings (see step 1)
GLAZE:
150 ml (5 fl oz) fruit juice and
10 ml (2 teaspoons) arrowroot
or
45 ml (3 tablespoons) fruit jelly (*see step 5*)

1 *For a soured cream topping, lightly beat the soured cream with sugar and flavourings, such as powdered ginger or cinnamon. Just before the end of the recommended cooking time, spoon this over the cake, then return it to the oven for the remaining cooking time. The sour cream will set.*

2 *To top a cheesecake with grapes, skin, halve and seed them. When the filling is set and cold, arrange the grapes in circles over the top.*

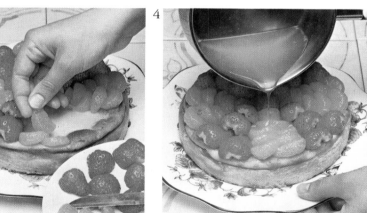

3 *Halved strawberries and segmented mandarin oranges or satsumas mixed together make a refreshing topping. Arrange the fruit in alternate concentric circles or in triangles over the top of the cooled filling.*

4 *To glaze, stir together 150 ml (5 fl oz) fruit juice and 10 ml (2 teaspoons) arrowroot. Bring to the boil over medium heat and boil for 1 minute. Allow to cool before pouring over the fruit. Alternatively, melt a little redcurrant, blackcurrant or apple jelly and spoon over the fruit.*

5 *Use poached fresh fruit or canned fruit for a substantial topping. Drain the fruit well and arrange it over the cooled, firm filling just before serving. Reserve the can juice or poaching syrup.*

6 *Measure up to 150 ml (5 fl oz) of the reserved juice. Stir in 10 ml (2 teaspoons) arrowroot and bring to the boil over medium heat, stirring. Boil for 1 minute, or until thickened. Cool slightly, then pour the thickened syrup over the fruit.*

Ricotta Cheesecake

Serves 6
225 g (8 oz) biscuits (e.g. digestives) made into crumbs
100 g (4 oz) butter
40 g (1½ oz) sugar
450 g (1 lb) Ricotta cheese
pinch salt
15 ml (1 tablespoon) plain flour
100 g (4 oz) soft brown sugar
2 eggs, separated
2.5 ml (½ teaspoon) saffron
5 ml (1 teaspoon) finely grated orange rind
25 g (1 oz) raisins
25 g (1 oz) candied orange peel, chopped
2.5 ml (½ teaspoon) ground cinnamon
30 ml (2 tablespoons) icing sugar

Preheat the oven to 180°C, 350°F, Gas 4. Grease a 20-cm (8-in) loose-bottomed cake tin and prepare a biscuit crumb base with the first 3 ingredients following the instructions on page 100. Remove from the oven and cool slightly.

Increase the oven temperature to 190°C, 375°F, Gas 5.

Beat the cheese until smooth, then mix it together with the salt, flour, brown sugar, egg yolks, saffron and grated orange rind. Stir in the raisins and orange peel.

Whisk the egg whites until they form stiff peaks. Fold them into the cheese mixture. Spoon the mixture into the prepared tin and smooth the surface with a palette knife. Bake for 30–35 minutes, or until firm.

Set aside to cool. Sprinkle with the cinnamon and icing sugar before serving.

Swedish Cheesecake

Serves 8
450 g (1 lb) cottage cheese
25 g (1 oz) plain flour
3 eggs, lightly beaten
40–50 g (1½–2 oz) caster sugar
425 ml (15 fl oz) single cream
50 g (2 oz) blanched, toasted and chopped almonds

Preheat the oven to 140°C, 275°F, Gas 1. Lightly grease a shallow 2.25-litre (4-pint) baking dish.

Beat the cottage cheese until it is smooth. Stir in the flour, eggs, sugar, cream and almonds. Pour the mixture into the prepared dish and bake for 1 hour, or until a skewer inserted in the centre comes out clean.

Italian Cheesecake

Serves 8–10
PASTRY:
225 g (8 oz) plain flour
1.5 ml (¼ teaspoon) salt
175 g (6 oz) butter, cut into small pieces
4 egg yolks, lightly beaten
30 ml (2 tablespoons) sugar
75 ml (5 tablespoons) Marsala
grated rind of 1 lemon
FILLING:
1.1 kg (2½ lb) Ricotta or whole curd cottage cheese, sieved
100 g (4 oz) sugar
30 ml (2 tablespoons) plain flour
1.5 ml (¼ teaspoon) salt
2.5 ml (½ teaspoon) vanilla essence
grated rind of 1 orange
grated rind and juice of 2 lemons
4 egg yolks
45 ml (3 tablespoons) raisins
30 ml (2 tablespoons) finely chopped candied peel
30 ml (2 tablespoons) slivered, blanched almonds
1 egg white, lightly beaten

Grease a 25-cm (10-in) spring-form tin and set aside.

To make the pastry, sift together the flour and salt and make a well in the centre. Add the butter, egg yolks, sugar, Marsala and lemon rind. Combine the ingredients with the fingertips and lightly knead the dough until it is smooth. Form it into a ball, wrap in foil and refrigerate for 1 hour.

Break off about one-quarter of the dough. Dust with flour, cover and return to the refrigerator. Form the remaining dough into a ball and then flatten into a circle. Sprinkle over a little flour and then roll out the dough into a circle 5 cm (2 in) larger than the prepared tin. Line the tin with the pasty taking it up the sides and trim the edges. Set aside.

Preheat the oven to 180°C, 350°F, Gas 4.

Beat together the cheese, sugar, flour, salt, vanilla essence, orange and lemon rind, lemon juice and egg yolks until thoroughly combined. Stir in the raisins and candied peel. Spoon the mixture into the pastry case and smooth the surface with the back of the spoon. Sprinkle over the almonds evenly.

Roll out the reserved pastry into a rectangle 25 cm (10 in) long and cut it into long strips. Arrange the strips over the filling in a lattice pattern. Brush the strips with egg white.

Bake for 1 hour or until the crust is golden brown and the filling is firm to the touch. Remove the outside rim of the tin and set the cake aside on a wire rack to cool. Serve cold.

Almond Cheesecake with Black Cherry Topping

Italian Cheesecake

Serves 8

175 g (6 oz) sweet shortcrust pastry (*see page 86*)
50g (2 oz) butter
75 g (3 oz) caster sugar
2 large eggs, separated
225 g (8 oz) curd cheese
50 g (2 oz) ground almonds
2–3 drops almond essence
25 g (1 oz) semolina

TOPPING:
225 g (8 oz) canned black cherries in syrup
10 ml (2 teaspoons) arrowroot

Preheat the oven to 200°C, 400°F, Gas 6.

Roll out the pastry and line a 20-cm (8-in) spring-form tin. Trim the edges, prick the base and bake blind for 15 minutes.

Cream together the butter and sugar until light and fluffy. Beat in the egg yolks, then gradually beat in the cheese, almonds, almond essence and semolina.

Whisk the egg whites until they form soft peaks. Fold them into the cheese mixture.

Pile the mixture into the pastry case and smooth the surface with a palette knife. Bake for 45 minutes, then turn off the heat and leave the cheesecake in the oven until cold.

Remove the cake from the tin. Drain the cherries and reserve 150 ml (5 fl oz) of the syrup. Arrange the cherries over the top of the cake.

Stir a little of the reserved syrup into the arrowroot and then stir this blended mixture into the syrup. Set over medium heat and bring to the boil, stirring. Boil for 1 minute and set aside to cool.

Spoon the thickened syrup over the cherries and leave to set before serving at room temperature.

Cooked Strawberry Cheesecake

Serves 4–5
175 g (6 oz) shortbread biscuits, crushed
finely grated rind of 1 orange
50 g (2 oz) caster sugar
50 g (2 oz) butter, melted
225 g (8 oz) cottage cheese, sieved
225 g (8 oz) full fat, soft cream cheese
1 egg, lightly beaten
225 g (8 oz) strawberries, hulled, washed and halved
30 ml (2 tablespoons) redcurrant jelly
15 ml (1 tablespoon) hot water

Preheat the oven to 180°C, 350°F, Gas 4. Lightly grease an 18-cm (7-in) loose-bottomed cake tin.

Mix together the biscuit crumbs, orange rind, 15 ml (1 tablespoon) of the sugar and the melted butter. Use to line the base and sides of the prepared tin. Bake for 10 minutes. Set aside to cool slightly.

Increase the oven temperature to 190°C, 375°F, Gas 5.

Beat together the sieved cottage cheese, cream cheese, egg and remaining sugar until smooth and creamy.

Pile the filling into the biscuit crumb base and smooth the surface with a palette knife. Bake for 40–45 minutes, or until the filling is firm. Set aside to cool.

Remove the cheesecake from the tin. Arrange the strawberries on top. Dissolve the redcurrant jelly in the water and brush over the strawberries to glaze. Allow to cool before serving.

Siphnos Cheese and Honey Pie

Serves 8
225 g (8 oz) flour
2.5 ml (½ teaspoon) salt
175 g (6 oz) butter, chilled and cut into very small pieces
45 ml (3 tablespoons) iced water
450 g (1 lb) unsalted curd or low fat soft cheese
4 eggs
10 ml (2 teaspoons) ground cinnamon
125–150 ml (4–5 tablespoons) clear honey

Sift together the flour and salt. Add the butter and very lightly rub it in with the fingertips or a pastry blender. Gradually add sufficient water to form a soft dough. Form the dough into a ball, wrap in foil and chill in the refrigerator for 30 minutes.

Preheat the oven to 180°C, 350°F, Gas 4.

Press the dough into the sides and bottom of a 25-cm (10-in) pie dish with your hands and bake for 10 minutes. Cool. Increase the oven temperature to 190°C, 375°F, Gas 5.

Mix together the cheese, eggs, half the cinnamon and honey to taste. Set aside.

Pour the cheese mixture into the cooled pastry shell and bake for 35 minutes or until the filling is firm and the top is golden. Remove from the oven, dust the pie with the remaining cinnamon and set aside to cool. Serve cold.

Yorkshire Curd Cheesecake

Serves 4
225 g (8 oz) sweet shortcrust pastry (*see page 86*)
225 g (8 oz) curd cheese
50 g (2 oz) caster sugar
finely grated zest of 1 lemon
30 ml (2 tablespoons) currants
15 g (½ oz) melted butter
2.5 ml (½ teaspoon) freshly grated nutmeg
2 eggs, plus 1 extra white

Preheat the oven to 220°C, 425°F, Gas 7. Make the pastry and use to line a 20-cm (8-inch) loose-bottomed flan tin. Lightly prick the base all over.

Mix together the cheese, sugar, lemon zest, currants, melted butter and half the nutmeg. Separate the whole eggs and beat the yolks into this mixture.

Whisk the egg whites until they form stiff peaks and fold these into the cheese mixture. Pour into the flan case and sprinkle the remaining nutmeg over the top.

Bake in the centre of the oven for 10 minutes, then lower the heat to 180°C, 350°F, Gas 4 and bake for 20 minutes more, until the pastry is crisp and the filling is set and golden brown. Cool slightly before removing from the tin. Serve warm or cold.

Yorkshire Curd Cheesecake

Ginger Cheesecake

Serves 6
50 g (2 oz) butter, melted
175 g (6 oz) digestive biscuits, crushed
350 g (12 oz) cream cheese
175 g (6 oz) sugar
1 egg, well beaten
7.5 ml (1½ teaspoons) ground ginger
350 ml (12 fl oz) soured cream
60 ml (4 tablespoons) canned pineapple, drained
and crushed

Preheat the oven to 180°C, 350°F, Gas 4. Lightly grease a 23-cm (9-in) loose-bottomed cake tin.

Mix together the biscuits and butter. Line the prepared cake tin with the crumb crust and set aside.

Beat together the cream cheese, half the sugar and the egg until smooth. Stir in 5 ml (1 teaspoon) of the ginger. Pour the mixture into the lined cake tin and bake for 25 minutes, or until the filling has set.

Meanwhile, beat together the soured cream, the remaining sugar and the remaining ginger, until the sugar has dissolved.

Turn off the heat. Spread the soured cream mixture evenly on top of the cake and return it to the oven for 5 minutes. Cool.

Arrange the crushed pineapple on top of the cake and chill for 1 hour before serving.

Redcurrant Cheesecake

Serves 6
225 g (8 oz) digestive biscuits, crushed
100 g (4 oz) butter, melted
5 ml (1 teaspoon) ground cinnamon
450 g (1 lb) cream cheese
50 g (2 oz) caster sugar
125 ml (4 fl oz) single cream
550 g (1¼ lb) redcurrants, trimmed
15 g (½ oz) gelatine,
30 ml (2 tablespoons) water
275 ml (½ pint) double cream
1 egg white, stiffly beaten

Lightly grease a 20-cm (8-in) loose-bottomed cake tin.

Combine the biscuits, butter and cinnamon and use to line the base of prepared tin. Set aside.

Beat together the cream cheese and sugar until the mixture is smooth and creamy. Stir in the single cream and 450 g (1 lb) of the redcurrants. Dissolve the gelatine in the water (*see page 28*) and beat it into the cheese mixture. Spoon this into the tin on top of the biscuit base, smooth over the surface and chill in the refrigerator for 30 minutes, or until set.

Whisk the double cream until it forms stiff peaks. Fold in the egg white and spoon over the cheesecake, making swirling patterns with the back of a spoon. Sprinkle over the remaining redcurrants and serve.

Blackcurrant Cheesecake

Serves 4–5
175 g (6 oz) digestive biscuits, crushed
75 g (3 oz) butter, melted
1.5 ml (¼ teaspoon) vanilla essence
juice of ½ lemon
30 ml (2 tablespoons) water
15 g (½ oz) gelatine
175 g (6 oz) cream cheese
2 large eggs, separated
50 g (2 oz) caster sugar
200 ml (7 fl oz) double cream
350 g (12 oz) canned blackcurrants, drained and with the
syrup reserved
10 ml (2 teaspoons) arrowroot

Preheat the oven to 200°C, 400°F, Gas 6.

Mix together the biscuits, butter and vanilla and use to line the base of an 18-cm (7-in) loose-bottomed cake tin. Bake for 15 minutes.

Set the crumb crust aside to cool completely and then line the sides of the tin with greaseproof paper oiled on both sides.

Mix the lemon juice and water together and sprinkle over the gelatine in a small saucepan. Set aside.

Beat together the cream cheese, egg yolks and sugar until smooth. Gradually add the cream and 60 ml (4 tablespoons) of the reserved canned syrup. Fold in half the drained blackcurrants.

Whisk the egg whites until the form stiff peaks. Fold them into the cheese and cream mixture.

Set the lemon juice and gelatine over low heat until the gelatine has dissolved. Stir it into the cheese and cream mixture. Pour the mixture into the prepared tin and chill in the refrigerator until set.

Mix the arrowroot with 30 ml (2 tablespoons) of the remaining syrup. Put the rest of the syrup in a pan over moderate heat and bring to the boil. Add the arrowroot and cook, stirring constantly, until the syrup is thick and transparent. Remove from the heat and stir in the remaining blackcurrants. Set aside to cool.

Remove the cheesecake from the tin carefully and slide it on to a serving plate. Carefully pour the thickened blackcurrant mixture evenly over the top. Chill until required, but remove from refrigerator 30 minutes before serving.

Strawberry Shortbread Cheesecake

Strawberry Shortbread Cheesecake

Serves 6–8
175 g (6 oz) shortbread biscuits, crushed
75 g (3 oz) butter, melted
225 g (8 oz) fresh strawberries, hulled
grated zest of ½ orange
30 ml (2 tablespoons) orange juice
15 g (½ oz) gelatine
45 ml (3 tablespoons) water
175 g (6 oz) curd cheese
75 g (3 oz) caster sugar
1–2 drops vanilla essence
30 ml (2 tablespoons) yoghurt
150 ml (5 fl oz) double cream, softly whipped
1 egg white
DECORATION:
halved strawberries

Preheat the oven to 180°C, 350°F, Gas 4. Lightly grease an 18-cm (7-in) loose-bottomed cake tin.

Stir together the shortbread biscuits and the melted butter and use to line the bottom of the prepared tin. Bake for 8–10 minutes until lightly browned. Put on one side to cool completely.

Put the strawberries in a bowl with the grated orange zest and juice and mash with a fork. Sprinkle the gelatine over the water in a small pan and leave for 5 minutes to soften.

Beat the curd cheese with a wooden spoon until soft, then gradually beat in the sugar, vanilla essence, yoghurt, cream and mashed strawberries.

Dissolve the gelatine (*see page 28*). Pour into the cheese mixture in a thin stream, stirring all the time.

Put the cheese mixture in a cool place for about 5 minutes then whisk the egg white until it forms soft peaks. Fold this into the cheese mixture and spoon over the biscuit base. Level the surface and cover with cling film or foil. Refrigerate for at least 3 hours.

When ready to serve, transfer the cheesecake onto a serving plate and decorate with halved strawberries.

Russian Easter Pudding

Serves 16

1.5 kg (3 lb 5 oz) cottage or curd cheese, drained in a
cheesecloth bag for 12 hours
100 g (4 oz) blanched almonds, chopped
100 g (4 oz) candied mixed peel, chopped
200 g (7 oz) seedless raisins, chopped
100 g (4 oz) glacé cherries, chopped
250 g (9 oz) butter, softened
3 eggs
200 g (7 oz) caster sugar
100 ml (3½ fl oz) clotted, thick or soured cream
5 ml (1 teaspoon) rosewater
DECORATION:
blanched almonds
glacé cherries
candied fruits
angelica

Line a new clay flower pot with two layers of cheesecloth. Rub the cheese through a strainer and stir in the
almonds, candied peel, raisins, cherries and butter. Mix
thoroughly.

Whisk together the eggs and sugar until the mixture
is pale and frothy. Whisk this into the cheese mixture,
followed by the cream and rosewater. Continue
whisking until the mixture is completely smooth. Turn
into the flower pot and fold the cheesecloth over the
top. Put a small plate on top to fit inside the rim and
place a heavy weight on it. Stand the pot upright on a
large saucer to catch the whey and chill in the
refrigerator for 12 hours.

Carefully unfold the cheesecloth and turn the
pudding out. Decorate with almonds, glacé cherries,
candied fruit and angelica and serve immediately.

Tipsy Raisin Cheesecake

Serves 6

100 g (4 oz) raisins
125 ml (4 fl oz) port
75 g (3 oz) digestive biscuits, crushed
75 g (3 oz) plain wheaten biscuits, crushed
75 g (3 oz) butter, melted
5 ml (1 teaspoon) mixed spice
225 g (8 oz) cottage cheese
275 ml (½ pint) plain yoghurt
30 ml (2 tablespoons) double cream

Soak the raisins in the port for 6 hours or overnight.

Combine the biscuits, butter and mixed spice and use
to line the base and sides of an 18-cm (7-in) loose-
bottomed cake tin. Chill while you make the filling.

Sieve the cottage cheese, then gradually beat in the
yoghurt and cream. Drain the raisins and fold them
into the cheese mixture.

Spoon the mixture into the tin and smooth the
surface with a palette knife. Chill in the refrigerator for
1 hour before serving.

Orange and Peach Cheesecake

Serves 6–8

225 g (8 oz) rich tea biscuits, crushed
100 g (4 oz) butter, softened
40 g (1½ oz) caster sugar
juice and grated rind of 1 orange
20 g (¾ oz) gelatine
45 ml (3 tablespoons) orange-flavoured liqueur
425 g (15 oz) full-fat soft cheese
90 ml (6 tablespoons) apricot jam
75 ml (3 fl oz) double cream, thickly whipped
400 g (14 oz) peaches, skinned, stoned and sliced

Preheat the oven to 180°C, 350°F, Gas 4. Grease and
line the base of a 22-cm (8-in) loose-bottomed cake tin.
Do not fit on the sides.

Combine the biscuits, butter and sugar. Spread the
mixture over the base of the tin and bake for 8 minutes.
Set aside for 1½ hours to cool completely before fitting
the sides of the tin.

Strain the orange juice into a measuring jug and add
sufficient warm water to bring the level up to 275 ml
(½ pint). Put in a saucepan and sprinkle over the
gelatine. Set aside for 5 minutes to soften. Put over a
very low heat for 3 minutes without stirring until the
gelatine has dissolved. Remove from the heat and stir in
the liqueur. Set aside.

Mix together the cheese, orange rind and 60 ml
(4 tablespoons) of jam. Beat until thoroughly blended.
Fold in the cream. Add the dissolved gelatine mixture,
stirring constantly. Chill in the refrigerator for 5–10
minutes, or until just beginning to thicken.

Spread the remaining jam over the biscuit base in the
tin. Pour over the cheese mixture, then chill in the
refrigerator for 2 hours or until set.

Just before serving, arrange the peach slices over the
top of the cheesecake.

Citrus Almond Cheesecake

(Illustrated on page 96)
Serves 6
275 g (10 oz) almond macaroons, crushed
75 g (3 oz) butter, melted
225 g (8 oz) curd cheese
150 ml (5 fl oz) yoghurt
2 eggs
30 ml (2 tablespoons) clear honey
15 g (½ oz) gelatine
grated zest of 1 orange
30 ml (2 tablespoons) orange or grapefruit juice
DECORATION:
25 g (1 oz) blanched almonds, toasted

Lightly grease a 20-cm (8-in) flan ring and stand on a flat, greased serving plate.

Mix together 225 g (8 oz) of the crushed macaroons with the melted butter and use to line the base and sides of the flan ring on the plate. Chill.

Beat together the cheese and yoghurt with a wooden spoon until they are quite smooth. Lightly beat the eggs with a fork, then beat them into the cheese mixture with the honey.

Sprinkle the gelatine over the orange or grapefruit juice in a small pan and leave for 5 minutes. Dissolve over a very low heat (*see page 28*). Let it cool slightly.

Pour the gelatine in a thin stream into the cheese mixture beating all the time. Stir in the grated orange zest and the remainder of the crushed macaroons.

Pour this into the biscuit case and chill for at least 2 hours. Just before serving, remove the flan ring very carefully and decorate the top with the toasted almonds.

Chocolate Cheesecake

Serves 6
40 g (1½ oz) butter
40 g (1½ oz) chocolate
175 g (6 oz) digestive biscuits, crushed
3 eggs, separated
75 g (3 oz) caster sugar
grated rind and juice of 1 orange
grated rind and juice of ½ lemon
350 g (12 oz) cottage cheese, sieved
20 ml (4 teaspoons) gelatine
150 ml (5 fl oz) double cream, thickly whipped
25 g (1 oz) chocolate

Melt the butter and chocolate together over low heat. Remove from the heat, stir in the biscuit crumbs and

use to line the base of an 18-cm (7-in) loose-bottomed cake tin. Chill in the refrigerator for 5 hours, or until firm.

Whisk together the egg yolks and sugar until thick and creamy. Stir in the orange and lemon rind, then the sieved cottage cheese.

Put the orange and lemon juice in a saucepan and sprinkle over the gelatine. Set aside for 5 minutes, then dissolve over very low heat (*see page 28*). Pour the gelatine mixture into the egg and cheese mixture in a continuous stream, stirring constantly. Fold in the cream.

Whisk the egg whites until they form stiff peaks. Fold them into the egg and cheese mixture. Spoon the filling into the tin and chill in the refrigerator for 4 hours or overnight.

Transfer the cheesecake to a serving plate. Melt the chocolate in a bowl over a pan of hot water. Using a piping bag made out of greaseproof paper, dribble the melted chocolate over the cheesecake in a decorative pattern. Leave to set.

Sicilian Cassata Cheesecake

Serves 6–8
1 × 20-cm (8-in) whisked sponge (*see page 114*)
700 g (1½ lb) Ricotta or cottage cheese, sieved
50 g (2 oz) caster sugar
50 g (2 oz) plain chocolate, grated
2.5 ml (½ teaspoon) almond essence
ICING:
1 large egg white
175 g (6 oz) icing sugar, sifted
10 ml (2 teaspoons) lemon juice
100 g (4 oz) mixed glacé fruit

Slice the cake horizontally into three equal layers and set aside.

Beat together the cheese and sugar until the mixture is smooth and the sugar has dissolved. Beat in the chocolate and the almond essence. Spread half the mixture over the bottom layer of sponge. Place the middle layer on top and spread with the remaining mixture. Top with the final layer of sponge.

Whisk the egg white until just stiff but not dry. Whisk in half the icing sugar, 15 ml (1 tablespoon) at a time. Stir in the lemon juice. Continue whisking in the icing sugar until the mixture has a coating consistency.

Spread the icing over the top of the cake with a palette knife. Decorate with the glacé fruit and set aside in a cool place for 1 hour to set.

Store Cupboard Cheesecake

Serves 6
2 tablets lemon jelly
60 ml (4 tablespoons) water
3 large eggs, separated
150 ml (5 fl oz) milk
grated rind and juice of 2 lemons
25 g (1 oz) caster sugar
1 × 17.5-cm (7-in) whisked sponge, cooked and cooled
(*see page 114*)
450 g (1 lb) cream cheese
150 ml (5 fl oz) double cream, lightly whipped
15 ml (1 tablespoon) icing sugar, sifted

Cut the jelly tablets into pieces and put them in a saucepan with the water over gentle heat. Dissolve, stirring constantly. Remove from the heat and set aside.

Beat together the egg yolks and milk and stir the mixture into the jelly. Place over low heat for 2 minutes, stirring constantly. Remove from the heat and stir in the lemon rind, juice and sugar. Set aside to cool until on the point of setting.

Cut the cake in half horizontally. Put the bottom layer in the base of a 17.5-cm (7-in) spring-form tin.

Beat the cream cheese until it is smooth. Beat in the jelly mixture, a little at a time, then fold in the cream.

Whisk the egg whites until they form stiff peaks. Fold them into the filling. Spoon the mixture into the tin and level the top. Top with the other layer of sponge cake. Chill in the refrigerator until firm.

Transfer the cheesecake to a serving plate and dust with the icing sugar before serving.

Jellied Cheesecake

Serves 6
225 g (8 oz) digestive biscuits, crushed
100 g (4 oz) butter, melted
15 g (½ oz) gelatine
60 ml (4 tablespoons) cold water
3 eggs
100 g (4 oz) plus 30 ml (2 tablespoons) sugar
50 ml (2 fl oz) milk
juice and grated rind of 1 lemon
350 g (12 oz) cottage cheese
150 ml (5 fl oz) double cream, stiffly whipped

Combine the biscuits and butter and use to line the base of a 20-cm (8-in) spring-form cake tin.

Sprinkle the gelatine over the water in a small saucepan and set aside for 5 minutes to soften. Dissolve over a low heat (*see page 28*).

Separate 2 of the eggs and beat the yolks with the whole egg, 100 g (4 oz) of the sugar and the milk. Pour the mixture into a saucepan and set over low heat. Cook, stirring constantly, for 3–4 minutes, or until it thickens. Do not let the mixture boil.

Remove the pan from the heat and stir in the dissolved gelatine. Set aside to cool to room temperature.

Mix in the lemon juice and rind, the cottage cheese and the remaining sugar. Fold in the cream.

Whisk the egg whites until they form stiff peaks, then fold them into the cheese mixture. Spoon the mixture into the tin and smooth the surface with a palette knife. Chill in the refrigerator for 2 hours, or until set.

Glazed Apricot Cheesecake

Serves 6–8
225 g (8 oz) digestive biscuits, crushed
100 g (4 oz) butter, melted
225 g (8 oz) dried apricots, soaked overnight
175 g (6 oz) cream cheese
225 g (8 oz) cottage cheese
60 ml (4 tablespoons) caster sugar
5 ml (1 teaspoon) vanilla essence
juice and grated zest of 1 lemon
2 eggs, separated
15 g (½ oz) gelatine
45 ml (3 tablespoons) water
275 ml (½ pint) double cream, softly whipped
1 extra egg white
TOPPING:
30 ml (2 tablespoons) apricot jam
5 ml (1 teaspoon) arrowroot
400 g (14 oz) canned apricot halves, drained

Preheat oven to 180°C, 350°F, Gas 4. Lightly grease a 20-cm (8-in) loose-bottomed tin.

Mix together the biscuits and melted butter and use to line the base and sides of the prepared tin. Bake for 8–10 minutes, then cool completely.

Put the apricots with their soaking juice into a saucepan. Add extra water to cover if necessary and cook for about 20 minutes, until tender. Drain, reserving the juice and purée the apricots in an electric blender or by rubbing them through a sieve. Leave to cool completely.

Beat together the cheeses, sugar and vanilla essence. Add the lemon juice and zest and the beaten egg yolks. Beat everything together until smooth.

Sprinkle the gelatine over the water in a small pan

Glazed Apricot Cheesecake

and leave to stand for 5 minutes. Dissolve over a very low heat (*see page 28*). Cool.

Pour the dissolved gelatine into the cheese mixture in a thin stream, beating all the time, then fold in the whipped cream, together with the apricot purée.

Whisk the egg whites (including the extra one) until they form soft peaks, then fold these into the cheese mixture. Spoon this over the biscuit base and chill in the refrigerator until set.

Measure and strain 275 ml (½ pint) of the reserved apricot cooking juice. Put in a saucepan and bring to the boil. Boil for 10–15 minutes, until reduced to half its original volume. Remove from the heat and add the apricot jam, stirring until it has melted.

Mix the arrowroot to a paste with 5 ml (1 teaspoon) more of the reserved juice. Tip a little of the syrup into this, then tip it back into the pan. Set over the heat again and bring back to the boil. Stir all the time, until the mixture has thickened. Leave to cool.

Arrange the drained apricot halves over the set cheesecake, then spoon over the cooled (it should be tepid) syrup to glaze. Chill again before serving.

Chocolate Cream Pie

Serves 6–8
350 g (12 oz) low-fat curd cheese
100 g (4 oz) cottage cheese
pinch salt
45 ml (3 tablespoons) brandy
75 g (3 oz) caster sugar
50 g (2 oz) bitter chocolate, grated
50 g (2 oz) preserved orange peel, finely chopped
45 ml (3 tablespoons) apricot jam
1 × 22-cm (8½-in) shortcrust pastry case, baked blind and cooled (*see page 83*)
30 ml (2 tablespoons) chocolate caraque

Sieve the cheeses and salt into a bowl. Stir in the brandy, sugar, grated chocolate and orange peel. Chill in the refrigerator for 1 hour.

Heat the apricot jam over low heat until it has melted. Brush the inside of the pastry case to glaze. Pile the cheese mixture into the pastry case and chill until required.

Before serving, scatter the chocolate caraque on top.

Gâteaux & Cakes

Dessert cakes and gâteaux are so luscious, extravagant and splendid, they are almost sinful. They positively invite you to indulge in a glorious orgy of fresh cream, fruit and chocolate. However, it must be one of the best kept culinary secrets in the world that you don't have to be an expert to make them. Time and care are the only special requirements, combined with a few helpful hints, and perhaps a willingness to stretch the household budget once in a while.

Few puddings are as spectacular, tempting, delicious and elegant as a really beautifully prepared and decorated gâteau. The combination of richness and a melt-in-the-mouth texture is irresistible except to the most iron-willed!

The majority of the finest tasting and most splendid dessert cakes are based on a whisked sponge, piled together in layers with flavoured cream, chocolate or fruit. While not difficult to make, it requires a light touch and plenty of time for the preparation.

The Sponge

Accurate measurement is essential when making a whisked sponge, so a good pair of scales and a set of measuring spoons are the first priority. The sponge gets its light, airy texture by being whisked and a balloon whisk achieves the best results here. An electric whisk is not quite as good although it saves a little time. The mixture is whisked over hot water, so you need an earthenware or glass bowl which can be set over a saucepan. Make sure that the bottom of the bowl does not touch the water in the saucepan.

Have all your ingredients ready and at room temperature and prepare the baking time before you begin making the sponge. Brush the tins with melted butter or vegetable oil, then line them with a circle of greaseproof paper and grease this. Sprinkle with flour and shake the tin lightly by tapping it against a hard surface to distribute the flour evenly. Tip out any excess. This will give the sponge a crisp outer edge and prevent it sticking.

Always preheat the oven to the recommended temperature for at least 15 minutes. Once the mixture is ready, it should be baked immediately. It is very delicate and, if it is kept waiting, some of the air—and thus some of its lightness—will be lost.

The sponge is made with eggs, sugar, flour and flavourings, but without fat. Sometimes other ingredients are added or substituted, but it is essential to follow the recipe precisely because disproportionate ingredients will give disappointing results. (Step-by-step instructions are given on page 114.)

The lightness of the texture is derived from the air trapped in the eggs as they are whisked. Always use large eggs for maximum volume and if they have been stored in the refrigerator, remove them at least 30 minutes beforehand.

The flour, salt and any powdered flavourings should be sifted together twice to aerate the ingredients as much as possible. Unless otherwise specified, use plain flour. (Some types of cakes will require the addition of a raising agent or the use of self-raising flour.) Add about one-quarter of the flour to the egg mixture at a time, sprinkling it over the surface and then fold it in with a metal spoon. Use a gentle figure-of-eight movement and make sure that each batch of flour is fully incorporated before adding the next. Never be tempted to stir or beat the mixture as this will result in a flat and heavy sponge. The volume of the mixture should be more or less the same as it was before the flour was added; this will depend on the lightness of your 'folding-in' technique.

Add any liquid flavourings at this stage, folding them in in the same way as the flour. The mixture should have a pouring consistency. Use a rubber spatula to scrape it from the sides of the bowl into the prepared tin (or tins). Cook in the centre of the oven.

As soon as the cake is ready (see overleaf), remove it from the oven and stand it, still in the tin, on a damp tea-towel for 30 seconds. This helps to loosen it. Invert the cake on to a wire cooling rack and carefully peel off the lining paper. Stand the cake the right way up and leave until it is cold.

Other Types of Cakes

Although a whisked sponge forms the basis of many dessert gâteaux as mentioned, other types of cakes can also be used. Angel cake is a feather-like confection made by a similar method to whisked sponge. This should ideally be cooked in an angel cake tin—a deep, round, metal tin, about 20-cm (8-in) in diameter with 10-cm (4-in) sloping sides and a funnel or tube in the centre, attached to a flat, removable base. However, you can also use a spring-form tin with a detachable tube base.

The cake can be decorated with simple toppings and frostings and the central hollow can be filled with fruit. A Surprise Angel Cake (see page 120) is very spectacular and well worth the effort needed in the preparation.

Choux pastry is sometimes used in making gâteaux and forms the basis of such classics as a pyramid of profiteroles (see page 122) and the delectable Gâteau St. Honoré (see page 125).

Fillings and Toppings

Fillings and toppings serve a double purpose. First, they are intended to add to the flavour of the cake, making it richer and often more moist. Second, they decorate the cake. Indeed it is the careful arrangement of sliced fruit, piped cream, chocolate caraque or flavoured frostings that give dessert gâteaux their mouth-watering appeal.

Double cream is undoubtedly the most popular choice for both fillings and toppings. Whisk it until it forms stiff peaks, keeping it plain or flavouring it with liqueurs, coffee, praline, orange or vanilla. Use it to sandwich cakes together as well as for piped decoration.

Fruit is often used in conjunction with cream, particularly those fruits which can be eaten raw, such as pineapple, raspberries, peaches and strawberries. Always use the freshest and best looking fruit for the final decoration and good quality fruit for a chopped filling.

Frostings are not only intended for tea-time cakes, but can also be used on dessert gâteaux. The softer, moister frostings, such as American frosting, caramel icing and chocolate ganache are the most suitable (see page 116). Once the cake is coated with any one of these, it is best to leave it plain or just decorate it very simply with halved walnuts or piping. Use the frostings immediately they are made and allow sufficient time for setting, but do not keep the decorated cake waiting about for too long before serving.

The sides of a multi-layered cake can be decorated with chocolate vermicelli or blanched and split almonds. Coat the sides smoothly with stiffly whipped double cream, then gently press the vermicelli or nuts on to the cream with a palette knife, turning the cake to make sure it is evenly coated.

Making a Whisked Sponge

75 g (3 oz) plain flour
dry flavouring such as 2.5 ml (½ teaspoon) cinnamon, ginger, mixed spice or nutmeg
or
grated rind from 1 orange or lemon or 2.5 ml (½ teaspoon) rose or orange water
3 large eggs
75 g (3 oz) caster sugar

1 *Preheat the oven to 190°C, 375°F, Gas 5 and prepare the baking tins (see introduction page 113). Half fill a large saucepan with water and heat to almost boiling. Sift the flour and any dry flavourings twice. Whisk the eggs in a large bowl. Add the sugar and place the bowl over the pan of hot water making sure it does not touch the water.*

2 *Whisk the eggs and sugar together until the mixture is pale coloured and thick enough to leave a trail when lifted with the whisk. This will take about 5 minutes with an electric whisk; 15 minutes with a balloon whisk. Remove the bowl and continue whisking until the mixture cools slightly.*

3 *Quickly fold in the flour and any other flavouring, one-quarter at a time, using a metal spoon. Pour the mixture into the prepared tins and bake for the required time (see chart below) in the centre of the oven. Do not bang the oven door because this can break down the bubbles in the mixture and prevent the cakes from rising.*

4 *Do not open the oven door until the end of the recommended cooking time. Then lightly press the surface of the cake with your fingertips. It should feel firm and your fingers should leave no impression. The cake should have shrunk very slightly from the side of the tin and there should be no sounds of bubbling. Turn out on to a wire rack to cool.*

Tin Sizes and Baking Times

Number of Eggs	Size of Tin	Baking Time
2	2 × 18 cm (7 in) sandwich	20–25 minutes
2	1 × 20 cm (8 in) sandwich	25–30 minutes
3	3 × 18 cm (7in) sandwich	20–25 minutes
3	2 × 20 cm (8 in) sandwich	25–30 minutes

Making and Using Simple Frosting

for a 17.5-cm (7-in) round cake
225 g (8 oz) icing sugar
1 large egg
2.5 ml (½ teaspoon) vanilla essence
15 ml (1 tablespoon) lemon juice
25 g (1 oz) unsalted butter

1 Prepare a double boiler and set it over low heat. Sift the icing sugar into the top of the boiler and make a well in the centre. Add the other ingredients.

2 As soon as the butter begins to melt, start beating the mixture with a wooden spoon. Continue beating, making sure that all the ingredients are thoroughly blended, until the frosting thickens to a 'spreading' consistency. This means it should easily coat the back of the spoon. Remove the top of the boiler from the heat.

3 Using a palette knife and working as quickly as you can, spread the warm frosting in swirls over a cooled, freshly made sponge cake. (It can be filled with jam or cream if you like.) Set aside for at least 1 hour, to allow the frosting to set.

4 As an alternative to making swirling patterns in the frosting, use a narrow-bladed knife to fluff it up into little peaks all over the top of the cake. Smooth the sides neatly with a warm, damp palette knife.

5 For a chocolate frosting, break 50 g (2 oz) chocolate into small pieces and melt with the other ingredients. Stir well to incorporate all melted chocolate from the sides of the pan.

6 Spread the icing over the cake as in step 3, smoothing it evenly with a palette knife.

Caramel Icing

for a 17.5-cm (7-in) cake
22.5 ml (1½ tablespoons) milk
22.5 ml (1½ tablespoons) single cream
75 g (3 oz) butter
30 ml (2 tablespoons) caster sugar
350 g (12 oz) icing sugar, sifted

Put the milk, cream and butter in a saucepan over low heat until melted. Stir to blend.

Put the caster sugar in a saucepan over low heat and cook until it has caramelized. Remove from the heat. Add the milk and butter mixture and stir until the caramel has dissolved. Stir in the icing sugar and beat until the mixture is cold, creamy and spreading in consistency. Use immediately, then leave the cake for at least 1½ hours to allow the icing to set.

Maple Satin Frosting

for a 17.5-cm (7-in) cake
75 g (3 oz) unsalted butter
350 g (12 oz) icing sugar, sifted
45 ml (3 tablespoons) maple syrup
few drops vanilla essence

Cream the butter until it is light and smooth. Beat in the icing sugar and maple syrup, a little at a time, until smoothly blended. Beat in the vanilla essence. Use immediately.

American Frosting

for a 20-cm (8-in) cake
225 g (8 oz) sugar
60 ml (4 tablespoons) water
pinch cream of tartar
1 egg white
pinch salt

Put the sugar and water in a pan over low heat. Stir constantly until the sugar has dissolved. Stir in the cream of tartar. Bring to the boil. Boil, without stirring, until the temperature registers 116°C (240°F) on a sugar thermometer. Brush down the sides of the pan with a wet brush to prevent crystals forming.

Meanwhile, whisk together the egg white and the salt until it forms stiff peaks.

Remove the syrup from the heat and allow the bubbles to subside. Then pour the syrup on to the egg white, whisking constantly at high speed. Continue whisking until the frosting thickens, turns opaque and will coat a spoon. Use immediately to decorate the cake, spreading the icing with a warm, wet palette knife.

Note: Add any liquid flavourings, such as essences, after beating the syrup in but before the frosting thickens. Add any solid flavourings, such as chopped nuts, just before spreading. Colour the icing with edible food colouring as you like (*see pic opposite*).

Syrup Frosting

for a 17.5-cm (7-in) cake
2 egg whites
30 ml (2 tablespoons) golden syrup

Put the egg whites and syrup in the top of a double boiler and whisk. Place over simmering water and whisk until the mixture thickens. Use to decorate the cake immediately.

Chocolate Ganache

for a 17.5-cm (7-in) cake
150 g (5 oz) plain, dark chocolate, broken into small pieces
75 ml (3 fl oz) strong, cold, black coffee
50 g (2 oz) unsalted butter, cut into small pieces
2 large egg yolks
10 ml (2 teaspoons) dark rum

Put the chocolate and the coffee in the top of a double boiler over simmering water. When the chocolate has melted, stir to blend thoroughly.

Remove from the heat and beat in the butter, one piece at a time. Then beat in the egg yolks and the rum.

Set aside, stirring occasionally, until cold and thick. Use as a filling or pipe over the top of a cake.

Chocolate Caraque

100 g (4 oz) dark, cooking chocolate

Break the chocolate into small pieces. Put them into a bowl and set over a pan of hot, but not boiling, water, until they have melted. Spread the chocolate on a cold surface with a palette knife, so that it is smooth and about 6 mm (¼ in) thick. Leave until set.

Using a sharp knife, shave the chocolate into curls and use for decoration.

Choux Pastry

makes 275 g (10 oz) pastry
75 g (3 oz) butter, cut into small pieces
5 ml (1 teaspoon) salt
pinch grated nutmeg
275 g (10 oz) plain flour
5 large eggs

Bring the water to the boil over moderate heat and add the butter, salt and nutmeg. When the butter has melted, remove the pan from the heat and beat in the flour. Continue beating until the mixture pulls away from the sides of the pan. Beat in the eggs, one at a time, adding just enough to keep the mixture thick and glossy. You may have a little egg left over.

It is now ready for use.

Ginger Nut Roll

Serves 6
225 g (8 oz) ginger nut biscuits
45 ml (3 tablespoons) sherry
225 ml (8 fl oz) double cream, stiffly whipped
6 glacé cherries
2.5 cm (1 in) piece angelica, cut into strips

Dip the biscuits in the sherry, one at a time. Spread each one with a little cream and sandwich them togther. Spread the remaining cream over the top and sides to cover completely. Decorate with the glacé cherries and angelica. Serve immediately (or no longer than an hour or so), cutting into slanting slices.

American Frosting, coloured pink

Rum and Orange Layer Cake

Serves 8
350 g (12 oz) plain flour
10 ml (2 teaspoons) baking powder
2.5 ml (¼ teaspoon) salt
2.5 ml (½ teaspoon) bicarbonate of soda
2.5 ml (½ teaspoon) ground cloves
2.5 ml (½ teaspoon) ground cinnamon
175 g (6 oz) butter, softened
350 g (12 oz) sugar
3 eggs, separated
5 ml (1 teaspoon) finely grated orange rind
125 ml (4 fl oz) fresh orange juice
50 ml (2 fl oz) dark rum
30 ml (2 tablespoons) orange-flavoured liqueur
2.5 ml (½ teaspoon) almond essence
5-cm (2-in) piece orange peel, finely shredded
FILLING:
225 g (8 oz) unsalted butter
100 g (4 oz) sugar
50 ml (2 fl oz) water
5 egg yolks, lightly beaten
30 ml (2 tablespoons) orange-flavoured liqueur

Prepare the filling. Cream the butter until it is light and fluffy. Set aside. Heat the sugar and water over low heat, stirring constantly, until the sugar has dissolved. Increase the heat and bring the syrup to the boil. Cover and boil for about 3–4 minutes. Cool slightly, then beat the syrup into the egg yolks, a little at a time. Stand the bowl in cold water and continue beating until the mixture is thick and cold.

Beat in the creamed butter, a little at a time. Stir in the liqueur, cover and chill in the refrigerator.

Preheat the oven to 180°C, 350°F, Gas 4. Line three 18-cm (7-in) sandwich tins with greaseproof paper and grease lightly.

Sift together the flour, baking powder, salt, bicarbonate of soda, cloves and cinnamon and set aside.

Cream the butter and sugar together until the mixture is smooth and creamy. Beat in the egg yolks, one at a time and add the orange rind.

Fold in a litttle of the flour mixture and a litle of the orange juice. Continue doing this until all the flour and orange juice are incorporated. Beat in the rum, orange-flavoured liqueur and almond essence and continue beating until all the ingredients are combined.

Whisk the egg whites until they form stiff peaks. Fold them into the cake batter. Divide the batter between the prepared tins and bake for 30–35 minutes.

Turn the cakes out on to wire racks to cool.

Sandwich the cold cakes together with the prepared filling and sprinkle over the orange peel.

Frosted Walnut Cake

Serves 6
225 g (8 oz) plain flour
2.5 ml (½ teaspoon) salt
10 ml (2 teaspoons) baking powder
75 g (3 oz) butter
225 g (8 oz) caster sugar
2.5 ml (½ teaspoon) vanilla essence
2 egg yolks
100 g (4 oz) walnuts, chopped
125 ml (4 fl oz) milk
2 egg whites
FROSTING:
2 egg whites
350 g (12 oz) sugar
75 ml (5 tablespoons) cold water
1.5 ml (¼ teaspoon) cream of tartar
2.5 ml (½ teaspoon) vanilla essence
50 g (2 oz) walnuts, finely chopped
DECORATION:
30 ml (2 tablespoons) walnut halves

Preheat the oven to 190°C, 375°F, Gas 5. Grease two shallow 20-cm (8-in) cake tins.

Sift the flour, salt and baking powder into a bowl. Set aside. Cream the butter until it is soft and gradually beat in the sugar and vanilla essence. Continue beating until the mixture is fluffy. Beat in the egg yolks with 50 g (2 oz) of the flour mixture. Mix in the walnuts, half the milk and a further 75 g (3 oz) of the flour mixture. Fold in the remaining flour mixture and mix in the remaining milk.

Whisk the egg whites until they form stiff peaks. Fold them into the cake mixture.

Divide the mixture between the two prepared tins and bake for 35–40 minutes.

Set the cakes aside in their tins for 5 minutes before turning them out on wire racks to cool completely.

To make the frosting, put the egg whites, sugar, water and cream of tartar in the top of a double boiler and whisk well. Set over boiling water over high heat and whisk constantly for 7 minutes.

Remove the container from the heat and beat in the vanilla essence. Continue beating until the frosting is thick enough to spread. Fold in the chopped walnuts.

Put one cake on a serving dish and spread with frosting. Top with the other cake and spread the remaining frosting over the top and sides. Decorate with walnut halves. Allow to set completely before cutting.

Frosted Walnut Cake

Surprise Angel Cake

Serves 10–12
75 g (3 oz) plain flour, sifted
25 g (1 oz) cornflour, sifted
pinch salt
225 g (8 oz) caster sugar, sifted
10 egg whites
15 ml (1 tablespoon) lemon juice
15 ml (1 tablespoon) hot water
5 ml (1 teaspoon) cream of tartar
5 ml (1 teaspoon) vanilla essence
PRALINE CREAM:
175 g (6 oz) hazelnuts
75 g (3 oz) caster sugar
575 ml (1 pint) Crème Chantilly (*see page 175*)

Preheat the oven to 180°C, 350°F, Gas 4.

Sift together the flour, cornflour and salt. Add about one-quarter of the sugar and sift the mixture three times. Set aside.

Lightly whisk together half the egg whites, half the lemon juice and half the water. When foamy, add half the cream of tartar and a little sugar. Continue whisking until the mixture forms stiff peaks. Do the same in another bowl with the remaining egg whites and other ingredients. Combine the whites and whisk in the rest of the sugar, 15 ml (1 tablespoon) at a time. Sift the flour mixture into the egg whites, 15 ml (1 tablespoon) at a time, and fold in.

Turn the mixture into a 20-cm (8-in) angel cake tin and smooth the surface with a palette knife. Draw the knife through the mixture to release any large pockets of air. Bake for 45 minutes.

Meanwhile, make the praline cream. Brown the nuts in a heavy frying-pan, without fat, over medium heat, shaking the pan constantly. When the skins begin to flake, remove from the heat ·and cool. When cool enough to handle, rub the nuts between the hands to remove the skins completely.

Put the sugar in a pan over medium heat. When it has melted and is light brown, return the nuts to the pan and stir until well coated. Pour the mixture on to a greased baking sheet or ·piece of foil and set aside to cool. When quite cold, grind to a coarse powder in a mill or grinder. Fold it into the Crème Chantilly and set aside.

Cool the cake in its tin on a wire rack for 1½ hours. Turn it out. Set toothpicks around it, 2.5 cm (1 in) from the top, to act as a cutting guide, then slice of the top layer in one piece. Cut round the inside of the cake 2.5 cm (1 in) from the inner edge and to within 2.5 cm (1 in) of the base. Repeat this 2.5 cm (1 in) from the outer edge. Scoop out the crumb from this 'channel'.

Fill the channel with praline cream. Replace the lid and cover the top and sides with the remaining praline cream. Serve.

Refrigerator Pineapple Cake

Serves 6–8
8 canned pineapple rings
225 g (8 oz) white marshmallows
125 ml (4 fl oz) plus 60 ml (4 tablespoons) medium
dry sherry
15 g (½ oz) gelatine
350 ml (12 fl oz) double cream, stiffly whipped
225 g (8 oz) digestive biscuits, crushed
25 g (1 oz) caster sugar
75 g (3 oz) butter, melted
4 fresh or glacé cherries

Lightly grease a 23-cm (9-in) loose-bottomed cake tin. Drain the pineapple rings, reserving 125 ml (4 fl oz) of the syrup.

Cut the marshmallows into small pieces and put in a pan with the 125 ml (4 fl oz) sherry and the reserved pineapple syrup. Set over a low heat and stir constantly until the marshmallows have melted. Dissolve the gelatine in the remainder of the sherry (*see page 28*) and leave to cool slightly.

Pour the gelatine into the marshmallow mixture and tip it into a bowl. Whisk in 275 ml (½ pint) of the cream and chill in the refrigerator until on the point of setting.

Meanwhile, mix together the biscuits, caster sugar and melted butter. Use this to line the base of the prepared cake tin. Cover with foil and chill for 20 minutes.

Arrange 4 pineapple rings on the biscuit crust. Spoon over the marshmallow mixture and smooth the top. Arrange the remaining pineapple rings on top and place a cherry in the centre of each one. Cover with foil and chill in the refrigerator for 6 hours or overnight.

Pipe the remaining cream around the edge of the pineapple rings before serving.

Devil's Food Cake

Serves 8–10
100 g (4 oz) dark cooking chocolate
225 ml (8 fl oz) milk
175 g (6 oz) light brown sugar
2 eggs, separated
1 extra egg yolk
275 g (10 oz) plain flour, sifted
5 ml (1 teaspoon) bicarbonate of soda
pinch salt
100 g (4 oz) butter
175 g (6 oz) caster sugar
50 ml (2 fl oz) water
5 ml (1 teaspoon) vanilla essence
CHOCOLATE FUDGE FROSTING:
225 ml (8 fl oz) single cream
450 g (1 lb) sugar
pinch salt
50 g (2 oz) dark cooking chocolate, grated
45 ml (3 tablespoons) butter
2.5 ml (½ teaspoon) vanilla essence
50 g (2 oz) walnuts, chopped

Preheat the oven to 180°C, 350°F, Gas 4. Lightly grease and line three 20-cm (8-in) sandwich tins.

Put the chocolate, milk, brown sugar and one egg yolk in a bowl set over a saucepan of hot water. Stir until the chocolate melts and the mixture thickens. Remove from the heat and set aside.

Sift together the flour, bicarbonate of soda and salt.

Cream the butter. Gradually beat in the caster sugar and continue beating until the mixture is light and fluffy. Beat in the remaining egg yolks, one at a time. Stir in one-third of the flour mixture and half the water. Add the remaining flour mixture and water and beat well until the batter is smooth. Stir in the vanilla essence. Gradually stir in the melted chocolate.

Whisk the egg whites until they form stiff peaks. Fold them into the cake batter. Divide the batter equally between the prepared tins and bake for 25 minutes.

Turn the cakes out on to wire racks to cool.

To make the frosting, bring the cream to the boil over moderate heat. Remove from the heat and stir in the sugar, salt and grated chocolate.. Return the pan to the heat and stir until the chocolate has melted. Cover and cook for 3 minutes. Uncover the pan and reduce the heat to low. Continue cooking until the temperature registers 114.5°C (238°F) on a sugar thermometer.

Remove the pan from the heat and plunge it into cold water. When the mixture has cooled to 43°C (110°F), beat in the butter and the vanilla. Continue beating until the frosting thickens and has a spreading consistency. Stir in the walnuts. Sandwich the three rounds of cake together with three-quarters of the frosting and spread the remainder over the top and sides.

Coffee and Walnut Ring

Serves 8–10
15 ml (1 tablespoon) instant coffee
15 ml (1 tablespoon) hot milk
100 g (4 oz) self-raising flour
5 ml (1 teaspoon) baking powder
100 g (4 oz) soft margarine
100 g (4 oz) caster sugar
2 eggs
FILLING:
10 ml (2 teaspoons) instant coffee
20 ml (4 teaspoons) hot milk
few drops almond essence
100 g (4 oz) icing sugar
40 g (1½ oz) butter, at room temperature
50 g (2 oz) walnuts, finely chopped
ICING:
30 ml (2 tablespoons) instant coffee
90 ml (6 tablespoons) hot milk
450 g (1 lb) icing sugar
50 g (2 oz) butter at room temperature
4 walnuts, halved

Preheat the oven to 160°C, 325°F, Gas 3. Grease and line with greaseproof paper a 20-cm (8-in) ring mould. Grease the paper.

Dissolve the coffee in the milk.

Sift the flour and baking powder together and add the margarine, sugar and eggs. Add the coffee mixture and beat until glossy and light. Turn the mixture into the prepared mould, spreading it out evenly, and bake for 35–40 minutes.

Leave to cool for 3 minutes before turning out on to a wire rack to cool completely.

Meanwhile, make the filling. Dissolve the coffee in the milk. Add the almond essence. Sift the icing sugar and beat in the butter, coffee mixture and nuts.

Cut the cake in half by pushing a knife through to the middle, holding it steady and turning the cake. Spread the cut halves with the filling and sandwich together again. Put on a rack over a tray.

To make the icing, dissolve the coffee in the milk. Sift the icing sugar into a bowl and add the butter with the coffee mixture. Set the bowl over a pan of simmering water and beat the mixture until smooth. Remove from the heat and set aside, beating occasionally, until it has a glossy look and a coating consistency.

Pour the icing over the cake and shake to smooth the surface. Repeat with the icing that has collected in the tray underneath. Decorate with the walnut halves and leave to set.

Profiterole Pyramid with Ice-cream and Chocolate

Serves 4
275 g (10 oz) choux pastry (*see page 117*)
1 egg, lightly beaten with 2.5 ml (½ teaspoon) water
450 ml (16 fl oz) vanilla ice-cream
100 g (4 oz) dark cooking chocolate, melted

Preheat the oven to 220°C, 425°F, Gas 7. Grease two baking sheets.

Fill a pastry bag, fitted with a 6-mm (¼-in) plain nozzle, with the pastry. Pipe 16 mounds, about 2.5 cm (1 in) in diameter and 12 mm (½ in) high, on the prepared sheets. Make sure that they are well spaced to allow room for expansion during cooking. Brush each puff with the egg and water mixture.

Bake for 10 minutes. Reduce the oven temperature to 190°C, 375°F, Gas 5 and bake for a further 15–20 minutes. Turn off the heat. Make a slit in the side of each puff to allow the steam to escape and return them to the oven for 10 minutes. Then transfer to a wire rack to cool.

Cut off and reserve the top of each choux puff. Fill the puffs with the ice-cream with a teaspoon. Replace the tops and arrange them on a chilled serving plate, piling them on top of each other to form a pyramid. Pour over the melted chocolate and serve immediately.

Doboz Torte

Serves 8
4 large eggs
175 g (6 oz) caster sugar
5 ml (1 teaspoon) vanilla essence
150 g (5 oz) plain flour, sifted
CARAMEL TOPPING:
175 g (6 oz) caster sugar
CRÈME AU BEURRE MERINGUÉE:
100 g (4 oz) plain chocolate, broken into small pieces
225 g (8 oz) butter, softened
175 g (6 oz) meringue cuite (*see page 56*)
DECORATION:
75 g (3 oz) chocolate vermicelli

Preheat the oven to 190°C, 375°F, Gas 5. Grease and line six baking sheets with non-stick baking paper and mark six 20-cm (8-in) circles. (Use the same baking sheet twice if necessary.)

Put the eggs, caster sugar and vanilla essence in a bowl over a saucepan of hot, but not boiling, water. Whisk until the mixture is thick and foamy, has doubled in size and will leave a ribbon trail when you lift the whisk. Remove from the heat and continue whisking until cold. Fold in the flour, a little at a time.

Spoon one-sixth of the mixture into the centre of each marked circle and spread it out with a spoon. Bake in two batches for 8–10 minutes, or until just firm.

Leave to cool on the sheets for 2 minutes and then transfer to wire racks to cool completely. When cool, trim, if necessary and select the best round for the top layer. Leave this on a greased wire rack.

To make the caramel topping, put the sugar in a saucepan over low heat until it has melted. Bring slowly to the boil and boil steadily, without stirring, until it turns a rich, brown colour. Pour the caramel over the top layer and spread quickly with an oiled knife. Mark the top of the caramel into eight sections with the knife before it hardens and leave to set.

To make the crème au beurre meringuée, melt the chocolate in a bowl over a saucepan of hot water. Set aside. Beat the butter well and then beat in the meringue cuite, a little at a time. Stir in the melted chocolate and set aside to cool.

Divide half of this cream between the five remaining cake rounds, spreading it out well. Sandwich them together and top with the caramel-covered layer. Reserve 30 ml (2 tablespoons) of the remaining crème and spread the rest over the sides of the cake. Coat the sides with the chocolate vermicelli, patting it on with a palette knife.

Use the remaining crème to pipe a swirl in the centre of the caramel.

Sachertorte

100 g (4 oz) butter
175 g (6 oz) caster sugar
6 eggs, separated
175 g (6 oz) plain chocolate, broken into small pieces
5 ml (1 teaspoon) vanilla essence
75 g (3 oz) plain flour, sifted
2 extra egg whites
pinch salt
GLAZE:
175 g (6 oz) apricot jam
10 ml (2 teaspoons) lemon juice
ICING:
100 g (4 oz) icing sugar
45 ml (3 tablespoons) cocoa powder
30 ml (2 tablespoons) water
75 g (3 oz) butter, cut into small pieces
2–3 drops vanilla essence

Preheat the oven to 180°C, 350°F, Gas 4. Lightly grease a 23-cm (9-in) cake tin and line with greaseproof

Sachertorte

paper. Grease again.

Beat the butter until it is soft and light. Add the sugar and cream the mixture until light and fluffy. Beat in the egg yolks, one at a time.

Put the chocolate in a bowl over a saucepan of hot, but not boiling, water. Stir until melted. Remove from the heat and cool slightly.

Beat the melted chocolate into the creamed mixture and then beat in the vanilla essence. Fold in the flour.

Whisk together the egg whites and salt until they form stiff peaks. Fold them into the creamed mixture. Put the mixture into the prepared tin and smooth the top. Bake for 1 hour, or until the cake is evenly risen.

Leave the cake in its tin for 5 minutes before turning out on to a wire rack to cool completely.

Cut the cold cake horizontally into two layers and place the bottom one on a wire rack.

Put the jam in a saucepan over low heat until it has melted. Stir in the lemon juice. Allow it to cool slightly and strain. Spread half of this over the bottom layer of the cake. Put the other layer on top and brush the top and sides with the remaining jam mixture.

To make the icing, put the sugar, cocoa and water in a saucepan and blend well. Place over moderate heat and bring to the boil. Boil for 1 minute, stirring constantly.

Remove the pan from the heat and beat in the butter, one piece at a time, and the vanilla essence. Allow to cool slightly and then coat the top and sides of the cake. Leave to set completely before serving.

Tipsy Cake

Serves 6

1 × 23-cm (9-in) slightly stale, whisked sponge (*see page 114*)
60 ml (4 tablespoons) raspberry jam
150 ml (5 fl oz) medium sherry
575 ml (1 pint) thick hot Crème Anglaise (*see page 176*)
225 ml (8 fl oz) double cream, softly whipped
50 g (2 oz) glacé cherries, halved
25 g (1 oz) angelica, cut into strips
50 g (2 oz) slivered almonds

Cut the cake horizontally into two even layers. Spread each cut half with the jam and sandwich together. Pour over the sherry. Pour over the Crème Anglaise to coat the top and sides. Cool and then chill in the refrigerator until set.

Spread the cream over the top and sides of the cake to cover the Crème Anglaise completely. Decorate with the cherries, angelica and almonds.

Brazil Nut Cake

Serves 8–10

100 g (4 oz) self-raising flour
100 g (4 oz) sugar
pinch salt
2.5 ml (½ teaspoon) ground ginger
225 g (8 oz) Brazil nuts, finely ground
225 g (8 oz) stoned dates, finely chopped
15 ml (1 tablespoon) finely chopped stem ginger
4 eggs
425 ml (15 fl oz) double cream, stiffly whipped
6 strawberries, hulled, washed and halved
1 peach, skinned, stoned and sliced

Preheat the oven to 180°C, 350°F, Gas 4. Lightly grease a 1.4-litre (2½-pint) loaf tin.

Sift together the flour, sugar, salt and ground ginger and stir in the nuts, dates and chopped ginger. Beat the eggs and add to the mixture, stirring thoroughly. Pour the mixture into the prepared tin and bake for

1½ hours, or until the top is lightly browned.

Cool for 5 minutes in the tin before turning out on to a wire rack to cool completely.

Slice the cake in half horizontally and spread one-third of the cream on the bottom half. Top with the other layer and spread half the remaining cream over the top of the cake. Pipe rosettes around the join and over the top with the remainder of the cream and decorate with the fruit.

Gâteau St. Honoré

Serves 8–10
100 g (4 oz) choux pastry (*see page 117*)*
37.5 ml (2½ tablespoons) orange-flavoured liqueur
125 ml (4 fl oz) Crème Chantilly (*see page 175*)
PÂTE SUCRÉE:
100 g (4 oz) plain flour
50 g (2 oz) unsalted butter, softened
30 ml (2 tablespoons) sugar
2 egg yolks plus 1 egg yolk, lightly beaten with 5 ml
(1 teaspoon) water
1.5 ml (¼ teaspoon) vanilla essence
CRÈME ST. HONORÉ:
275 ml (½ pint) milk
1 vanilla pod
4 eggs, separated
100 g (4 oz) sugar
30 ml (2 tablespoons) plain flour
15 g (½ oz) gelatine, softened in 45 ml (3 tablespoons)
water (*see page 28*)
CARAMEL SYRUP:
100 g (4 oz) sugar
50 ml (2 fl oz) water

First prepare the pâte sucrée. Sift the flour on to a board or marble slab and make a well in the centre. Add the butter, sugar, 2 egg yolks and vanilla essence and mix them with the fingertips until well blended. Gradually draw in the flour and knead the dough until it is smooth. Cover with cling wrap and chill in the refrigerator for 30 minutes.

Preheat the oven to 220°C, 425°F, Gas 7. Lightly grease two baking sheets.

Roll out the dough into a circle 20 cm (8 in) in diameter and about 6 mm (¼ in) thick. Transfer it to one of the prepared baking sheets. Using a plain nozzle, pipe a ring of choux pastry, 12 mm (¼ in) wide, around the pastry circle, about 6 mm (¼ in) from the edge.

Pipe the remaining choux pastry into eight small puffs on to the other baking sheet. Brush the choux pastry with the egg yolk and water to glaze and set aside.

Tipsy Cake

Bake the pastry circle for 10 minutes, or until the choux pastry ring is puffed up and light brown. With a sharp knife, prick the bubbles that have formed in the pastry circle. Reduce the oven temperature to 190°C, 375°F, Gas 5 and bake for a further 15 minutes. Carefully transfer the pastry circle to a wire rack to cool and then transfer to a serving dish.

Meanwhile, increase the oven temperature to 220°C, 425°F, Gas 7. Bake the choux puffs for 10 minutes or until puffed up and lightly browned. Pierce each puff with a sharp knife. Reduce the oven temperature to 190°C, 375°F, Gas 5 and bake for a further 10 minutes.

Transfer the puffs to a wire rack to cool.

To prepare the Crème St. Honoré, put the milk and vanilla pod in a saucepan over moderate heat and bring to just below boiling point. Remove from the heat, cover and set aside for 15 minutes to infuse.

Beat the egg yolks in a bowl set over a pan of hot water until they are thick and pale. Gradually beat in the sugar and continue beating until the mixture has thickened and will leave a ribbon trail.

Remove the vanilla pod from the milk. Gradually beat the milk into the egg yolk mixture. Beat in the flour. Strain the mixture into a saucepan and set over moderate heat. Cook, stirring constantly, for 2–3 minutes, or until the custard thickens and will coat the spoon. Remove the pan from the heat and stir in the gelatine. Continue stirring until it has completely dissolved. Set aside to cool.

Whisk the egg whites until they form stiff peaks. Fold them into the cooled custard.

Fill the choux puffs with about one-quarter of the Crème St. Honoré. Reserve the remainder.

To prepare the caramel syrup, dissolve the sugar in the water over low heat, stirring constantly. Increase the heat to high and bring to the boil. Boil for 5 minutes, or until the syrup turns pale gold. Remove the pan from the heat and set it over a bowl of hot water. Dip the tops and bottoms of the choux puffs in this caramel and arrange them on top of the choux pastry ring on the pastry circle. If the caramel becomes too hard, return it to low heat and re-melt.

Fill the centre of the gâteau with the reserved Crème St. Honoré. Chill in the refrigerator for 1–2 hours, or until the Crème has set.

Beat the liqueur into the Crème Chantilly and pipe stars in between the choux puffs. Serve as soon as possible.

* 100 g (4 oz) choux pastry means 100 g (4 oz) flour; adjust other ingredients accordingly.

Peach Gâteau

(Illustrated on page 112)
Serves 6–8
SPONGE:
3 eggs
100 g (4 oz) caster sugar
15 g (½ oz) cornflour
40 g (1½ oz) butter, melted
TOPPING:
800 g (1 lb 12 oz) canned peaches
250 ml (9 fl oz) double cream
90 ml (6 tablespoons) brandy
5 ml (1 teaspoon) arrowroot
25–50 g (1–2 oz) flaked almonds, toasted

Preheat the oven to 190°C, 375°F, Gas 5. Line and grease two 18-cm (7-in) sandwich tins and dust with flour.

Beat the eggs and sugar together in a bowl set over a saucepan of hot, but not boiling, water, until the mixture is thick and light.

Remove from the heat. Sift the flour and cornflour and fold into the egg mixture. Fold in the melted butter.

Pour the mixture into the prepared tins and smooth the tops. Bake for 20 minutes, or until well risen. Leave to cool for 5 minutes before turning out on to wire racks.

A maximum of 1 hour before serving, drain the peaches and reserve 150 ml (5 fl oz) of the juice. Reserve 7 peach halves for decoration and chop the remainder.

Whisk together the cream and 30 ml (2 tablespoons) of the brandy until it forms stiff peaks. Sprinkle the remaining brandy over the sponge circles.

Put one sponge circle on a serving plate and spread it with one-quarter of the cream. Add the chopped peaches. Spoon over a further quarter of the cream. Top with the other sponge circle and arrange the reserved peach halves on top.

Blend the arrowroot with a little of the reserved can juice. Mix with the remainder and put in a saucepan set over low heat. Cook, stirring constantly, until the mixture thickens. Brush the glaze over the peaches and set aside to cool.

Spread half the remaining cream over the sides of the cake and press the almonds on to it with a palette knife. Pipe the remaining cream around the top of the cake in rosettes and decorate each one with an almond.

Coffee and Brandy Gâteau

Serves 8
1 × 23-cm (9-in) whisked sponge (*see page 114*)
200 ml (7 fl oz) strong Italian coffee
10 ml (2 teaspoons) coffee essence
100 ml (3½ fl oz) brandy
CUSTARD:
3 egg yolks
100 g (4 oz) caster sugar
45 ml (3 tablespoons) plain flour
500 ml (18 fl oz) milk
2.5 ml (½ teaspoon) vanilla essence
DECORATION:
275 ml (½ pint) double cream, stiffly whipped
30 ml (2 tablespoons) finely ground coffee
coffee beans

First make the custard. Beat the egg yolks and sugar together in a bowl until the mixture is pale and creamy. Beat in the flour, 15 ml (1 tablespoon) at a time.

Set the milk over low heat and bring to just below boiling point. Stir it into the egg mixture. Rinse out the pan and pour the custard back into it. Set over low heat and cook, stirring constantly, until the mixture thickens. Do not let it boil. Remove from the heat, stir in the vanilla essence and set aside to cool.

Cut the cake vertically into 12-mm (½-in) slices. Line the bottom of a 15 × 20 cm (6 × 8 in) deep cake tin with a layer of cake, patching, if necessary, for a good fit.

Mix together the coffee, coffee essence and brandy and brush over the cake slices. Spoon over a layer of custard. Continue making layers in this way with the sponge, coffee mixture and custard until all these ingredients are used up, finishing with a layer of cake. Chill in the refrigerator for 6 hours.

Turn the gâteau out on to a serving dish. Pipe cream around the base. Sprinkle the ground coffee over the top. Pipe cream decoratively in the centre of the cake and decorate with the coffee beans.

Coffee and Brandy Gâteau

Gâteau Mille Feuille

Serves 6
450 g (1 lb) puff pastry dough (*see page 86*)
FILLING:
225 g (8 oz) strawberry jam
275 ml (½ pint) Crème Chantilly (*see page 175*)
ICING:
100 g (4 oz) icing sugar
1.5 ml (¼ teaspoon) vanilla essence
15 ml (1 tablespoon) hot water
50 g (2 oz) blanched almonds, slivered

Prepare the pastry and follow the rolling, folding and chilling process outlined on page 86. If time is at a premium, you need only complete these processes 3 times, instead of 6. However, the more times you roll, fold and chill the pastry, the lighter and 'flakier' it will be.

Preheat the oven to 220°C, 425°F, Gas 7.

Cut the dough into four pieces. Roll out each piece into a rectangle 10 × 30 cm (4 × 12 in). Transfer one rectangle to a damp baking sheet and prick with a fork. Bake for 10–12 minutes in the centre of the oven, until golden brown. Transfer to a wire rack to cool. Cook the remaining rectangles in the same way, keeping them in the refrigerator until the oven is free.

When all the layers are cooked and cooled, spread 3 of them with the jam and top each with the Crème Chantilly. Carefully sandwich them together and top with the remaining layer, smooth side uppermost.

Stir together the icing sugar, vanilla essence and hot water until smooth. Pour on top of the pastry and smooth with a warm, wet knife. Sprinkle the almonds on top and let the icing set before cutting and serving the gâteau.

Strawberry Gâteau

Serves 8–10
3 large eggs, lightly beaten
75 g (3 oz) caster sugar
75 g (3 oz) plain flour, sifted twice
15 ml (1 tablespoon) warm water
FILLING:
425 g (15 oz) strawberries, hulled, washed and halved
275 ml (½ pint) double cream, stiffly whipped
50–75 g (2–3 oz) toasted, flaked almonds

Preheat the oven to 180°C, 350°F, Gas 4. Grease and line a deep 15-cm (6-in) round cake tin. Dust with flour, tipping out any excess.

Put the eggs in a bowl over a pan of hot water and add the sugar. Whisk until the mixture is pale, thick and foamy and will form a ribbon trail. Remove the bowl from the heat and continue whisking for 5 minutes, until cool. Fold in the flour, one-quarter at a time, then fold in the water. Turn the mixture into the prepared tin and bake for 25 minutes. Reduce the oven temperature to 170°C, 325°F, Gas 3 and bake for a further 40 minutes, until the sponge is firm.

Turn the sponge out on a wire rack to cool.

Reserve 10 strawberry halves for decoration and chop the remainder.

Slice the cake horizontally into three even layers. Spread the bottom layer with about 45 ml (3 tablespoons) of the cream and sprinkle over half the chopped strawberries. Place the centre layer on top and spread with a further 45 ml (3 tablespoons) of the cream and the rest of the chopped strawberries. Top with the final layer. Coat the top and sides of the cake with all but 45 ml (3 tablespoons) of the cream. Press the almonds around the sides of the cake.

Use the remaining cream to pipe stars round the cake and decorate with the reserved strawberries.

Black Forest Gâteau

Serves 12
180 g (6½ oz) plain chocolate
210 g (7½ oz) butter
7 egg whites
180 g (6½ oz) icing sugar, sifted
180 g (6½ oz) plain flour
FILLING:
700 g (1½ lb) black cherries
90 ml (6 tablespoons) icing sugar
30 ml (2 tablespoons) caster sugar
5 ml (1 teaspoon) vanilla essence
225 ml (8 fl oz) Kirsch
500 ml (18 fl oz) double cream
50 g (2 oz) chocolate (optional)

Preheat oven to 180°C, 350°F, Gas 4. Grease a 25-cm (10-in) round cake tin and dust with flour.

Break the chocolate into pieces and melt in a bowl over hot, but not boiling, water. Remove and cool.

Beat the butter until fluffy. Beat in the melted chocolate when it is just barely warm.

Whisk the egg whites until stiff, then whisk in the sifted icing sugar. Tip the butter and chocolate on to this mixture together with the flour and fold in with a metal spoon. Turn into the prepared cake tin and bake in the centre of the oven for 1 hour. Test to see if the

cake is cooked; it should be well risen and springy to the touch. Leave it in the tin for 5 minutes, then turn on to a wire rack to cool completely (preferably overnight).

Make the filling. Reserve 13 whole, stoned cherries for decoration, then stone and halve the rest. Put all the cherries in a bowl and sprinkle over 60 ml (4 tablespoons) icing sugar, 15 ml (1 tablespoon) caster sugar and 2.5 ml (½ teaspoon) vanilla essence. Pour over half the Kirsch, cover the bowl and leave for 3–4 hours.

Strain the liquid from the cherries into a small pan. Stir over a low heat. Do not boil. Pour it over the cherries again and leave overnight.

The next day, slice the chocolate cake horizontally into 3 layers. Put these on 3 separate plates.

Strain off the liquid from the cherries and measure it. If there is more than 200 ml (7 fl oz), reduce it in a small pan. Add half the remainder of the Kirsch and spoon over the cake layers. Leave to soak for 30 minutes.

Black Forest Gâteau

Whip the cream until fairly stiff, then whisk in the remainder of the icing sugar, caster sugar, vanilla essence and the Kirsch. If any more liquid has strained off the cherries, whip this into the cream, too.

Reserve the whole cherries. Keep the bottom layer of the cut cake for the top of the gateau. Spread one of the other layers with a third of the whipped cream and cover with half the cut cherries.

Put the second layer of cake on top of this and repeat the cream and cherry layers.

Put the top layer of the cake on top (bottom—i.e. not cut-side-up) and cover this and the sides of the gâteau with the remaining whipped cream. Decorate with the whole cherries. If desired, shave the 50 g (2 oz) chocolate into strips with a potato peeler and use to decorate the sides. Chill the gâteau for about 1 hour.

Pancakes, Crêpes & Batter Puddings

The ease of making batter belies its amazing versatility. The same ingredients can be combined to make traditional pancakes, melt-in-the-mouth crêpes, wickedly tempting fritters and any number of tasty batter puddings. Don't neglect these desserts as so many people do: pancakes and crêpes in particular, whether served simply with lemon and sugar, or made into elaborate meringue-covered gâteaux, add a touch of festivity to any meal.

Almost every kitchen must have a permanent stock of flour, eggs and milk—the combination of which forms the foundation of an immense variety of really splendid desserts. Pancakes, crêpes, blintzes, waffles and fritters can be as plain and simple or as elaborate and elegant as you like. What is even more appealing is that the batters are all quick, easy and economical to make and you don't even have to splash out on expensive fillings to turn them into a scrumptious treat. Don't forget that plain English pancakes served with lemon juice and sugar, syrup or an easy sauce are a wonderful standby—when guests arrive unexpectedly, for example.

English Pancakes

Making pancake batter is ridiculously easy (*see step-by-step instructions, page 132*). Always use plain flour; strong, white flour (used for bread-making) gives the best flavour. To obtain the right consistency, use large eggs. If you prefer to use skimmed rather than full cream milk, this will not affect the finished result. Fat is added to the batter to prevent it becoming leathery during cooking. Use melted butter or a flavourless oil.

There is no need to set the batter aside to rest before cooking, as was once recommended, although it can be prepared in advance. Whisk again before use to restore aeration.

Cooking pancakes is a little more difficult than making the batter, but if you follow a few simple rules, you should have no problems (*see page 132*). They key to success is the right frying-pan. The easiest size to handle is one with a diameter of about 17.5 cm (7 in). If you use anything larger, you may find tossing the pancake almost impossible. The pan should be quite heavy to ensure an even dispersal of heat. Rounded sides make it easier to loosen the pancake with a palette knife before turning. Special crêpe pans which meet all these requirements are available.

Strictly speaking, pancakes are not fried, but are cooked by dry heat. However, a very little fat in the pan is necessary to prevent the batter from burning or sticking. Use clarified butter or flavourless oil. Swill it round the hot pan to coat the sides and bottom with a thin layer and pour off any excess before adding the batter. Re-grease the pan before cooking another pancake.

Pancakes have to be cooked on both sides and this means that they must be turned during cooking. Tossing the pancake is traditional and requires nothing more than a deft flick and a certain amount of self-confidence! If you don't feel brave enough to do this, use a palette knife or fish slice.

Crêpes

Crêpes are the French equivalent of English pancakes. While using the same basic ingredients, they have a subtle Gallic delicacy which makes them extra special.

Always use plain flour and, once again, strong plain flour produces the best taste. Use medium-sized eggs and melted butter, but both in a higher proportion than in English pancakes (*see page 134*). Allow the butter to cool slightly before adding it to the mixture, or it will cook the eggs. The liquid ingredient is usually a mixture of milk and water.

To ensure that there are no lumpy particles, strain the batter before using it. Unlike English pancake batter, crêpe batter should be set aside to rest for at least 2 hours before cooking. In fact, it can be prepared up to 8 hours in advance. This resting period is essential for obtaining tender, light results. Set the batter aside, in a covered jug, somewhere cool, such as a larder, but do not refrigerate as this would make the butter solidify.

As with English pancakes, the key to success is the pan. A traditional French iron crêpe pan, measuring 18 cm (7 in), is the ideal choice but any small, heavy frying-pan will serve.

Crêpes are cooked in a similar way to English pancakes. Brush the pan with just enough clarified butter or oil to prevent the batter from sticking. The pan should be very hot.

Crêpes are thinner than pancakes so less batter is required for each one. Many cooks find it easier to pour the batter from a jug, rather than spooning it into the pan. When the pan is hot, remove it from the heat and pour a maximum of 45 ml (3 tablespoons) batter into the centre. Quickly tilt the pan in all directions to spread a thin film over the base. Pour any batter not adhering to the base back into the jug. Cook over moderately high heat until the crêpe becomes opaque and small air bubbles form under the surface.

You can turn the crêpe with a flexible spatula, or even toss it, if you feel very brave. However, it is perhaps easiest to turn crêpes by hand. Shake the pan to check that the crêpe is not sticking. Then pick up the crêpe edge nearest you in your fingers, lifting it towards you and drop it over top side down. Cook it very briefly on the second side.

This second side never looks as attractive or evenly coloured as the first side. (This is also true of English pancakes but it is less noticeable.) Therefore, when stuffing and rolling, or folding crêpes in quarters, make sure the second side goes inside.

Keep crêpes warm over hot water or in the oven in the same way as English pancakes (*see page 133*).

Crêpes can be cooked in advance and re-heated to serve. Stack the cooked crêpes, interleaved with kitchen or greaseproof paper, on a plate and cover them lightly with foil. Keep in the refrigerator for up to three days.

To reheat, place the plate of crêpes over a small pan of hot water and cover both with a bowl.

Fritters

Making fritter batter is very similar to making pancakes or crêpes. However, the difference is that fritter batter is used to give a light crisp coating to deep fried fruit or other foods. It needs, therefore, to be extra light and to achieve this, extra air is incorporated by adding whisked egg white. Also, oil rather than melted butter, is used to make the batter, as this gives a lighter result; similarly, the liquid ingredient is always water, rather than milk.

The basic batter is made by the same method as pancake batter (*see recipe page 133*). However, it should be set aside for 30 minutes to rest. As it does not include melted butter, it can be put in the refrigerator. The egg whites should not be added to the batter until just before it is used, otherwise some or all of the aeration will be lost.

Making and Cooking Pancakes

100 g (4 oz) plain flour
pinch of salt
1 egg, beaten
275 ml (½ pint) milk
15 ml (1 tablespoon) melted butter or oil
30 ml (2 tablespoons) clarified butter or oil, for cooking

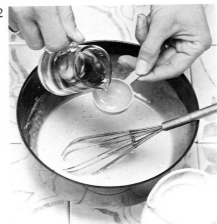

1 *Sift the flour and salt into a bowl and make a well in the centre. Add the egg and about one-quarter of the milk. Gently beat the egg and milk together and keep stirring to incorporate the flour gradually. Continue beating until the batter is smooth and the consistency of double cream.*

2 *Add the melted butter or flavourless oil to the batter and beat well. Gradually beat in the remaining milk. Keep beating the batter until small bubbles appear on the surface and the batter is completely smooth, the consistency of single cream.*

3 *Set a heavy-based frying-pan, 17.5 cm (7 in) in diameter, over high heat for 2 minutes. When the pan is hot, add 2.5 ml (½ teaspoon) clarified butter or oil. Swirl it round so that a thin film coats the bottom and sides of the frying-pan. Pour off any excess.*

4 *Remove the pan from the heat. Quickly pour about 15 ml (1 tablespoon) batter into the centre of the pan and about 15 ml (1 tablespoon) batter at the edge. Swirl the pan so that the batter joins to make a solid circle. Return to medium heat.*

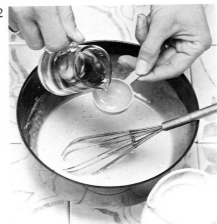

5 *Cook the pancake for 1–2 minutes, until little bubbles appear on the surface. Shake the pan from time to time to keep the bottom of the pancake loose. To toss, loosen the edges with a palette knife, lift the pan with both hands and give a quick flick. Catch the pancake!*

6 *Alternatively, turn the pancake with a fish slice or palette knife. Cook the second side of the pancake for a few seconds only. Tip the pancake out of the pan and keep warm (see opposite). Re-grease the pan before repeating this cooking process.*

Using Pancakes

1 *Keeping pancakes hot: pancakes which are to be stuffed and rolled need to remain flexible while the remaining batter is cooked. Stack them in layers, interleaved with sheets of kitchen or greaseproof paper on a heatproof plate. Set the plate over a pan of hot water.*

2 *Pancakes for layering can be kept warm in the oven. This gives a crisper texture. Stack the pancakes, interleaved with kitchen or greaseproof paper, in a buttered dish. Keep warm in an oven preheated to 110°C, 225°F, Gas ¼.*

3 *Filling pancakes: if filling is thick, such as sliced or chopped fruit, put 30–45 ml (2–3 tablespoons) of the filling on one edge. Carefully roll up the pancake so that the filling is in the centre. Avoid uneven lumps which spoil the appearance.*

4 *If using a thin filling such as fruit purée or jam, to stuff pancakes, spoon over 30 ml (2 tablespoons). Spread the filling evenly over the surface and roll up. Avoid fillings which are very runny, as these will leak out and make the pancakes soggy.*

Making Fritter Batter

100 g (4 oz) plain flour plus a pinch of salt
15 ml (1 tablespoon) caster sugar
30 ml (2 tablespoons) olive oil
150 ml (5 fl oz) water
2 egg whites

1 *To make a sweet fritter batter, sift the flour and salt into a bowl. Stir in the sugar and make a well in the centre and pour in the olive oil and water. Gradually mix in the flour from the sides until it is all incorporated into the liquid.*

2 *Mix the batter until it is smooth and the consistency of double cream. Rest in a cool place for 30 minutes. Just before using the batter, whisk the egg whites until they are stiff but not dry. Fold the batter into the egg whites. Use the batter at once.*

Crêpe Batter

Makes 425 ml (15 fl oz)—10–15 crêpes
225 g (8 oz) plain flour
pinch of salt
20 ml (4 teaspoons) caster sugar
4 eggs
200 ml (7 fl oz) water
225 ml (8 fl oz) milk
60 ml (4 tablespoons) melted butter, cooled

Sift the flour and salt into a mixing bowl and stir in the sugar. Make a well in the centre.

Beat together the eggs, water and milk. Slowly pour the egg mixture into the well, beating them into the dry ingredients. Continue beating until smooth. Gradually beat in the melted butter.

Strain the batter into a jug. Cover and set aside in a cool place for 2–8 hours to rest.

Before using, beat the batter again.

Buttermilk Pancakes

Serves 4–6
225 g (8 oz) plain flour
5 ml (1 teaspoon) baking powder
5 ml (1 teaspoon) bicarbonate of soda
5 ml (1 teaspoon) salt
2 eggs, beaten
450 ml (16 fl oz) buttermilk
60 ml (4 tablespoons) melted butter
45 ml (3 tablespoons) oil

Sift together the flour, baking powder, bicarbonate of soda and salt into a mixing bowl.

Beat together the eggs and buttermilk and fold into the flour mixture. Stir in the melted butter, mixing thoroughly to make a smooth batter.

Preheat the oven to 110°C, 225°F, Gas ¼.

Heat a small frying-pan and brush with a little oil. Pour in about 125 ml (4 fl oz) batter, tilting the pan to coat evenly. Cook until bubbles start to appear on the surface. Toss or turn the pancake with a flexible spatula. Cook until the pancake is golden on both sides.

Slide the pancake out and keep warm in the oven while you cook the remaining batter in the same way Serve immediately.

Note: These pancakes are somewhat thicker than conventional English pancakes or crêpes.

Pancakes with Coconut Filling

Makes 14–16 pancakes
150 g (5 oz) plain flour
4 ml (¾ teaspoon) salt
3 eggs, lightly beaten
45 ml (3 tablespoons) melted butter
225 ml (8 fl oz) milk
60 ml (4 tablespoons) clarified butter or oil
FILLING:
225 ml (8 fl oz) water
75 g (3 oz) brown sugar
100 g (4 oz) desiccated coconut
5-cm (2-in) cinnamon stick
pinch of salt
5 ml (1 teaspoon) lemon juice

Sift the flour and salt into a bowl. Make a well in the centre and pour in the eggs and melted butter. Gradually incorporate the flour into the egg mixture and stir until smooth. Gradually add the milk, beating thoroughly. Strain into a jug and set aside for 2 hours.

To make the filling, put the water and sugar in a saucepan and stir until the sugar has dissolved. Bring to the boil. Add the coconut, cinnamon and salt and simmer gently until the coconut has absorbed all the water. Add the lemon juice and cook, stirring constantly, for 1 minute. Remove from the heat, set aside and keep warm while you make the pancakes.

Heat a 12–18-cm (5–7-in) pan and brush with a little clarified butter or oil. Pour in just enough batter to coat the bottom of the pan thinly and evenly. Cook for 1 minute. Using a flexible spatula or palette knife, turn the pancake and cook for 1 minute.

Slide the pancake out and keep warm while you cook the remaining batter, greasing the pan before cooking each pancake.

Discard the cinnamon stick from the filling, then place 15 ml (1 tablespoon) of the prepared filling in each pancake and roll them up. Serve immediately.

Glazed Apple Pancakes

Glazed Apple Pancakes

Makes 12
5 ml (1 teaspoon) butter
275 ml (½ pint) basic pancake batter (*see page 132*)
60 ml (4 tablespoons) clarified butter or oil
275 ml (½ pint) double cream
FILLING AND GLAZE:
900 g (2 lb) cooking apples, peeled, cored and sliced
225 g (8 oz) sugar
30 ml (2 tablespoons) water
finely grated rind of 1 lemon
15 ml (1 tablespoon) apricot jam
25 g (1 oz) walnuts, chopped

First make the filling. Put the apples, sugar and water in a saucepan. Cover and cook over low heat for 15–20 minutes, until the apples are very soft.

Drain the apples, then return them to the pan and stir in the lemon rind. Set aside but keep warm.

Preheat the oven to 180°C, 350°F, Gas 4. Grease an ovenproof dish with the butter and set aside.

Using the batter, cook 12 pancakes, greasing the pan with the clarified butter or oil. Stack the pancakes interleaved with greaseproof paper, as you cook them and keep warm.

Spread 15 ml (1 tablespoon) of the apple filling over one half of each pancake. Fold the pancakes in half and then in quarters. Arrange the pancakes in the prepared dish and heat through in the oven for 10 minutes.

Meanwhile, put the jam in a small saucepan over low heat until bubbling.

Remove the pancakes from the oven. Brush with the jam, sprinkle over the walnuts and serve immediately with the cream.

Apple Pancake Gâteau

Serves 8
1.4 kg (3 lb) apples
15 g (½ oz) butter
1.25 ml (¼ teaspoon) ground cinnamon
grated rind and juice of 2 oranges
sugar (see recipe)
75 g (3 oz) raisins soaked in 45 ml (3 tablespoons) vodka
or rum
425 ml (15 fl oz) basic crêpe batter (*see page 134*)
75 ml (5 tablespoons) apricot jam
225 ml (8 fl oz) water
15 ml (1 tablespoon) cornflour

Peel, core and slice the apples.

Melt the butter in a large saucepan. Add the apples, cinnamon, grated rind and juice of 1 orange and sugar to taste. Cook gently for about 10 minutes, until the apples are soft and pulpy. Stir in the raisins and vodka or rum. Set aside.

Lightly grease a crêpe pan with a little oil and cook as many crêpes as possible using the batter. Set them on a wire rack as they are cooked.

Put 1 crêpe on an ovenproof serving plate and cover with a layer of the apple mixture. Continue making layers in this way until you have used all the crêpes and the apple mixture. Cover with foil and keep warm while you make the sauce.

Put the jam, the orange rind and juice from the remaining orange and the water in a small saucepan and heat, stirring to dissolve the jam. Mix the cornflour with the remaining orange juice and add to the pan. Simmer, stirring, for 3 minutes, keeping the sauce smooth.

Spoon a little sauce over the crêpe gâteau and bake for 10 minutes. Serve hot, cut into wedges, with the remaining sauce served separately.

Party Pancake Layer

Serves 4–6
60 ml (4 tablespoons) clarified butter or oil
250 ml (9 fl oz) basic pancake batter (*see page 132*)
3 egg whites
pinch of salt
175 g (6 oz) caster sugar
350 g (12 oz) strawberries, washed, hulled and sliced
45 ml (3 tablespoons) brandy (optional)
50 g (2 oz) icing sugar, sifted
25 g (1 oz) split blanched almonds

Preheat the oven to 110°C, 225°F, Gas ¼.

Lightly grease a shallow, ovenproof dish with the butter or oil. Set aside.

Make 12 pancakes with the batter, using the remainder of the butter or oil to grease the pan. Transfer the pancakes to the prepared dish, separating them with greaseproof paper and put in the oven to keep warm.

Whisk the egg whites with the salt until they form stiff peaks. Whisk in one-quarter of the caster sugar. Fold in the remainder in 2 batches.

Remove the pancakes from the oven and increase the temperature to 200°C, 400°F, Gas 6.

Place 1 pancake on an ovenproof plate. Cover with a thin layer of strawberries. Sprinkle over a little brandy, if using, and dredge with icing sugar. Continue making layers in this way, finishing with a pancake.

Spread the meringue over the pile of pancakes to coat completely. Scatter over the almonds.

Bake for 5 minutes. Remove the plate from the oven and serve immediately.

Anisette Crêpes

Serves 4
300 g (11 oz) plain flour
pinch of salt
100 g (4 oz) caster sugar
1 egg
350 ml (12 fl oz) milk
60 ml (4 tablespoons) oil
50 ml (2 fl oz) anisette

Sift the flour and salt into a mixing bowl and stir in the sugar. Make a well in the centre.

Beat together the egg and milk and pour into the well. Add 15 ml (1 tablespoon) of the oil and the anisette, beating the liquid ingredients well together. Continue beating, gradually incorporating the flour. Continue beating until the batter is smooth and creamy. Set aside for 2 hours.

Heat a 12–15-cm (5–6-in) frying-pan and brush with a little oil. Pour in enough batter to coat the bottom of the pan thinly and evenly. Cook the pancake for 1 to 2 minutes. With a flexible spatula or palette knife, turn the pancake and cook for 1 minute.

Slide the pancake out of the pan and cook the remaining batter in the same way. Serve immediately.

Apple Pancake Gâteau

Old-fashioned Jam Crêpes

Serves 6
50 g (2 oz) plus 10 ml (2 teaspoons) butter, softened
50 g (2 oz) caster sugar
2 eggs
50 g (2 oz) strong plain white flour
425 ml (15 fl oz) milk
90 ml (6 tablespoons) jam
150 ml (5 fl oz) double cream, whipped

Preheat the oven to 190°C, 375°F, Gas 5.

Cream the 50 g (2 oz) butter well and then beat in the sugar until the mixture is light and fluffy.

Beat in the eggs, one at a time, with 5 ml (1 teaspoon) flour. Beat in the remaining flour. Blend in the milk.

Grease 6 large saucers with the remaining butter. Beat the batter again and divide it between the prepared saucers, taking care not to overfill them.

Transfer the saucers to baking sheets and bake the crêpes for 15–20 minutes.

Remove from the oven and top each crêpe with 15 ml (1 tablespoon) jam and cream. Serve immediately.

Crêpes Suzette

Serves 4–6
3 egg yolks
150 ml (5 fl oz) milk
150 ml (5 fl oz) water
30 ml (2 tablespoons) orange liqueur (optional)
100 g (4 oz) plain flour, sifted
30 ml (2 tablespoons) caster sugar
60 ml (4 tablespoons) melted butter, cooled
clarified butter for cooking
30 ml (2 tablespoons) brandy
SAUCE:
65 g (2½ oz) unsalted butter
45 ml (3 tablespoons) caster sugar
finely grated rind of 1 orange
150 ml (5 fl oz) orange juice
30 ml (2 tablespoons) orange liqueur

First make the crêpes. Whisk together the egg yolks, milk, water and liqueur, if using. Gradually whisk in the flour and 15 ml (1 tablespoon) of the sugar. Beat in the melted butter. Strain the batter into a jug and set aside in a cool place for 2–8 hours.

Preheat the oven to 110°C, 225°F, Gas ¼. Heat an 18-cm (7-in) frying-pan until very hot.

Brush the pan lightly with a litle clarified butter. When hot, remove pan from the heat.

Pour a little batter into the pan and swill round to coat the base. Pour off any excess.

Cook the crêpe until golden and set. Toss or turn with a fish slice. Alternatively, pinch the crêpe between your fingers and flick it over. Cook the second side for 30 seconds.

Fold the crêpe in half, the second side inside, and in half again. Keep warm in the oven while you cook 11 more in the same way.

Melt the butter for the sauce in a large frying-pan. Add the sugar, orange rind, juice and liqueur. Cook gently until the sugar has melted.

Add 1 folded crêpe and turn to coat with the sauce. Slide it to one side of the pan, while you coat the next and so on until all the crêpes are coated and hot.

Sprinkle over the remaining caster sugar. Add the brandy and ignite. Serve when the flames have died down.

Lemon Soufflé Crêpes

Serves 6
5 ml (1 teaspoon) butter
12 crêpes made with 425 ml (15 fl oz) crêpe batter
(*see page 134*)
30 ml (2 tablespoons) brandy
FILLING:
25 g (1 oz) plain flour
50 g (2 oz) caster sugar
4 eggs, separated
150 ml (5 fl oz) milk
grated rind of 2 lemons
juice of 1 lemon

Preheat the oven to 220°C, 425°F, Gas 7. Grease a large, shallow, ovenproof dish with the butter and set aside.

To make the filling, mix together the flour and sugar. Beat in 2 of the egg yolks and 60 ml (2 tablespoons) of the milk.

Bring the remaining milk to the boil and gradually blend it into the flour mixture.

Pour the mixture into a saucepan and set over low heat. Cook, stirring constantly, for 3 minutes. Do not boil. Remove the pan from the heat.

Beat the lemon rind and juice into the mixture. Beat in the remaining egg yolks.

Stiffly whisk the egg whites and fold into the mixture.

Divide the mixture between the prepared crêpes, spooning it on to one half only. Fold the other over and smooth the filling towards the edges with your hands.

Transfer the pancakes to the prepared dish and bake for 10 minutes.

Heat a ladle and pour in the brandy. Remove the crêpes from the oven. Ignite the brandy and pour over. Serve as soon as the flames have died down.

Fruity Batter Pudding

Serves 4–6
10 ml (2 teaspoons) butter
225 g (8 oz) can pineapple rings, drained and quartered
425 g (15 oz) can apricot halves, drained
2 × 215 g (7½ oz) cans red cherries, drained and stoned
50 g (2 oz) seedless raisins
275 ml (½ pint) water
50 g (2 oz) plain flour
2.5 ml (½ teaspoon) ground mixed spice
pinch of salt
75 g (3 oz) caster sugar
3 eggs
150 ml (5 fl oz) milk
150 ml (5 fl oz) single cream

Preheat the oven to 180°C, 350°F, Gas 4. Grease a 1-litre (2-pint) ovenproof dish with the butter.

Mix together the pineapple, apricots and cherries. Spread the mixture over the bottom of the dish.

Fruity Batter Pudding

Put the raisins and water in a small saucepan over medium heat. Bring to the boil and boil for 1 minute. Drain and sprinkle the raisins over the other fruit. Set aside.

Sift together the flour, spice and salt into a mixing bowl. Stir in 50 g (2 oz) of the sugar and make a well in the centre. Break the eggs into the well. Beat the eggs, gradually incorporating the flour mixture until smoothly blended. Gradually beat in the milk and cream a little at a time.

Pour the batter over the fruit. Bake for 1–1¼ hours, until the batter is firm at the centre, slightly puffed at the edges and golden brown all over.

Remove the pudding from the oven and set aside to cool for 15 minutes.

Sprinkle the remaining sugar over the top of the pudding and serve warm.

American Waffles

Makes 8
100 g (4 oz) plain flour
10 ml (2 teaspoons) baking powder
pinch of salt
15 ml (1 tablespoon) caster sugar
1 egg, separated
200 ml (7 fl oz) milk
30 ml (2 tablespoons) melted butter
2.5 ml (½ teaspoon) vanilla essence

Set the waffle iron over low heat, turning occasionally to heat both plates.

Sift together the flour, baking powder and salt into a mixing bowl. Stir in the sugar and make a well in the centre. Pour the egg yolk, milk, butter and vanilla essence into the well and beat them together, gradually incorporating the flour. Continue beating until the batter is thick and smooth.

Stiffly whisk the egg white and fold it into the batter.

Pour just enough batter over the surface of the heated waffle iron to cover it. Close the iron and cook for 2–3 minutes. Turn the iron and cook for a further 2–3 minutes, until crisp and golden. Cook the remaining batter in the same way and serve immediately.

Chocolate Waffles

Makes 15
225 g (8 oz) plain flour
15 ml (1 tablespoon) baking powder
50 g (2 oz) plain chocolate, grated
125 ml (4 fl oz) milk
3 eggs, lightly beaten
100 g (4 oz) caster sugar
1.5 ml (¼ teaspoon) salt
50 g (2 oz) plus 10 ml (2 teaspoons) butter, melted
2.5 ml (½ teaspoon) vanilla essence

Sift together the flour and baking powder into a mixing bowl. Make a well in the centre.

Place the chocolate and milk in a small saucepan over low heat. Cook, stirring constantly, until the chocolate has melted. Transfer the mixture to a bowl. Beat in the eggs, a little at a time. Stir in the sugar, salt, the 50 g (2 oz) butter and vanilla essence.

Pour the chocolate mixture into the well in the flour. With a wooden spoon gradually incorporate the flour until a thick batter is formed.

Lightly brush a heated waffle iron with melted butter. Pour over just enough batter to cover the surface. Close the iron and cook for 2–3 minutes. Turn the iron and cook for a further 2–3 minutes, until the waffle is crisp and well risen. Cook the remaining batter in the same way and serve immediately.

Apricot and Buttermilk Waffles

Makes 6
100 g (4 oz) plain flour
10 ml (2 teaspoons) baking powder
pinch of salt
15 ml (1 tablespoon) caster sugar
2 eggs, separated
150 ml (5 fl oz) buttermilk
45 ml (3 tablespoons) melted butter
100 g (4 oz) canned apricots, drained and puréed
50 g (2 oz) canned apricots, drained and chopped
150 ml (5 fl oz) double cream
2.5 ml (½ teaspoon) vanilla essence

Set the waffle iron over low heat, turning occasionally to heat both plates.

Sift together the flour, baking powder and salt into a mixing bowl. Stir in the sugar and make a well in the centre. Pour the egg yolks, buttermilk and butter into the well and beat them together, gradually incorporating the flour. Continue beating until the batter is thick and smooth. Fold in the apricot purée.

Stiffly whisk the egg whites and fold them into the batter.

Pour just enough batter over the surface of the heated waffle iron to cover it. Close the iron and cook for 3 minutes. Turn the iron and cook for a further 2–3 minutes, until crisp and golden brown. Cook the remaining batter in the same way.

Place the chopped apricots in a bowl. Whisk together the cream and vanilla essence until stiff. Fold the cream into the apricots.

Serve the waffles with the apricot cream.

Beery Batter Puffs

Serves 6
150 ml (5 fl oz) pale ale
100 g (4 oz) plain flour
25 g (1 oz) sugar
15 g (½ oz) butter, melted
2 eggs, separated
oil for deep frying
60 ml (4 tablespoons) caster sugar

Pour the beer into a saucepan and set over a low heat until just warm. Remove the pan from the heat.

Sift the flour into a mixing bowl and stir in the sugar. Make a well in the centre and pour in the beer, butter and egg yolks. Beat together, gradually incorporating the flour. Continue beating until a smooth batter is formed. Set aside for 1 hour.

Preheat the oven to 110°C, 225°F, Gas ¼. Heat the oil in a deep fryer to 180–190°C (350–375°F), or until it will brown a cube of bread in 32 seconds.

Stiffly whisk the egg whites and fold them into the batter.

Drop spoonfuls of batter into the oil and cook, turning once, for 4 minutes or until puffed and golden. Drain on kitchen paper and keep warm in the oven while you cook the remaining batter.

Pile the puffs on to a serving plate, sprinkle with the caster sugar and serve immediately.

Chinese Toffee Apples and Bananas

Serves 4
1 dessert apple
3 bananas
15 ml (1 tablespoon) lemon juice
150 ml (5 fl oz) plus 15 ml (1 tablespoon) water
15 ml (1 tablespoon) peanut oil
225 g (8 oz) sugar
oil for frying
15 ml (1 tablespoon) sesame seeds
BATTER:
100 g (4 oz) rice flour
75 g (3 oz) plain flour
15 ml (1 tablespoon) baking powder
15 ml (1 tablespoon) semolina
200 ml (7 fl oz) water

Peel the bananas and cut into chunks. Peel and core the apple and cut into chunks. Put the fruit in a bowl. Mix together the lemon juice and the 15 ml (1 tablespoon) water and pour this over the fruit. Set aside.

To make the batter, sift the rice flour, flour, baking powder and semolina into a bowl. Make a well in the centre, pour in the water and blend to a coating consistency.

With a perforated spoon, remove the fruit from the bowl and drain on kitchen paper.

Make the syrup. Stir together the remaining water, peanut oil and sugar in a saucepan set over a low heat until the sugar has dissolved. Bring to the boil and continue boiling until pale golden in colour. Set aside.

Heat the oil for frying to 180–190°C (350–375°F), or until it will brown a cube of bread in 32 seconds. Dip the fruits in the batter and fry for 2 minutes, until golden. Drain on kitchen paper.

Stir the sesame seeds into the syrup.

Using 2 oiled spoons, dip the fritters into the syrup and immediately into a bowl of iced water. Serve immediately.

Swiss-fried Cherry Clusters

Serves 4–5
900 g (2 lb) dark ripe cherries, with stalks
oil for deep frying
45 ml (3 tablespoons) caster sugar
BATTER:
100 g (4 oz) plain flour
pinch of salt
1 egg
150 ml (5 fl oz) milk
30 ml (2 tablespoons) oil or melted butter
15 ml (1 tablespoon) caster sugar

Tie the cherries in clusters of 4 or 5 with thread. Wash and pat dry with kitchen paper. Set aside.

To make the batter, sift the flour and salt into a mixing bowl. Make a well in the centre and pour in the egg. Add one-quarter of the milk and stir, gradually incorporating the flour. Beat in the oil or melted butter. Beat in the remaining milk and the sugar.

Heat the oil in a deep fat fryer to 180–190°C (350–375°F), or until it browns a cube of bread in 30 seconds. Preheat the oven to 110°C, 225°F, Gas ¼.

Suspend 3 or 4 of the cherry clusters on a long skewer. Dip them into the batter to coat well and then fry until golden brown and crisp. Drain on kitchen paper towels. Keep warm in the oven while you cook the remaining cherries in the same way.

Transfer the cherries to a serving plate. Remove and discard the tying threads. Sprinkle over the caster sugar and serve immediately.

Cream Cheese Blintzes

Serves 8
150 g (5 oz) plain flour
5 ml (1 teaspoon) salt
4 eggs, lightly beaten
275 ml (½ pint) milk
oil for frying
30 ml (2 tablespoons) icing sugar, sifted
150 ml (5 fl oz) double cream, stiffly whipped
FILLING:
100 g (4 oz) cottage cheese
100 g (4 oz) full fat cream cheese
2 egg yolks
30 ml (2 tablespoons) caster sugar
pinch of cinnamon
75 g (3 oz) seedless raisins or sultanas

First make the filling. Sieve the cottage cheese into a bowl. Beat in the cream cheese. Gradually beat in the egg yolks. Beat in the sugar, cinnamon and raisins or sultanas. Set aside.

To make the blintzes, sift together the flour and salt into a mixing bowl. Make a well in the centre.

Beat together the eggs and milk and pour into the well. Beat, gradually incorporating the flour.

Brush a 15-cm (6-in) frying-pan with a little oil and set over medium heat.

Pour in enough batter to make a thin layer, tilting the pan to coat the base evenly. Cook over low heat until the top of the pancake is dry and blistered.

Transfer to a heatproof dish set over hot water to keep warm, while you make 15 more blintzes.

Lay 1 pancake, raw side down and spread 30 ml (2 tablespoons) of the prepared filling along the centre. Fold the sides inwards and fold the ends over. Fill the remaining pancakes in the same way.

Preheat the oven to 110°C, 225°F, Gas ¼.

Heat a little oil in a large frying-pan. Put 2 blintzes in the pan, seam side down, and cook for 2 minutes. turn and continue frying until golden brown. Keep warm in the oven while you cook the remaining blintzes.

Transfer the blintzes to a serving dish. Dredge with the icing sugar and top with the cream. Serve immediately.

Orange Fritters

Serves 4–6
4 large oranges, peeled, pith removed and cut
into segments
few drops vanilla essence
60 ml (4 tablespoons) dry white wine
425 ml (15 fl oz) sweet egg white fritter batter (*see page 133*)
oil for frying

Arrange the orange segments in a single layer in a shallow dish. Mix together the vanilla essence and the wine. Pour over the oranges and set aside for 20 minutes.

Heat the oil to 180–190°C (350–375°F), or until it will brown a cube of bread in 32 seconds.

Dip the orange segments in the batter and deep fry until golden brown.

Drain quickly on kitchen paper and serve immediately.

Pineapple Fritters with Lemon Batter

Serves 4
275 g (10 oz) canned pineapple rings, drained and patted dry
30 ml (2 tablespoons) caster sugar
30 ml (2 tablespoons) Kirsch
oil for frying
15 ml (1 tablespoon) icing sugar, sifted
BATTER:
100 g (4 oz) plain flour
pinch of salt
2 eggs, separated
grated rind and juice of 1 lemon
15 ml (1 tablespoon) olive oil
150 ml (5 fl oz) water

First make the batter. Sift together the flour and salt into a bowl and make a well in the centre. Stir in the egg yolks, lemon rind and juice and the oil. Beat in the water. Set aside for 30 minutes.

Arrange the pineapple slices in a single layer in a shallow dish. Sprinkle over the caster sugar and the Kirsch. Set aside, turning the fruit from time to time, for 30 minutes.

Heat the oil to 180–190°C (350–375°F), or until it will brown a cube of bread in 32 seconds.

Stiffly whisk the egg whites. Fold batter into them.

Dip the pineapple slices into the batter and deep fry until they are golden brown all over.

Drain quickly on kitchen paper. Dredge with the icing sugar and serve immediately.

Mincemeat Fritters

Serves 4
60 ml (4 tablespoons) butter
8 slices stale white bread, crusts removed
120 ml (8 tablespoons) mincemeat
425 ml (15 fl oz) sweet fritter batter (*see page 133*)
oil for frying

Butter one side of each slice of bread. Divide the mince-meat between 4 of the slices and spreading it evenly over the butter. Top with the remaining slices, butter side inwards. Cut each sandwich into 4.

Heat the oil in a deep fat fryer to 180−190°C (350−375°F), or until it will brown a cube of bread in 32 seconds.

Dip the sandwiches into the batter. Fry for 4 minutes, until the batter is golden and puffy.

Drain quickly on kitchen paper and serve immediately.

Clafoutis aux Cerises

Clafoutis aux Cerises

Serves 4
15 g (½ oz) butter
225 g (8 oz) black cherries, washed and stoned
65 g (2½ oz) plain flour
pinch of salt
50 g (2 oz) caster sugar
3 eggs, beaten
275 ml (½ pint) milk
a few drops vanilla essence
30 ml (2 tablespoons) icing sugar, sifted

Preheat the oven to 180°C, 350°F, Gas 4. Lightly grease an 18.5-cm (7½-in) ovenproof dish with the butter. Arrange the cherries in the base and set aside.

Sift the flour and salt into a bowl. Stir in the sugar. Make a well in the centre and add the eggs.

Add one-quarter of the milk. Whisk the eggs and milk together and then slowly incorporate the flour.

Add the vanilla essence to the remaining milk and beat this into the batter.

Pour the batter over the cherries and bake for 1 hour.

Remove the dish from the oven and set aside for 15 minutes to cool. Dredge with icing sugar and serve.

Traditional Puddings

Here's your chance to indulge in a little culinary nostalgia. One of the things that made 'the old days' so good, was the excellence of the puddings. In those days nobody worried about calories or 'fighting the flab'. Forget such things yourself every once in a while and take a gourmet's trip down memory lane. Sample the ageless delights of Steamed Marmalade Sponge, Figgy Pudding, Trifle, Apple Charlotte and Fruit Crumbles, to name but a few of these memorable traditional puddings. Your family will be thrilled that you have turned back the clock!

The traditional puddings that are part of our heritage were once a basic part of any skilled cook's repertoire. These days, however, they tend to be somewhat neglected, perhaps because they evoke bad memories of school meals or because they are considered to be too full of fats and calories for today's health and weight conscious cooks!

By and large, they do not deserve such neglect and can certainly be incorporated into any sensible eating plan. Properly made, milk puddings are creamy and delicious; a selection of delectable toppings—caramel, brûlée, jam and meringue—will take the humble rice pudding, for example, out of the nursery and on to the family dining table. Suet sponges should be light, fluffy and packed with flavour; there is certainly little more tempting and appetizing on a cold, wintry evening than a meltingly sweet baked jam roll or a subtly flavoured, light orange sponge.

Why 'traditional'

Puddings, like anything else, only become traditional because they have been around for quite a long time. In the course of their history, many have moved from country to country as people have migrated from their homes to new lands. The well-known saying, 'As American as apple pie,' is, no doubt, a valid one, but both the English and the Dutch will put in claims for originating that particular treat. Some of the traditional recipes in the following pages are 'classics' from one particular country, while others are now popular in many countries.

The recipe for Christmas Pudding (*see page 156*) is the one used every year for the British Royal Family and was first served to George I on Christmas Day in 1714. Another royal note is struck by Riz a l'Impératrice (*see page 154*), created for the Empress Josephine, wife of Napoleon Bonaparte. Berry Grunt (*see page 153*), on the other hand, is as synonymous with republican New England as clam chowder.

A well-known song has the lines:
We all want some figgy pudding,
So bring some out here!
Figgy Pudding (*see page 153*) has an even more venerable association with Christmas festivities in England than the, now, better known Christmas Pudding. The North of England, long recognized as the home of good, no-nonsense cooking, is represented by Plum Dowdy (*see page 148*) and the deceptive simplicity that characterizes French cuisine is beautifully illustrated by Crème Brûlée (*see page 154*).

Suet Puddings

It is probably true to say, however, that steamed or baked suet puddings remain the most traditional of all traditional puddings. They are not at all difficult to make, but they do require time and first-class ingredients.

The basic suet sponge mixture can be used to make three kinds of puddings, all equally good, but each slightly different in preparation and appearance. In its simplest form this pudding is a flavoured sponge, steamed in a pudding basin and then turned out and served with a separately prepared sauce. A popular variation is to line the bottom of the basin with another ingredient, usually jam, before adding the suet mixture. When the pudding is turned out after steaming, it has a sweet topping. The third type is made by pouring the suet mixture over a filling and baking it in the oven.

The main ingredients of all three types are suet, sugar and flour. Suet is what gives the sponge its distinctive flavour and crumbly texture. Caster sugar is the best sweetener to use because its fine crystals dissolve easily, but for a richer flavour, you can use soft brown sugar. Demerara sugar, however, is not suitable as the larger crystals do not dissolve so easily.

Alternative sweeteners to sugar are honey and golden syrup. These can replace up to half the sugar and will make the pudding sweeter and richer. Reduce the liquid (*see right*) accordingly.

For the flour, most recipes specify self-raising flour, but you can use plain flour, if you add baking powder as a raising agent. Whatever flour you use, sift it to give maximum lightness.

For puddings with an especially light texture, breadcrumbs can replace up to half the quantity of flour. They should be very fine and made from fresh bread.

Liquid is required to bind the sponge mixture to a soft, dropping consistency and the steam produced by the liquid during cooking helps to make the sponge rise. Milk or eggs or both provide this liquid content. Always use medium-sized eggs.

Both dry and liquid flavourings can be incorporated into the sponge mixture. Dry flavourings, such as cocoa powder, should be sifted with the flour and the amount of flour reduced accordingly. Dried fruit, nuts and grated citrus rind can be stirred in after the suet and sugar have been added. Liquids, such as concentrated essences, should be added with the milk and eggs.

Toppings can be used instead of, or in addition to, such flavourings. Jam is traditional but other possibilities include golden syrup, treacle, honey, marmalade and lemon curd. You can also use fruit, cut into walnut-sized pieces. The best fruits are hard, tart ones which will not disintegrate during cooking, such as rhubarb, gooseberries and cooking plums.

The fillings in baked sponges are similar to these toppings, although jams are not suitable as they tend to make a pool in the bottom of the dish and are liable to burn. A thick layer of fruit, about 5 cm (2 in) deep, is ideal. Fresh, frozen and drained, canned fruit are all suitable; pack the fruit tightly.

Both earthenware and glass pudding basins are suitable for steamed puddings. You can also use dariole moulds for individual puddings. Always use the size recommended in the recipe to allow room for the pudding to rise. Grease the basin thoroughly with melted butter or margarine or brush it with flavourless vegetable oil. You can, if you like, coat the base and sides with biscuit crumbs, desiccated coconut, brown sugar or finely ground nuts.

Spoon the mixture into the basin. It should be two-thirds full. Grease a large circle of foil and make a 2.5-cm (1-in) pleat in the centre to allow for expansion. Tie this securely over the basin. Stand it in a steamer or on a trivet in a large saucepan. Add sufficient boiling water to come halfway up the sides and cover with a well-fitting lid. Steam for the time specified, topping up the water level as necessary.

Making Milk Puddings

45 g (1¾ oz) large grains, such as rice, sago or tapioca*
40 g (1½ oz) small grains, such as flaked or ground rice or semolina*
575 ml (1 pint) milk and about 75 g (3 oz sugar)
flavourings such as a vanilla pod or essence, lemon or orange rind etc.
*these quantities are for hot puddings; allow 7 g (¼ oz) more for cold puddings

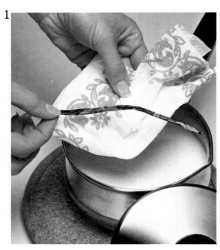

1 *Baked milk puddings are all cooked in similar ways. If you want to flavour the milk first, set it over low heat, adding citrus rind or a vanilla pod and bring to just below boiling point. Cover and set aside for 20 minutes to infuse. Remove the flavouring.*

2 *Generously grease an ovenproof baking dish with butter or margarine and sprinkle in the grain. Stir the sugar into the milk and pour over the grain. Add some dried fruit, if liked, and leave everything to soak for 3 hours. Alternatively, soak the grain separately, and then tip it over a layer of jam or fruit put in the dish.*

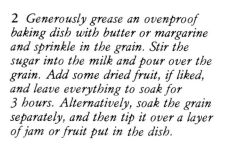

3 *Position a shelf in the centre of the oven and preheat to 150°C, 300°F, Gas 2. Dot the surface of the soaked grain and milk with small pieces of butter and, if desired, sprinkle over ground cinnamon, grated nutmeg or finely chopped glacé fruit.*

4 *For a pudding with a skin, place the dish uncovered in the centre of the oven and bake for 3 hours. The pudding should be thick and creamy with a golden skin on top. Serve straight away. For a pudding without a skin, cover the dish with oiled foil before baking. Cook for 3 hours.*

5 *To enrich a pudding without a skin, remove it from the oven and set aside for 10 minutes to cool slightly. Lightly beat together two large egg yolks. Stir them into the pudding and return it to the oven for about 5 minutes. Serve at once.*

6 *Fruit can be added to a pudding without a skin. After cooking, stir in a little fresh or canned fruit. Or add 30–45 ml (2–3 tablespoons) of freshly squeezed or canned fruit juice and stir this in carefully. Fruit syrup may be served separately or poured on top.*

Covering and Turning out a Steamed Pudding

1 Cut a piece of foil or greaseproof paper at least 7.5 cm (3 in) larger all round than the top of the pudding basin you have used. Grease a circle in the centre of this, a little larger than the diameter of the basin.

2 Make a 12-mm (½-in) pleat across the centre of the greased circle. This allows room for the pudding to rise.

3 Place the foil or paper over the basin, greased side down. Fold the foil down and tie securely with string under the rim of the basin.

4 Make a double strip of foil long enough to go under the basin, leaving sufficient foil either side to hold firmly. Use to lower the basin into the saucepan and to remove it when the pudding is cooked.

5 When the pudding is cooked, remove from the pan and leave to stand for 5 minutes to allow it to shrink away from the sides. Remove string and covering, then run a knife round the pudding. Using thick oven gloves put a plate over the pudding, then invert with the basin.

6 Carefully lift the basin off the pudding, leaving it whole on the plate.

Quantities for Turned-out Steamed Puddings

Basin	Flour	Servings	Cooking Time
1.1 litre (2 pint)	225 g (8 oz)	8	2¼–2½ hours
850 ml (1½ pint)	175 g (6 oz)	6	2 hours
575 ml (1 pint)	100 g (4 oz)	4	1½ hours
400–550 ml (¾–1 pint)	75 g (3 oz)	3	1–1¼ hours
6 dariole moulds	100 g (4 oz)	6	30–40 minutes

Note: Take care when using a thick topping that the mixture still only comes two-thirds of the way up the basin. Leave one-third free to allow the pudding to rise.

Plum Dowdy

Serves 4
6 slices stale, white or brown bread
75 g (3 oz) butter
700 g (1½ lb) purple cooking plums, washed, halved
and stoned
30 ml (2 tablespoons) golden syrup
30 ml (2 tablespoons) water
50 g (2 oz) soft brown sugar

Preheat the oven to 190°C, 375°F, Gas 5. Grease a deep baking dish. Spread the slices of bread with the butter on one side only. Line the base and sides of the dish with half of these, butter side upwards. Place the plums in the centre of the dish, cut sides upwards.

Put the syrup and water in a pan over low heat. Heat, stirring constantly, until the mixture is smooth and runny. Pour the syrup over the plums.

Cover with the rest of the bread slices, butter side up. Sprinkle over the brown sugar.

Bake in the centre of the oven for 1½ hours. Serve warm or cold with cream or custard (*see page 176*).

Bread Pudding

Serves 6–8
8 slices white or brown bread, crusts removed
275 ml (½ pint) milk
350 g (12 oz) mixed dried fruit
50 g (2 oz) mixed, candied peel
1 cooking apple, peeled, cored and grated
25 g (1 oz) soft brown sugar
45 ml (3 tablespoons) rich cut orange marmalade
2 eggs, lightly beaten
5 ml (1 teaspoon) lemon juice
5 ml (1 teaspoon) ground cinnamon
100 g (4 oz) butter

Break the bread into small pieces. Pour over the milk and set aside for 45 minutes, until the bread has absorbed all the milk. Stir in all the ingredients except for the butter. Mix thoroughly.

Preheat the oven to 150°C, 300°F, Gas 2.

Melt the butter in a small saucepan over low heat. Brush a baking tin, about 20 × 15 cm (8 × 6 in) and 10 cm (4 in) deep with a little of the melted butter.

Stir half the remaining butter into the bread pudding mixture. Turn the mixture into the prepared tin and smooth the surface with a palette knife. Pour over the remaining butter. Set aside for 5 minutes.

Bake in the centre of the oven for 1½ hours. Increase the temperature to 180°C, 350°F, Gas 4 and bake for a further 30 minutes. Serve hot or cold.

Apple Charlotte

Serves 4
900 g (2 lb) cooking apples, peeled, cored and
thinly sliced
1 quince (optional), peeled, cored and grated
grated rind and juice of 1 lemon
150 g (5 oz) unsalted butter
100 g (4 oz) caster sugar
1.5 ml (¼ teaspoon) ground cloves
30 ml (2 tablespoons) ground almonds
6–8 large slices white bread, crusts removed

Preheat the oven to 160°C, 325°F, Gas 3.

Put the apples, quince, if using it, lemon rind and juice in a flameproof casserole. Cover and bake in the oven for 30 minutes, until tender but not disintegrating.

Strain the fruit and return it to the casserole. Beat with a balloon whisk to form a light and fluffy purée. Beat in 25 g (1 oz) of the butter, the sugar and the cloves. Set over moderately low heat and cook, stirring frequently, for 15 minutes, until the purée is thick. Remove from the heat, stir in the almonds and set aside to cool.

Cut a circle from one of the slices of bread to fit the bottom of an 850-ml (1½-pint) ovenproof pudding basin. Cut a second, larger circle to fit the top.

Melt half the remaining butter in a frying-pan over low heat. Fry the smaller circle until it is crisp and pale gold. Remove it from the pan and cut it into 4 triangles. Arrange them in the bottom of the basin.

Melt the remaining butter. Cut the remaining slices of bread into strips 3–4 cm (1¼–1½ in) wide. Dip them in the butter, one at a time, to coat both sides. Arrange them around the sides of the basin, slightly overlapping, so that it is completely lined.

Spoon the apple purée into the basin, packing it in firmly and doming the top. Fold over the protruding strips of bread. Dip the remaining bread circle in the butter and place on top of the pudding. Dribble any remaining butter over the top of the pudding.

Cover the top of the pudding with greaseproof or waxed paper and weigh it down with a plate. Set aside for 10 minutes.

Preheat the oven to 220°C, 425°F, Gas 7.

Remove the weight and paper from the pudding. Stand the basin on a baking sheet and cook for 30 minutes, until the bread has turned crisp and golden. Remove the pudding from the oven and set aside for 10 minutes to cool slightly. Invert the pudding on to a serving plate. It should slide easily out of the basin. If it does not slide out easily, cool for a further 5 minutes. Serve immediately.

Bread and Butter Pudding

Serves 4

6 slices white bread, crusts removed
65 g (2½ oz) butter
100 g (4 oz) mixed dried fruit
2 eggs
50 g (2 oz) caster sugar
575 ml (1 pint) milk
2.5 ml (½ teaspoon) grated nutmeg

Lightly grease a 700-ml (1¼-pint) baking dish.

Spread the bread thinly with the butter, on one side only. Cut each slice into four triangles. Arrange triangles around the sides and over the bottom of the prepared dish. Sprinkle over a layer of diced fruit and cover with more triangles. Continue making layers until all the ingredients are used up, ending with a layer of bread.

Whisk together the eggs and sugar until the mixture is pale. Put the milk in a saucepan over heat and bring to just below boiling point. Pour the milk over the egg mixture and beat thoroughly. Pour the mixture over the bread and set aside for 30 minutes to soak.

Preheat the oven to 200°C, 400°F, Gas 6.

Sprinkle the nutmeg over the top of the pudding and bake in the centre of the oven for 35–40 minutes, or until the top is golden brown. Serve immediately.

Bread and Butter Pudding

Apple Brown Betty

Serves 4
700 g (1½ lb) cooking apples, peeled, cored and
thinly sliced
175 g (6 oz) stale white breadcrumbs
100 g (4 oz) soft brown sugar
5 ml (1 teaspoon) ground cinnamon
50 g (2 oz) butter, cut into small pieces

Preheat the oven to 190°C, 375°F, Gas 5. Lightly grease a 1.1-litre (2-pint) deep pie dish.

Put a layer of apple slices, about 5 cm (2 in) deep in the bottom of the prepared dish. Mix together the breadcrumbs, sugar and cinnamon. Cover the apples with a layer of this mixture about 12 mm (½ in) thick. Continue making layers in this way until all the ingredients are used up, ending with a layer of breadcrumbs. Dot the butter over the top.

Bake for 40–45 minutes, until the apples are tender. Serve warm or cold with cream or custard (*see page 176*).

Steamed Marmalade Sponge

(Illustrated on page 142)
Serves 4
225 g (8 oz) self-raising flour
100 g (4 oz) shredded beef suet
pinch of salt
100 ml (3½ fl oz) water
120 ml (8 tablespoons) orange marmalade
60 ml (4 tablespoons) fresh white breadcrumbs
30 ml (2 tablespoons) golden syrup

Lightly grease an 850-ml–1-litre (1½–2-pint) pudding basin. It should measure 15 cm (6 in) across the top. Grease a circle of foil large enough to cover the basin with a 2.5-cm (1-in) pleat in the centre.

Sift the flour into a bowl and stir in the suet and salt. Make a well in the centre and add the water gradually, adding just enough to make a firm dough.

Turn the dough onto a lightly floured surface and knead it briefly. Roll out to a thickness of 5mm (¼ in). Using saucers as guides and re-rolling the trimmings as necessary, cut 4 circles of dough the following sizes: 15 cm (6 in), 12.5 cm (5 in), 10 cm (4 in) and 9 cm (3½ in).

Mix together the marmalade, breadcrumbs and syrup.

Put the smallest circle of dough into the prepared basin, pushing it into the base. Spoon over one-third of the marmalade mixture. Top with the 10-cm (4-in) circle and another third of the filling. Repeat with the 12.5-cm (5-in) circle, the remainder of the filling and the largest circle.

Cut a 15-cm (6-in) circle of greaseproof paper, grease it and put it on top of the pudding. Cover with the foil and tie securely over the basin.

Put in the prepared steamer or saucepan and steam over a low heat for 3 hours. Top up with more boiling water if necessary.

Lift the basin out of the pan using oven gloves. Leave to stand for 5 minutes, then remove the foil and grease-proof paper. Turn the pudding out onto a warmed plate and serve with cream or Mousseline Sauce (*see page 178*).

Castle Puddings

Serves 4
10 ml (2 teaspoons) desiccated coconut, lightly toasted
30 ml (2 tablespoons) jam
100 g (4 oz) self-raising flour
pinch salt
50 g (2 oz) shredded suet
50 g (2 oz) caster sugar
1 egg, lightly beaten
30–45 ml (2–3 tablespoons) milk

Oil 4 dariole moulds. Grease 4 circles of foil large enough to cover each of the moulds with a 12-mm (½-in) pleat in the centre.

Put 2.5 ml (½ teaspoon) coconut in each mould. Turn and shake the moulds so that they are evenly coated. Spoon the jam into the base of each mould and set aside.

Sift together the flour and salt. Stir in the suet and sugar. Make a well in the centre and add the egg and 30 ml (2 tablespoons) milk. Mix together gently; the mixture should have a soft dropping consistency. Add more milk if necessary. Divide the mixture equally between the prepared moulds. They should be two-thirds full.

Make a 12-mm (½-in) pleat in the centre of each foil circle and tie them securely over the moulds. Prepare a steamer or a saucepan of boiling water. Steam for 30–40 minutes.

Remove the moulds from the steamer and uncover. Invert on to a warm serving plate, tap the top of each mould gently and lift off. Serve at once.

Rhubarb and Apple Crumble

Rhubarb and Apple Crumble

Serves 4–6
900 g (2 lb) rhubarb, washed and trimmed into 5-cm
(2-in) lengths
450 g (1 lb) cooking apples, peeled, cored and thinly sliced
60 ml (4 tablespoons) soft brown sugar
5 ml (1 teaspoon) ground cinnamon
TOPPING:
150 g (5 oz) plain flour
75 g (3 oz) sugar
75 g (3 oz) butter
2.5 ml (½ teaspoon) ground cinnamon
2.5 ml (½ teaspoon) grated nutmeg

Preheat the oven to 180°C, 350°F, Gas 4. Grease a
1.7-litre (3-pint) baking dish.

Arrange the rhubarb and apples in the prepared dish
and sprinkle over the brown sugar and the cinnamon.

To make the topping, put the flour and sugar into a
bowl. Add the butter and cut it into the flour with a
knife. Rub the butter into the flour and sugar mixture
with the fingertips until the mixture resembles coarse
breadcrumbs. Stir in the cinnamon and nutmeg.

Spread the topping over the fruit to cover it completely. Bake in the centre of the oven for 45 minutes.
Serve warm or cold with cream or custard (*see page
176*).

Black Cherry Roll

Serves 4
225 g (8 oz) plain flour
2.5 ml (½ teaspoon) salt
100 g (4 oz) shredded suet
150 ml (5 fl oz) cold water
60 ml (4 tablespoons) black cherry jam

Sift together the flour and salt. With a knife blade, stir in the suet and water to form a firm dough. Form it into a ball, cover and chill in the refrigerator for 10 minutes.

Preheat the oven to 200°C, 400°F, Gas 6.

Roll out the suet pastry on a lightly floured surface into a rectangle 20 × 25 cm (8 × 10 in). Trim the edges, Spread the jam over the pastry to within 1 cm (½ in) of the edges. Turn in the edges of the pastry, fold the corners neatly and roll up from one short edge.

Oil a large piece of foil and put the suet roll on it, seam side down. Bring the edge of the foil over the roll to form a loose parcel, leaving sufficient room inside for the pastry to expand. Place on a baking sheet and cook for 1¼ hours, unwrapping the top 5 minutes before the end of cooking time to brown the pastry.

Unwrap the roll and transfer to a serving dish. Serve at once with cream or custard (*see page 176*).

Berry Grunt

Serves 6
700 g (1½ lb) blueberries or 450 g (1 lb) blackberries, washed
200 g (7 oz) caster sugar
200 g (7 oz) plain flour, sifted
15 ml (1 tablespoon) baking powder
pinch salt
25 g (1 oz) butter
milk (*see recipe*)
275 ml (½ pint) single cream

Prepare a steamer or a saucepan of boiling water. Generously grease a 1.7-litre (3-pint) pudding basin. Grease a circle of foil large enough to cover the basin with a 2.5-cm (1-in) pleat in the centre.

Put the berries into the prepared basin and sprinkle half the sugar over them. Set aside.

Sift together the remaining sugar, the flour, baking powder and salt. Add the butter and rub it into the flour with your fingertips until the mixture resembles bread-crumbs. Stir in just enough milk to form a soft dough. Shape the dough into a circle and place it on top of the berries.

Make a 2.5-cm (1-in) pleat in the centre of the foil circle and tie it securely over the basin. Prepare a steamer or a saucepan of boiling water. Steam the pudding for 1½ hours.

Remove the pudding from the steamer and turn out on to a serving plate. Serve immediately with the cream.

Figgy Pudding

Serves 6
150 g (5 oz) plain flour
65 g (2½ oz) shredded suet
175 g (6 oz) dried figs, chopped
pinch grated nutmeg
2.5 ml (½ teaspoon) ground cinnamon
2.5 ml (½ teaspoon) ground ginger
2.5 ml (½ teaspoon) bicarbonate of soda
150 ml (5 fl oz) golden syrup
1 large egg, lightly beaten
150 ml (5 fl oz) milk

Grease a 575-ml (1-pint) pudding basin. Grease a circle of foil large enough to cover the basin with a 2.5-cm (1-in) pleat in the centre.

Sift the flour and stir in the suet, figs, spices and bicarbonate of soda.

Put the syrup in a saucepan over low heat and warm through until it is runny. Add this together with the egg and milk to the dry ingredients and stir thoroughly to mix.

Spoon the mixture into the prepared pudding basin. Make a 2.5-cm (1-in) pleat in the centre of the foil circle and tie it securely over the basin. Prepare a steamer or a saucepan of boiling water. Steam for 2 hours.

If you are not going to eat the pudding immediately, remove it from the steamer and uncover (but leave it in the basin). Set aside to cool. When the pudding is cold, cover it with a clean foil circle and store in a cold, dark place for up to 2 weeks.

To serve the pudding, steam for 1 hour to heat it through. Remove from the steamer and uncover. Set aside for 5 minutes. Run a knife around the inside of the basin and invert the pudding on to a warm serving plate and serve with custard (*see page 176*).

Black Cherry Roll

Crème Brûlée

Serves 4
275 ml (½ pint) double cream
1 vanilla pod
4 large egg yolks, lightly beaten
45 ml (3 tablespoons) icing sugar, sifted
30–45 ml (2–3 tablespoons) caster sugar

Put the cream and vanilla pod in a saucepan over low heat and bring to just below boiling point. Remove from the heat, cover and set aside for 15 minutes to infuse. Remove the vanilla pod.

Put the egg yolks in the top of a double boiler. Beat in the cream. Set the top of the boiler over the bottom and put on a low heat. Stir in the icing sugar. Cook, stirring constantly, for about 10 minutes, until the mixture thickens.

Pour the mixture into a 575-ml (1-pint) flameproof dish and set aside to cool. Then chill in the refrigerator for 8 hours or overnight.

Preheat the grill to high.

Sprinkle the caster sugar evenly and thickly over the surface of the crème. Grill until the sugar caramelizes and turns a deep golden brown. Set aside to cool and chill for 2 hours before serving.

Crème Caramel

Serves 6
575 ml (1 pint) milk
90 g (3½ oz) sugar
½ vanilla pod
2 eggs
2 extra egg yolks
CARAMEL:
100 g (4 oz) sugar
75 ml (5 tablespoons) water

First make the caramel. Put the sugar and water in a saucepan over low heat and stir constantly until the sugar has dissolved. Increase the heat to moderately high and bring the syrup to the boil. Boil until it turns light brown. Remove the pan from the heat and divide the syrup equally between 6 ramekins.

Put the milk, sugar and vanilla pod into a saucepan over moderate heat and stir to dissolve the sugar. When the sugar has dissolved, remove the pan from the heat. Cover and set aside for 20 minutes.

Preheat the oven to 170°C, 325°F, Gas 3.

Beat together the eggs and egg yolks until thick and pale. Strain the milk and gradually beat it into the eggs. Stir the mixture well and strain into the ramekins.

Put the ramekins in a deep baking tin and add sufficient boiling water to come halfway up the sides. Bake in the lowest part of the oven for 20–25 minutes, until the centre of the crème is firm when pressed with the finger. Do not allow the water to simmer during the baking. If it does, reduce the oven temperature.

Remove the ramekins from the baking tin and set aside to cool. Then chill in the refrigerator for at least 1 hour.

To serve, run a knife around the edge of each crème and invert on to a plate.

Bakewell Tart

Serves 6
125 g (4 oz) shortcrust pastry (*see page 84*)
30 ml (2 tablespoons) jam
50 g (2 oz) self-raising flour
2.5 ml (½ teaspoon) baking powder
2 eggs, lightly beaten
50 g (2 oz) soft margarine
50 g (2 oz) caster sugar
50 g (2 oz) ground almonds

Preheat the oven to 190°C, 375°F, Gas 5.

Roll out the pastry and line a 20-cm (8-in) pie plate. Spread the jam over the pastry base and set aside.

Sift together the flour and baking powder into a warm bowl. Add the eggs, margarine, sugar and almonds and mix together for 2–3 minutes, until light and glossy. Spoon the mixture over the jam and smooth the surface.

Bake in the centre of the oven for 35–40 minutes, or until a skewer inserted into the filling comes out clean. Serve warm or cold with cream.

Riz a l'Impératrice

Serves 8
275 ml (½ pint) milk
150 ml (5 fl oz) single cream
1 vanilla pod
75 g (3 oz) pudding rice
50 g (2 oz) caster sugar
275 ml (½ pint) Crème Anglaise (*see page 176*)
100 g (4 oz) mixed, chopped glacé and crystallized fruit
150 ml (5 fl oz) double cream
45 ml (3 tablespoons) redcurrant jelly
15 ml (1 tablespoon) brandy

Lightly oil a 1.1-litre (2-pint) plain mould.

Put the milk, cream and vanilla pod in a saucepan over low heat and bring to just below boiling point.

Remove from heat, cover and leave for 15 minutes.

Prepare a double boiler. Remove the vanilla pod from the milk. Pour the milk and cream into the top of the boiler. Stir in the rice and sugar. Set the top over the bottom over low heat and cook, stirring constantly, until thick. Remove from the heat and set aside to cool.

Fold the Crème Anglaise and the fruit, reserving a little for decoration, into the rice mixture. Whip the cream until it will just hold its shape and fold into the rice mixture.

Put the redcurrant jelly and brandy into a saucepan over low heat. Stir until thin and thoroughly blended, then pour into the prepared mould. Spoon the rice mixture on top and chill for at least 2½ hours.

Run a knife around the inside of the mould and invert the pudding on to a serving plate. Decorate with the reserved fruit.

Rich Rice Pudding

Rich Rice Pudding

Serves 6
50 g (2 oz) pudding rice
700 ml (1¼ pints) milk
75 g (3 oz) raisins
25 g (1 oz) caster sugar
25 g (1 oz) butter, cut into small pieces
pinch ground nutmeg
jam for serving

Lightly butter an ovenproof dish. Put the rice in the dish and pour over the milk. Add the raisins and sugar and set aside for 8 hours or overnight.

Preheat the oven to 150°C, 300°F, Gas 2.

Dot the butter over the dish and sprinkle over the nutmeg. Bake on the lowest shelf of the oven for 2–2½ hours, until the pudding is thick and creamy with a golden skin on top. Serve at once, passing a bowl of jam separately.

Sago Cream

Serves 4

575 ml (1 pint) diluted evaporated milk, made up following
the manufacturer's instructions
1 vanilla pod
45 g (1¾ oz) sago
15 g (½ oz) caster sugar
2 large egg whites
60 ml (4 tablespoons) double cream
25 g (1 oz) toasted almonds
30 ml (2 tablespoons) apricot jam
45 ml (3 tablespoons) orange juice

Put the milk and the vanilla pod in a saucepan over low heat and bring to just below boiling point. Remove the pan from the heat, cover and set aside for 20 minutes to infuse.

Remove the vanilla pod. Return the pan to the heat and bring to simmering point. Sprinkle over the sago, stirring constantly. Stir in the sugar. Cook, stirring occasionally, for 35 minutes, until the mixture is thick.

Remove from the heat and set aside for 15 minutes to cool.

Whisk the egg whites until they form stiff peaks. Whisk the cream until it will hold its shape. Fold the whites and the cream into the sago mixture. Set aside to cool completely. Sprinkle over the almonds.

Put the apricot jam in a saucepan and stir over low heat until melted and thin. Stir in the orange juice. Pour the hot apricot sauce into a jug and serve separately with the cold pudding.

Flummery

Serves 4

100 g (4 oz) pudding rice, washed, soaked in cold water for
30 minutes and drained
275 ml (½ pint) milk
275 ml (½ pint) double cream
50 g (2 oz) sugar
15 ml (1 tablespoon) grated lemon rind
5 ml (1 teaspoon) ground cinnamon

Put all the ingredients in the top of a double boiler. Set the top over the bottom and put on a low heat. Cover and cook, stirring occasionally, for 50–55 minutes.

Turn the mixture into a serving dish and set aside to cool. Then chill in the refrigerator for 3 hours, or until set. Serve straight from the refrigerator.

Christmas Pudding

Makes 2 puddings (see note below right)

225 g (8 oz) shredded suet
100 g (4 oz) stoned prunes
100 g (4 oz) chopped mixed peel
100 g (4 oz) seedless raisins
100 g (4 oz) sultanas
100 g (4 oz) currants
100 g (4 oz) plain flour, sifted
100 g (4 oz) dark soft brown sugar
100 g (4 oz) brown breadcrumbs
100 g (4 oz) chopped, mixed nuts
pinch ground nutmeg
pinch ground ginger
pinch ground cinnamon
pinch ground cloves
grated rind of ½ lemon
225 g (8 oz) eggs, weighed in their shells
150 ml (5 fl oz) plus 15 ml (1 tablespoon) brandy
juice of ½ lemon
15–30 ml (1–2 tablespoons) milk
TO SERVE:
30 ml (2 tablespoons) brandy per pudding

Put the suet, prunes, peel, dried fruit, flour, sugar, breadcrumbs, nuts, spices and lemon rind in a large bowl. Thoroughly mix together. Make a well in the centre.

Beat together the eggs, 150 ml (5 fl oz) of the brandy and the lemon juice and pour into the well. Stir vigorously until thoroughly mixed. If the mixture seems stiff and dry, add a little milk.

Cover the bowl with foil and set aside in a cool place for at least 12 hours.

Lightly grease two 575-ml (1-pint) pudding basins and two circles of foil, large enough to cover them with a 2.5-cm (1-in) pleat in the centre of each.

Spoon the mixture into the prepared basins, packing it down firmly. Leave a 2.5-cm (1-in) space at the top. Make a 2.5-cm (1-in) pleat in the centre of each foil circle and tie them securely over the basins. Prepare a double steamer or two large saucepans of boiling water. Steam the puddings for 1½ hours.

Remove the puddings from the steamer and discard the foil circles. Set aside to cool completely. Prick the surface of the puddings and brush with the remaining brandy. Cover with clean foil circles and store in a cool, dark place until required. (They will keep for several months—see note below.)

To serve the pudding, steam for 45 minutes to warm them through. Run a knife blade around the inside of the basin and invert the pudding on to a serving plate.

Heat the serving brandy in a small saucepan, until it is warm but not boiling. Pour the brandy over the pudding and ignite. Serve while still flaming, spooning the brandy from the plate back over the top of the pudding until the flames die out.

Note: This quantity can also be made into three 450-g (1-lb) puddings, one 1.1-kg (2-lb) pudding plus two 225-g (½-lb) puddings, or one 1.4-kg (3-lb) pudding, according to your family's requirements. A 450-g (1-lb) pudding serves 6–8. Allow 1 hour steaming time per 450 g (1 lb) of pudding for the initial cooking and 30 minutes steaming time per 450 g (1 lb) of pudding before serving.

The puddings will keep for up to two years. If keeping for two years, brush with brandy every month. If keeping for one year, brush with brandy every two months. If keeping for 3 months, brush with brandy once after a month and a half.

Christmas Pudding

Peach Trifle

Peach Trifle

Serves 6
6 trifle sponges
45 ml (3 tablespoons) strawberry jam
150 ml (5 fl oz) sweet sherry
575 ml (1 pint) milk
1 vanilla pod
4 egg yolks
15 ml (1 tablespoon) caster sugar
6 large peaches, blanched, peeled, halved and stoned
275 ml (½ pint) double cream
DECORATION:
angelica

Trim the sponges to fit snugly in to the base of a glass dessert dish, 20 cm (8 in) in diameter at the widest part. Then split the sponges in half and spread with the jam. Sandwich them together again and place in the dish. Sprinkle over the sherry and set aside for 3 hours to allow the sponge to absorb the sherry.

Put the milk and vanilla pod in a saucepan over low heat and bring to just below boiling point. Remove from the heat, cover and set aside for 15 minutes to infuse. Remove the vanilla pod from the milk.

Whisk together the egg yolks and sugar in the top of a double boiler, until light and thick. Pour over the milk, set the top of the boiler over the bottom and put on a low heat. Cook, beating constantly, until the custard is thick and will coat the back of a spoon. Remove the custard from the heat, strain, cover and set aside to cool.

Slice the peaches, catching the juice on a plate. Arrange the slices on top of the sponges and pour over the juice. Stir the custard and pour over the peaches.

Whip the cream until it forms soft peaks. Spread two-thirds of the cream over the custard, using a spatula. Put the remainder in a piping bag and pipe rosettes round the edge and in the centre. Decorate with pieces of angelica cut into diamond shapes.

Boodle's Orange Trifle

Serves 4
4 trifle sponges, split in half lengthways
60 ml (4 tablespoons) orange marmalade
120 ml (8 tablespoons) orange-flavoured liqueur
4 oranges and 2 lemons
30 ml (2 tablespoons) caster sugar
575 ml (1 pint) double cream

Sandwich the sponges together with the marmalade and arrange them in the bottom of a dish about 20 cm (8 in) in diameter and 10 cm (4 in) deep. Pour over the liqueur and set aside in a cool place for 3 hours.

Grate the rinds of 2 oranges and 1 lemon. Squeeze the juice from all the fruit and mix with the rind and the sugar. Whisk the cream until it forms soft peaks and fold it into the fruit juice mixture. Whisk again for a minute or two. Pour the cream over the sponges, cover and chill for at least 10 hours. Remove from the refrigerator 30 minutes before serving.

Queen of Puddings

Serves 6
575 ml (1 pint) milk
50 g (2 oz) butter
finely pared rind and juice of 1 lemon
150 g (5 oz) caster sugar
100 g (4 oz) stale sponge cake, crumbled
2 eggs, separated
pinch of salt
45 ml (3 tablespoons) apricot or strawberry jam

Preheat the oven to 180°C, 350°F, Gas 4. Grease an 850-ml (1½-pint) ovenproof dish with a little butter.

Put the milk, butter and lemon rind into a medium saucepan and bring to the boil over medium heat. Remove from the heat and stir in 25 g (1 oz) of the sugar until it has dissolved. Stir in the lemon juice, cover and set aside for 10 minutes.

Arrange the cake crumbs in the bottom of the prepared dish. Lightly beat the egg yolks and stir them into the milk mixture. Strain the egg and milk over the crumbs and stir well so all the crumbs are saturated.

Bake for 20 minutes, or until set. Remove from the oven and increase the heat to 200°C, 400°F, Gas 6.

Meanwhile, whisk together the egg whites and salt until they form stiff peaks. Whisk in half the remaining sugar, then fold in the rest.

Spread the jam over the top of the pudding. Cover with the meringue and bake for 10 minutes, or until the meringue is puffy and golden. Serve immediately.

Syllabub

Serves 6
50 g (2 oz) caster sugar
50 ml (2 fl oz) lemon juice
275 ml (½ pint) double cream
50 ml (2 fl oz) brandy
50 ml (2 fl oz) sherry

Combine the sugar and lemon juice in a bowl and stir until the sugar has dissolved.

Whisk the cream until it stands in soft peaks. Gradually whisk in the brandy, sherry and sweetened lemon juice.

Divide among 4 glasses and chill in the refrigerator for 2–3 hours before serving.

Sack Posset

Serves 4
2 large eggs, separated
275 ml (½ pint) double cream
45 ml (3 tablespoons) sweet or medium sherry
50 g (2 oz) caster sugar

Whisk the egg whites until they form stiff peaks, but not until they are dry.

Whip the cream until it is thick, but not stiff, then whisk in the egg yolks. Gradually whisk in the sherry and the sugar. Continue whisking until the mixture is very thick.

Fold the egg whites into the cream mixture. Spoon the posset into 4 glasses or custard cups and serve as soon as possible.

Lemon Posset

Serves 4
grated rind and juice of 1 lemon
60 ml (4 tablespoons) white wine
50 g (2 oz) caster sugar
275 ml (½ pint) double cream
2 egg whites
4 thin slices lemon

Put the lemon rind and juice, the wine and sugar in a bowl and stir until the sugar has dissolved. Add the cream and whisk the mixture until it forms stiff peaks. Set aside.

Whisk the egg whites until they form stiff peaks and fold them into the cream mixture. Turn the posset into 4 glasses, decorate with the lemon slices and serve.

Slimmers' Desserts

This is the chapter that helps you to atone for many of the others in this book! When the scales and ever-tightening waist-bands—not to mention your family—tell you the time has come for a temporary cut-down, simply substitute these low-calorie, but just as scrumptious 'Slimmers Specials'. You will soon discover that there is no reason why slimming should also be a punishment; that a sweet-tooth can be indulged without paying the price on the bathroom scales the next morning. And any dieting dinner guests will thank you, too!

Desserts are always a major problem for the slimmer and are doubly difficult for the cook on a diet. Even if you promise yourself that you will nibble an apple while the rest of the family tucks into ice-cream or rice pudding, the temptation is generally too much. It becomes absolutely unbearable and irresistible at dinner parties—particularly your own. After lavishing hours of loving care and attention on the preparation of a chocolate gâteau or cream-laden soufflé, it takes a will of iron not to sample the results. Yet even a thin slice or the tiniest helping is crammed full of unwanted and sinful calories.

Unfortunately, no food is, in itself, slimming. Virtually everything that you eat and drink, with a very few exceptions, contains calories. The art of losing weight, as every successful dieter knows, is to eat fewer calories than you 'burn up' as energy. Sadly, most of the typical ingredients for desserts—cream, butter, sugar, flour, chocolate and liqueurs, to name only a few—are very high in calories. So, for anyone with a sweet tooth and a weight problem, desserts constitute a 'red-alert'.

The only truly 'slimming' dessert is to go without altogether, but this makes dieting a dreary business, unfair on the family (quite apart from you) and simply not practical if you have dinner guests. The solution to this difficult dilemma is to prepare 'Slimmers' Specials'. Low-calorie desserts do not *have* to be boring. The recipes which follow are all designed to delight the palates of slimmers and non-slimmers alike, while not putting too many extra bulges on the waistline.

Some of the recipes are ideal desserts for everyday meals. They are tasty, not too demanding to make and very low in calories. For example, Pear and Prune Dessert (*see page 171*), a delightful and unusual mixture of chilled, poached fruit, contains about 120 calories per serving. Apple Yoghurt Fool (*see page 166*) is just as mouthwatering as a conventional fool made with double cream, but contains just over 100 calories per serving. Melon with Raspberries (*see page 170*) has a mere 65 calories per serving.

More elaborate desserts, suitable for a dinner party or a family celebration,

are also included. These tend to be more calorie-packed than the simpler Slimmers' Specials, but, even so, they are nothing like as 'fattening' as the rich cakes, soufflés, meringues, cheesecakes and ice-creams described elsewhere. For example, Ambrosia (*see page 172*), which really *is* fit to serve to the gods, contains about 270 calories in all and Pineapple Sorbet (*see page 172*) contains about 225 calories per serving. Sorbets and water ices are particularly good desserts for slimmers, which is why we have included a few recipes here. Don't neglect those in Chapter One however; they are equally 'non-sinful' and will help to give you variety.

Slimmers' Soufflé (*see page 171*) is a real dinner party treat; it contains only 70 calories per serving, yet it looks and tastes every bit as good as other richer, more 'fattening' soufflés and your guests will never imagine it is a Slimmers' Special, unless you tell them! Slimmers' Strawberry Chantilly (*see page 164*) is a mouthwatering combination of fresh strawberries and soured cream, flavoured with Kirsch. Rich-tasting and absolutely delicious by anyone's standards—slimmers and non-slimmers alike—it contains only 55 calories per serving.

Yoghurt Puddings

The classic dessert above all for dieters is yoghurt. Tasty and nourishing, it is low in calories; a normal, commercial carton weighing

150 ml (5 fl oz) contains only 75 calories. However, why not try making your own? Not only is it more economical, but it tastes much better. Simple step-by-step instructions are given on page 162. No special equipment is required and there is certainly no need to invest in a special yoghurt maker.

You can make as little or as much as you want, whenever you want, within a few hours. If you are fed up with the taste of plain yoghurt, flavour what you make with fresh fruit purée or pieces of chopped fruit. Because you know exactly what the ingredients are, you will be able to calculate the calorie content much more easily than you can that of commercial varieties. Also, the combination of homemade yoghurt and fresh fruit or fruit juice is infinitely superior both from the point of view of taste and nourishment.

Use homemade yoghurt as a dessert sauce instead of cream, custard or any other of the more conventional and calorie-packed sauces. It goes especially well with fruit salads and, if you simply must indulge in something more wicked, such as a sponge pudding or pastry, at least it will wreak less havoc on your waistline than jam sauce or ice-cream. Its tangy, slightly sharp flavour is refreshing and has the additional advantage of helping to re-educate the taste buds of the sweet-toothed. Use it to fold into fruit purées (sweetened with artificial sweetener) to make fools.

Approximate Calorie Values of Some Common Dessert Ingredients

Ingredients	Calories	Ingredients	Calories
Apple (one)	40	Nuts (chopped, mixed)—	
Apricots (dried)—25 g (1 oz)	40	25 g (1 oz)	125
Banana (one)	80	Orange (one)	40
Butter—25 g (1 oz)	260	Orange juice—150 ml	
Cherries—100 g (4 oz)	45	(5 fl oz)	60
Coconut (fresh)—25 g (1 oz)	170	Peach (one)	30
(desiccated)—		Pear (one)	35
25 g (1 oz)	180	Pineapple—175 g (6 oz)	65
Cottage cheese—25 g (1 oz)	45	Prunes—50 g (2 oz)	75
Cream cheese—25 g (1 oz)	145	Raisins—50 g (2 oz)	125
Egg (one)	90	Soured cream—25 ml (1 fl oz)	55
Egg white (one)	16	Strawberries—100 g (4 oz)	30
Grapes—100 g (4 oz)	60	Sugar (brown)—25 g (1 oz)	100
Ginger syrup—25 ml (1 fl oz)	80	(white)—25 g (1 oz)	110
Liqueurs—25 ml (1 fl oz)	75	White wine—125 ml (4 fl oz)	70
Melon—25 g (1 oz)	4	Yoghurt—150 ml (5 fl oz)	75

Making your own Yoghurt

575 ml (1 pint) pasteurized or homogenized milk
or
575 ml (1 pint) UHT milk
or
575 ml (1 pint) pasteurized or homogenized milk plus 100 g
(4 oz) dried skimmed milk powder
or
100 g (4 oz) dried skimmed milk powder plus 575 ml
(1 pint) water
or
275 ml (½ pint) evaporated milk plus water
30 ml (2 tablespoons) unpasteurized natural yoghurt

1 *Boil pasteurized, homogenized or UHT milk for 5 minutes. If using pasteurized or homogenized milk plus powder, boil the milk for 15 minutes and then mix. If using powdered milk alone, mix with 575 ml (1 pint) boiling water. Mix evaporated milk with its own volume of boiling water.*

2 *Cover and cool until the heated milk registers 46°C (115°F) on a thermometer. Place the yoghurt in a sterilized bowl or jug.*

3 *Warm a blanket and rinse out a bowl with hot water. Dry thoroughly. Alternatively, rinse out a vacuum flask with hot water. When the milk has cooled to the correct temperature, stir a little of it with the yoghurt. Whisk this into the rest of the milk.*

4 *Transfer the mixture to the warmed bowl or the vacuum flask. Cover the bowl with cling film and wrap it in the warmed blanket. Transfer to a warm place for at least 3 hours.*

5 *When a curd has formed, remove the bowl from the blanket and transfer it to a cool place until the yoghurt reaches room temperature. Cool a vacuum flask by holding it upright in a bowl of cold water for 5 minutes.*

6 *If you used a vacuum flask, tip out the yoghurt when it is cold into a clean bowl. Cover with cling film. Put the bowl in the refrigerator and chill for at least 1½ hours before using. The yoghurt will keep for up to a week.*

Flavouring and Thickening Yoghurt

Flavourings can be added to yoghurt either by infusing them with the yoghurt, or simply by mixing them in with a spoon or whisk. To infuse flavourings such as orange, lemon or grapefruit rind, or a vanilla pod, heat the yoghurt very slightly with the flavouring, then remove from the heat and leave for an hour or so. If you split open the vanilla pod, the flavour will be stronger. Spicy flavoured yoghurt complements many fruit puddings; simply mix in powdered cinnamon or nutmeg, and perhaps a little sugar. Or fold a spoonful or two of cider or wine into yoghurt, to serve with steamed sponge puddings, for example.

Yoghurt can be sweetened with icing, caster, granulated or soft brown sugar, or honey or golden syrup. Chopped fresh or canned fruit, concentrated fruit juice or fruit purée can all be mixed into yoghurt to make a fresh, satisfying pudding. Try also, mixing in desiccated coconut, crushed meringues or chopped sweets—such as marshmallows or a nut brittle—for a different taste.

1 *Thickened yoghurt is used in recipes which call for the yoghurt to be added before cooking. Line a strainer with a single layer of butter muslin or a double layer of cheesecloth. Place the strainer over a bowl.*

2 *Put the yoghurt in the strainer and set aside for 3 hours to drip. Do not squeeze the muslin or cheesecloth. For 'dry' yoghurt, set aside to drip for 6 hours. Transfer the yoghurt from the muslin or cheesecloth into a medium-sized, clean, dry mixing bowl.*

3 *To thicken yoghurt artificially, mix together 7.5 ml (½ tablespoon) cornflour with 15 ml (1 tablespoon) milk to form a smooth paste.*

4 *Stir the cornflower and milk mixture into the yoghurt. Transfer the mixture to a heavy-based saucepan and set over low heat.*

5 *Bring the yoghurt mixture to the boil slowly, stirring all the time. Simmer the mixture for 10 minutes, stirring occasionally. Remove the pan from the heat.*

6 *Tip the yoghurt into a bowl and set aside to cool to room temperature, stirring occasionally. The yoghurt is now ready for use. Store in the refrigerator until required.*

Slimmers' Strawberry Chantilly

Serves 4
350 g (12 oz) strawberries, washed and hulled
15 ml (1 tablespoon) Kirsch
150 ml (5 fl oz) plain yoghurt
liquid or granular artificial sweetener
1 large egg white

Slice the strawberries and put them in a bowl. Sprinkle over the Kirsch, then set aside for 1 hour, turning from time to time.

Stir together the yoghurt and artificial sweetener to taste. Whisk the egg white until it forms stiff peaks and fold the white into the yoghurt. Fold the strawberries into the yoghurt mixture.

Divide the mixture among 4 individual serving dishes and chill in the refrigerator for 2 hours.

No. of calories: 55 kcal per serving.

Maple Syrup and Orange Mousse

Serves 4
3 eggs, separated
1 orange
175 g (6 oz) maple syrup
15 g (½ oz) gelatine
575 ml (1 pint) plain yoghurt

Lightly beat the egg yolks in the top of a double boiler. Grate the rind of half the orange and add this to the egg yolks. Set over the bottom of the boiler and put on a low heat. Cook, stirring constantly, until the yolks thicken. Remove the pan from the heat. Stir in the maple syrup and set aside.

Squeeze the juice from the orange into a small saucepan. Dissolve the gelatine in it (*see page 28*) and allow to cool slightly. Pour the gelatine on to the egg yolk mixture in a thin stream, stirring constantly. Set aside until the mixture is on the point of setting.

Whisk the egg whites until they form stiff peaks. Stir the yoghurt into the egg yolk mixture and then fold in the egg whites. Pour the mousse into a serving dish and refrigerate for at least 2 hours, or until set.

No. of calories: 285 kcal per serving.

Apricot Lemon Cream

Serves 4
2 lemons
275 ml (½ pint) apricot yoghurt
150 ml (5 fl oz) soured cream
75 g (3 oz) icing sugar
2 egg whites
DECORATION:
julienne strips of lemon peel
sprigs of mint

Grate the zest from 1 lemon and pare the rind from the other with a potato peeler for the julienne strips (*see below*). Squeeze the juice from both lemons.

Whisk together the yoghurt and soured cream until the mixture is smooth and creamy. Whisk in the strained lemon juice and the icing sugar (to taste).

Whisk the egg whites until they form soft peaks. Fold the lemon mixture into these. Pile into 4 individual glasses and refrigerate for 1 hour.

Prepare the julienne strips of lemon. Cut the pared lemon rind into thin strips and put in a small pan. Cover with cold water, set over a gentle heat and bring to the boil. Drain, cover with cold water again and bring to the boil again. Simmer gently for 15 minutes, then drain and refresh under cold water.

Just before serving, decorate each glass with lemon strips and mint sprigs.

No. of calories: 233 kcal per serving.

Blackcurrant Whip

Serves 4
225 g (8 oz) frozen blackcurrants, defrosted
275 ml (½ pint) natural yoghurt
10 ml (2 teaspoons) gelatine
15 ml (1 tablespoon) water
artificial sweetener
2 egg whites

Rub the fruit through a sieve to make a smooth purée, then fold in the yoghurt.

Sprinkle the gelatine over the water in a small pan. Leave for 5 minutes, then dissolve over a low heat (*see page 28*).

Fold the gelatine into the blackcurrant and yoghurt and sweeten to taste with the artificial sweetener. Chill until on the point of setting.

Whisk the egg whites until they form soft peaks. Fold the blackcurrant mixture into the egg whites, and divide between 4 glasses. Refrigerate until set.

No. of calories: 63 kcal per serving.

Plum Snow

Serves 6
350 g (12 oz) red dessert plums, halved and stoned
275 ml (½ pint) water
100 g (4 oz) caster sugar
15 g (½ oz) gelatine
3 egg whites
DECORATION:
1–2 plums
crystallized rose petals (optional)

Put 45 ml (3 tablespoons) water into a small saucepan and set aside.

Put the prepared plums into a large saucepan with the remaining water, bring to the boil over a moderate heat, then cover and simmer gently for about 15 minutes, until the plums are very soft.

Stir the sugar into the plums, until it has dissolved. Leave to cool.

Sprinkle the gelatine over the water in the small pan and leave for 5 minutes to soften. Dissolve over a gentle heat (*see page 28*). Put the plums and their syrup into an electric blender and purée until smooth. Rub through a sieve.

Pour the gelatine into the plum purée in a thin stream, stirring to blend thoroughly. Refrigerate until on the point of setting.

Whisk the egg whites until they form stiff peaks. Fold the setting purée into them, and tip into a glass serving bowl.

When ready to serve, decorate the top of the snow with the reserved plums, neatly sliced and the rose petals, if using.

No. of calories: 105 kcal per serving.

Plum Snow

Sweet Saffron Yoghurt

(Illustrated on page 160)
Serves 6
575 ml (1 pint) plain yoghurt
350 g (12 oz) caster sugar
a few strands of saffron
15 ml (1 tablespoon) milk
pinch freshly grated nutmeg

Put the yoghurt in a large square of double cheesecloth and suspend over a bowl for 5 minutes to let the liquid drain off.

Tip the yoghurt into a bowl and add the sugar. Stir thoroughly until the sugar has dissolved.

Crush the strands of saffron using a pestle and mortar or the back of a wooden spoon. Heat the milk so it is just warm then add it to the saffron and leave for about 10 minutes to infuse.

Strain the milk into the sweetened yoghurt. Add the nutmeg and stir everything together. Chill for 2 hours and serve in individual dishes with fresh fruit in season.

No. of calories: 281 kcal per serving.

Apple Yoghurt Fool

Serves 6
450 g (1 lb) cooking apples, peeled, cored and chopped
50 g (2 oz) raisins
30 ml (2 tablespoons) water
2.5 ml (½ teaspoon) mixed spice
425 ml (15 fl oz) plain yoghurt
few drops green food colouring
DECORATION:
15 ml (1 tablespoon) Demerara sugar
15 ml (1 tablespoon) chopped nuts
(optional—strict slimmers, omit)

Put the apples, raisins, water and mixed spice in a saucepan over low heat. Bring to the boil and simmer for 10 minutes, or until the apples are tender.

Transfer the apples to a bowl and set aside to cool. Then chill in the refrigerator for 1 hour.

Stir the yoghurt into the apples. Stir in a few drops of food colouring.

Turn the mixture into 6 individual serving dishes. Sprinkle over the sugar and nuts, if wished.

No. of calories: 101 kcal per serving.

Instant Yoghurt Pudding

Serves 4
3 bananas, peeled and thinly sliced
3 large oranges, peeled, pith removed and separated into segments
575 ml (1 pint) plain yoghurt
60 ml (4 tablespoons) brown sugar

Preheat the grill to high.

Mix together the bananas, oranges and yoghurt and spoon into a medium-sized, flameproof dish. Smooth the surface and sprinkle with the sugar.

Place under the grill and cook for 3–4 minutes, or until the sugar caramelizes.

Serve immediately, if serving hot. If serving cold, set aside to cool to room temperature. Then chill in the refrigerator for 1 hour.

No. of calories: 241 kcal per serving.

Ginger Fruit Compôte

Serves 1
3 dried prunes
4 dried apricots
grated rind and juice of 1 small orange
30 ml (2 tablespoons) ginger syrup

If the prunes have stones, remove them by rubbing them between the thumb and forefinger until the stones pop out. Put the prunes and apricots in a bowl and add the orange rind and juice. Pour over sufficient warm water to raise the level of liquid in the bowl to 2.5 cm (1 in) above the fruit. Add the ginger syrup.

Cover and set aside to soak for 8 hours or overnight.

Transfer the fruit and any remaining liquid to a saucepan, cover and set over low heat. Simmer gently for 10 minutes. Turn into a bowl and cool. Chill for 1 hour before serving.

No. of calories: 152 kcal per serving.

Rhubarb and Gooseberry Compôte

Serves 4
225 g (8 oz) young or forced tender rhubarb
225 g (8 oz) gooseberries, topped and tailed
225 g (8 oz) caster sugar
275 ml (½ pint) water

Wash the rhubarb, trim the ends and cut into 2.5-cm

Rhubarb and Gooseberry Compôte

(1-in) lengths. Wash the gooseberries and put the fruits together in a heatproof bowl. Stir them to mix, but take care not to crush the fruit.

Put the sugar in a large saucepan with the water. Heat gently, stirring, to dissolve the sugar. Then raise the heat and boil for about 15 minutes, without stirring.

Cool the syrup for 1 minute. While it is still hot pour it over the fruits. Cover and leave in a cool place for 1 hour.

Chill the compôte for at least 2 hours (or overnight for the best flavour).

No. of calories: 234 kcal per serving.

Autumn Compôte

Serves 6
450 g (1 lb) fresh blackberries
275 g (10 oz) caster sugar
150 ml (¼ pint) water
225 g (8 oz) greengages, halved and stoned
225 g (8 oz) dessert plums, halved and stoned
2 large green dessert apples, washed
juice of 1 lemon

Put the blackberries in a large bowl and sprinkle 100 g (4 oz) caster sugar over them. Cover and leave to stand for 1 hour, stirring them over occasionally.

Put the water and the remainder of the sugar in a large heavy-based saucepan. Stir over a low heat until the sugar has dissolved. Raise the heat and bring to the boil. Boil for 1 minute, then remove from the heat and strain in the lemon juice.

Add the prepared greengages and plums to the syrup. Quarter and core the apples, but do not peel them. Slice them thinly into the syrup with the greengages and plums.

Mix the fruits carefully together and add the blackberries. Mix gently again, then cover and leave to stand for at least 1 hour in order to cool and give the flavours a chance to blend.

No. of calories: 257 kcal per serving.

Grape Cream

Serves 6
450 g (1 lb) seedless grapes, peeled
125 ml (4 fl oz) soured cream
125 ml (4 fl oz) plain yoghurt
50 g (2 oz) soft brown sugar

Mix together the grapes, cream, yoghurt and sugar and chill in the refrigerator for 2 hours.

Transfer to 6 individual glasses before serving.

No. of calories: 90 kcal per serving.

Peach Surprise

Serves 4
275 g (10 oz) peaches, skinned, stoned and sliced
10 ml (2 teaspoons) lemon juice
225 g (8 oz) cottage or curd cheese

Reserve 12 peach slices for decoration and brush with the lemon juice. Rub the remaining slices through a sieve to form a smooth purée.

Rub the cheese through the sieve into the purée and beat the mixture until thoroughly combined. Chill in the refrigerator for 1 hour.

Divide the mixture equally between four individual dishes. Decorate with the reserved peach slices.

No. of calories: 77 kcal per serving.

Tropical Fruit Salad

Serves 8
1 pawpaw
1 mango
16 lychees
2 Chinese gooseberries (kiwi fruit)
1 pineapple
juice of 1 lime
150 ml (5 fl oz) white wine

Halve the pawpaw and remove the seeds. Scoop out the flesh with a melon baller.

Cut thick slices from either side of the mango stone and then scoop out the flesh from the skin in chunks. Cut away the flesh that remains around the stone.

Peel the lychees. Loosen the flesh from the stone at the rounded end and gradually ease it away.

Peel and slice the Chinese gooseberries. Peel, core and dice the pineapple.

Mix all the fruit together in a serving dish and pour over the lime juice and white wine.

No. of calories: 85 kcal per serving.

Red Fruit Salad

Serves 4
225 g (8 oz) redcurrants, trimmed
45–60 ml (3–4 tablespoons) caster sugar
pinch ground cinnamon
grated rind and juice of 1 orange
100 g (4 oz) red dessert cherries, stoned
100 g (4 oz) strawberries, washed, hulled and halved
100 g (4 oz) raspberries, washed
15 ml (1 tablespoon) lemon juice

Put the redcurrants, sugar, cinnamon and orange rind in a saucepan. Pour over 30 ml (2 tablespoons) of the orange juice. Cover and shake. Set the pan over low heat and cook for 5–7 minutes, or until the sugar has dissolved and the currant juices have begun to flow. Add the cherries, re-cover the pan and turn off the heat.

When the contents of the pan are barely tepid, add the strawberries, raspberries, the remaining orange juice and the lemon juice. Mix lightly but thoroughly.

Turn the mixture into a serving bowl, cover and set aside in a cool place for at least 4 hours to macerate.

No. of calories: 96 kcal per serving.

Green and Cream Fruit Salad

Serves 4
2 small ogen melons
225 g (8 oz) white grapes, peeled and seeded
30–45 ml (2–3 tablespoons) caster sugar
juice of 1 lemon
2 small bananas
1 Chinese gooseberry (kiwi fruit)

Halve the melons and scoop out the seeds. Scoop out the flesh with a melon baller. Reserve the melon shells.

Put the melon balls and grapes in a bowl and sprinkle over the sugar and half the lemon juice. Cover and set aside in a cool place for 1–1½ hours.

Shortly before serving, add any juice that has collected in the melon shells to the bowl of fruit. Peel and slice the bananas. Sprinkle over the remaining lemon juice and add them to the bowl. Toss the mixture lightly and divide it between the four melon shells.

Peel the Chinese gooseberry and cut the flesh into slices. Divide the slices equally between the four shells and serve immediately.

No. of calories: 140 kcal per serving.

Redberry Dessert

Redberry Dessert

Serves 4
350 g (12 oz) redcurrants, stripped of the stalks
350 g (12 oz) raspberries
75–100 g (3–4 oz) caster sugar (see recipe)
25 ml (1 tablespoon) cornflour
finely grated zest of ½ orange
DECORATION:
split blanched almonds (optional)

Reserve a few redcurrants for decoration, and purée the remainder with the raspberries in an electric blender. Rub the purée through a sieve to extract the seeds.

Tip the purée into a heavy-based saucepan and sweeten to taste with the caster sugar. Heat gently, stirring from time to time.

Blend the cornflour to a smooth paste with a little water, then stir in a few spoonfuls of the hot purée. Pour the mixture back into the saucepan and bring slowly to simmering point, stirring all the time to keep the mixture smooth as it thickens.

Remove from the heat and stir in the orange rind. Divide between 4 individual serving glasses and leave in a cool place until quite cold. Refrigerate for about 30 minutes before serving.

Decorate with the blanched almonds and reserved redcurrants.

No. of calories: 134 kcal per serving.

*Strict slimmers should omit the blanched almond decoration, and could also sweeten the purée with artificial sweetener instead of sugar.

Strawberry Delight

Serves 4
150 g (5 oz) cottage cheese
30 ml (2 tablespoons) caster sugar
grated rind and juice of 1 orange
350 g (12 oz) strawberries, washed and hulled

Rub the cottage cheese through a strainer. Stir in the sugar and the grated orange rind.

Reserve about one-third of the strawberries for decoration and roughly chop the remainder. Mix these with the orange juice and stir the mixture into the cottage cheese.

Divide the mixture between 4 individual serving bowls and top with the reserved strawberries.

No. of calories: 97 kcal per serving.

Wine Jelly Melon Cups

Serves 4
2 small sweet melons, such as ogen
25 g (1 oz) gelatine
350 ml (12 fl oz) plus 30 ml (2 tablespoons) water
100 g (4 oz) sugar
500 ml (18 fl oz) medium dry white wine
juice of 1 lemon

Using a sharp knife cut the melons in half making deep zig-zag cuts through the flesh. Pull the halves apart and carefully scoop out the seeds. Refrigerate the melon halves.

Sprinkle the gelatine over the 30 ml (2 tablespoons) water. Leave to stand for 5 minutes.

Put the remaining water in a saucepan with the sugar, wine and lemon juice. Heat gently. Add the softened gelatine, and stir over a very low heat until the gelatine has dissolved. Leave the mixture to cool.

When the mixture is on the point of setting, pour all but about 225 ml (8 fl oz) into the melon halves. Refrigerate these and the remaining jelly.

Just before serving, whisk the reserved jelly until it is frothy. Divide it between the melon halves and serve at once.

No. of calories: 237 kcal per serving.

Melon with Raspberries

Serves 6
450 g (1 lb) raspberries, washed
45 ml (3 tablespoons) caster sugar
15 ml (1 tablespoon) Kirsch
1 medium-sized melon

Sprinkle the raspberries with the sugar and Kirsch and set aside in a cool place for 4 hours.

Cut a slice from the top of the melon and scoop out the seeds. Scoop out the flesh with a melon baller and mix it with the raspberries.

Pile the fruit mixture and juice into the melon. Refrigerate until required for serving.

No. of calories: 65 kcal per serving.

Wine Jelly Melon Cups

Slimmers' Soufflé

Serves 4
350 g (12 oz) cooking apples, peeled, cored and thinly sliced
15 ml (1 tablespoon) water
thinly pared rind of ½ lemon
few drops liquid artificial sweetener
2 eggs, separated
1 extra egg white

Preheat the oven to 170°C, 325°F, Gas 3. Lightly grease a 1.1-litre (2-pint) soufflé dish.

Put the apples, water and lemon rind in a saucepan and set over low heat. Cover and simmer for about 10 minutes or until the apple is soft.

Remove the pan from the heat. Remove and discard the lemon rind. Beat in sweetener to taste and continue beating until the apple is smooth. Set aside to cool.

Lightly beat the egg yolks together. Then beat them into the apple.

Whisk the egg whites until they form stiff peaks and fold into the apple mixture.

Turn the mixture into the prepared soufflé dish and bake for 30 minutes, or until the top is lightly browned and firm to the touch. Serve immediately.

No. of calories: 70 kcal per serving.

Slimmers' Cheesecake

Serves 6
100 g (4 oz) starch-reduced digestive biscuits, crushed
25 g (1 oz) low-fat margarine, melted
225 g (8 oz) cottage cheese, sieved
150 ml (5 fl oz) lemon-flavoured yoghurt
grated rind and juice of 1 large lemon
15 g (½ oz) gelatine
water (*see recipe*)
artificial sweetener
2 egg whites

Lightly grease a 15-cm (6-in) loose-bottomed cake tin.

Mix 75 g (3 oz) of the crushed biscuits with the melted margarine and use to line the base and sides of the tin.

Beat together the sieved cottage cheese, the lemon-flavoured yoghurt and the grated rind of the lemon until smooth and evenly mixed.

Make the juice of the lemon up to 150 ml (5 fl oz) water water. Put in a small pan and sprinkle the gelatine on top. Leave for 5 minutes, then dissolve (*see page 28*). Cool slightly.

Add the cooled gelatine to the cheese and lemon mixture, stirring to mix thoroughly. Add artificial sweetener to taste. Chill until on the point of setting.

Whisk the egg whites until they form soft peaks and fold the cheese mixture into them. Pour on to the biscuit base and refrigerate until set.

When ready to serve, remove the cheesecake from the tin on to a serving plate. Press the remaining crumbs on to the edges of the cheesecake in a rim about 15 mm (½ in) in from the outside edge.

No. of calories: 166 kcal per serving.

Pear and Prune Dessert

Serves 6
225 g (8 oz) prunes
50 g (2 oz) sugar
10 ml (2 teaspoons) lemon juice
700 g (1½ lb) small pears, peeled

Put the prunes in a bowl and add just enough water to cover. Set aside to soak for 8 hours or overnight.

Drain the prunes and reserve the liquid. Set the prunes aside.

Put the soaking liquid in a saucepan and add the sugar and lemon juice. Set over medium heat and bring to the boil, stirring constantly. Boil, stirring occasionally, for 5 minutes. Add the prunes and the pears. Cover and simmer for 10–15 minutes, or until the pears are tender.

Remove the pan from the heat. Carefully transfer the pears to a serving dish and spoon over the prunes and the syrup. Set aside to cool. Then chill in the refrigerator for 2 hours.

No. of calories: 127 kcal per serving.

Cream Cheese Cloud

Serves 4
450 g (1 lb) curd cheese
75 g (3 oz) sugar
2 egg whites
45 ml (3 tablespoons) chopped angelica

Beat curd cheese until smooth, then beat in the sugar.

Whisk the egg whites until they form stiff peaks. Fold them into the cheese mixture. Fold in the chopped angelica.

Line a strainer with muslin or cheesecloth and turn the mixture into it. Set aside in a cool place to drain for 3–4 hours, before transferring to a serving dish.

Serve with fresh fruit in season.

No. of calories: 264 kcal per serving.

Ambrosia

Serves 4
3 large oranges, peeled and with pith removed
1 small pineapple, peeled, cored and sliced
50 g (2 oz) caster sugar
150 g (5 oz) fresh coconut, coarsely grated
or
150 g (5 oz) coarse, desiccated coconut, soaked in
125 ml (4 fl oz) water for 30 minutes and drained

Cut the oranges into thin slices and remove the pips. Cut each of the pineapple slices into 8 cubes.

Mix together the sugar and the coconut.

Arrange a layer of orange slices in the bottom of a serving bowl. Sprinkle over a little of the sugar and coconut mixture. Top with a layer of pineapple chunks and sprinkle over a little of the sugar and coconut mixture. Continue making layers in this way until all the ingredients are used up, ending with a layer of the sugar and coconut mixture. Chill in the refrigerator for at least 2 hours before serving.

No. of calories: 268 kcal per serving.

Pineapple Sorbet

Serves 4
1 medium-sized pineapple
175 g (6 oz) caster sugar
400 ml (15 fl oz) water
2 egg whites

Set the refrigerator at its lowest setting. Chill an ice tray.

Cut a thin slice off the bottom of the pineapple. Cut off the spiky top. Cut the flesh loose and turn it out on to a plate to catch the juice. Cut into slices and remove the 'eyes', then chop roughly and purée with any juice that collected in the saucer in an electric blender.

Wrap the pineapple shell and top in foil and place in the bottom of the refrigerator until required (*see below*).

Put the sugar and water into a saucepan and set over medium heat. Bring to the boil, stirring constantly. Lower the heat and simmer for 5 minutes. Remove from the heat and set aside to cool.

Strain the cold syrup into a jug and chill, but do not freeze, for 30 minutes.

Mix together the pineapple purée and syrup. Pour the mixture into the ice tray, cover and freeze for 1 hour, or until slushy.

Just before removing the ice from the refrigerator, whisk the egg whites until they form stiff peaks.

Turn the ice into a bowl and stir. Whisk the ice into the egg whites, 15 ml (1 tablespoon) at a time.

Return the ice to the tray, cover and freeze for 1½–2 hours, or until firm.

Turn the ice into a bowl and beat for 3–4 minutes. Return it to the tray, cover and re-freeze for 1 hour.

When the ice is firm, re-set the refrigerator and store the ice in the freezer compartment.

To serve, remove the ice from the freezer compartment 15 minutes before serving. Unwrap the pineapple and pile the sorbet into the centre.

No of calories: 226 kcal per serving.

Mint Water Ice

Serves 4
850 ml (1½ pints) water
thinly pared rind and juice of 3 large lemons
200 g (7 oz) caster sugar
575 ml (1 pint) mint leaves, washed and drained
2–3 drops green food colouring
1 small egg white

Set the refrigerator at its lowest setting if necessary (*see page 9*). Chill an ice tray.

Put the water, lemon rind and juice and sugar into a saucepan. Put on a medium heat and bring to the boil, stirring constantly. Lower the heat and simmer for 5 minutes. Remove the pan from the heat.

Reserve a few mint leaves for decoration. Add the remainder to the syrup and stir to ensure that they are all well soaked. Cover and set aside for 30 minutes to infuse.

Strain the liquid, squeezing the leaves to extract all the flavour. Stir in the green colouring. Chill, but do not freeze, in the refrigerator for 30 minutes.

Pour the mixture into the ice tray, cover and freeze for 30 minutes, or until slushy.

Just before removing the ice from the refrigerator, whisk the egg white until it forms soft peaks.

Remove the ice from the refrigerator and turn into a bowl. Stir the ice and then beat it into the egg white, 15 ml (1 tablespoon) at a time, using an electric or rotary whisk.

Return the ice to the tray, cover and freeze for 1½ hours, or until firm.

Turn the ice into a bowl and beat again. Return it to the tray, cover and re-freeze until firm.

When the ice is firm, re-set the refrigerator and store the ice in the freezer compartment. Remove and set aside at room temperature 15 minutes before serving.

No. of calories: 215 kcal per serving.

Exotic Tropical Dessert

Exotic Tropical Dessert

Serves 6
1 small pineapple
1 ripe papaya
1 ripe mango
2 kiwi fruit
100 g (4 oz) strawberries, hulled and sliced
2 passion fruit
10 mint leaves
juice of 3 oranges
juice of 1 lemon
icing sugar (optional) .

Cut off both ends of the pineapple and remove the thick outer skin. Cut the flesh into quarters and remove the cores. Reserve one-quarter, and cut the remainder into thin slices.

Peel the papaya, cut in half and discard the pips. Put on one side. Cut half the flesh into small pieces, and reserve the remainder.

Peel the mango, and slice the flesh discarding the stone. Reserve about one-third of the flesh and dice the remainder into bite-sized pieces.

Peel the kiwi fruit and slice thinly. Put in a bowl with all the rest of the prepared fruit (except for the reserved pieces). Add half the sliced strawberries.

Put the reserved pineapple, papaya and mango into an electric blender. Cut the passion fruit in half and spoon the flesh and seeds into the blender. Add half the mint leaves and the juice of the oranges and lemons. Blend, then rub through a sieve into a bowl. Add more orange juice if the mixture seems too thick. Taste it, and add icing sugar if you find it too sharp.

Pour this mixture over the prepared fruit, cover the bowl and chill for about 2 hours.

About 45 minutes before serving, remove the fruit from the refrigerator, toss it lightly with a metal spoon and divide between 6 individual glass bowls. Top with the remainder of the strawberries.

Cut the rest of the mint leaves into strips and sprinkle these over the fruit. Serve at room temperature.

No. of calories: 92 kcal per serving.

Dessert Sauces

To serve some desserts without a sauce would be rather like serving a cake without icing. A tasty sauce is what adds the extra special sparkle that turns an ordinary meal into a dinner party. A clever choice of mix-and-match flavours and textures makes this part of the meal as individual as your signature. Experiment with traditional classics and unusual combinations to please the eye as well as the taste buds.

It has been said that what distinguishes the first class chef from the run of the mill cook is his or her sauces. Although this criterion is more usually applied to. the preparation of savoury sauces as accompaniments to meat, fish and vegetables, it is just as valid when thinking about desserts and puddings. A clever choice of dessert sauce can turn an ordinary pudding into something really special and an elaborate dessert into a masterpiece. Sauces can also help when things do not go exactly as planned. Although a sauce can never disguise an overcooked pudding, an unset mould or the taste of less-than-fresh ingredients, it can help mask one or two minor catastrophes, such as a slightly unappealing colour or a collapsed pudding.

As important as the choice of sauce is the choice of the dessert with which you are serving it. As a general rule, any plain dessert, whether a baked milk pudding, steamed sponge, plain cheesecake or single flavoured ice-cream, will be enhanced by serving it with a sauce. It hardly needs saying that serving a sauce with a rich gâteau already smothered in cream and fresh fruit is gilding the lily and plainly unnecessary. However, in between these two extremes, there is tremendous scope for the imaginative cook, combining unusual flavours, different textures and hot and cold sauces and desserts.

For example, try a sauce with a subtle but distinctive taste, such as Coconut Sauce (*see page 181*) with apple pie. Ginger Syrup Sauce (*see page 181*) will make a delightful change with both plain and filled crêpes and pancakes. Jam Sauce (*see page 179*) is almost a 'classic' with steamed pudding, but try it with ice-cream, too. Use different flavoured jams for different flavoured ice-creams.

Although breaking the 'rules' by combining unexpected flavours and textures can produce the most delicious results, there are one or two guidelines to bear in mind. A strong flavour will always mask a subtle one, so if you are serving a strongly flavoured dessert, a delicate flavour sauce is utterly wasted. If a sauce is required, you would be much more sensible to prepare something smooth and complementary in

a rather bland way, such as a Crème Anglaise (*see page 176*). The same rule applies in reverse. A delicate, lemon-flavoured pudding, for example, would be destroyed by Toffee Sauce. Serve a Lemon Sauce to enhance the flavour already prevalent in the pudding.

By the same token, strong flavours of both pudding and sauce will simply be at war with each other. Pick out the flavour of the pudding in the sauce so it enhances it—Marmalade Sauce (*see page 179*) with an orange pudding or a chocolate-flavoured sauce with a chocolate or coffee pudding.

Some combinations of desserts and sauces have become classics because the flavour, texture and appearance is precisely right. Even if you don't always stick to these, at least bear them in mind.

Crème Anglaise (literally English cream) is a true custard made with egg yolks, sugar and milk and flavoured with vanilla. (*Step-by-step instructions are given on page 176.*) It bears little relation to custard made from commercial powders and its rich, creamy taste is well worth the extra time and effort involved. As well as forming the basis of many desserts, such as trifles, ice-cream and fruit creams, it is a delicious sauce to serve with steamed puddings, cooked fruit and pies.

Crème Chantilly, a sweetened, vanilla-flavoured cream, is a little bit more special than simply serving plain cream with cold desserts and fruit salads. It is also thick and rich enough to use for sandwiching layered gâteaux and for piping decoratively over trifles and moulds. Make Crème Chantilly by whisking 275 ml (½ pint) chilled double cream in a bowl until it begins to thicken. Add 5 ml (1 teaspoon) each of vanilla essence and caster sugar and continue beating until the cream forms soft peaks. You can also flavour cream for sandwiching or decorating gâteaux with a liqueur.

A rich, fruity Christmas pudding is somehow incomplete without Brandy or Rum Butter. A hard sauce, it should be well chilled before serving, so that it melts deliciously over each slice. The ingredients and method for making traditional Cumberland Rum Butter are given on page 177. Make brandy butter

in the same way, by creaming unsalted butter with an equal amount of caster sugar and then beating in brandy, a little at a time. 100 g (4 oz) butter and an equal amount of sugar will take about 60 ml (4 tablespoons) of brandy.

Melba Sauce (*see page 178*) was invented by the great French chef, Escoffier, in honour of the Australian singer, Dame Nellie Melba. It is so easy to make, yet its delicate, refreshing taste can turn a simple ice-cream into a memorable treat. Serve it with fresh fruit—it is lovely with melon.

Chocolate Sauce (*see page 180*) is an eternal favourite with both adults and children. Rich, smooth and glossy, it is traditionally served hot with ice-cream and poached pears, but it can also be served with other fruit, as well as steamed and baked puddings.

Serving Sauces

It is wise to remove cold sauces from the refrigerator 10–15 minutes before serving so that the full flavour can develop. Hot sauces are best made at the last possible moment, so that they are not allowed to become either lukewarm, overcooked or even curdled by being kept too long. It is not always convenient to keep your guests waiting while you make the sauce to accompany the dessert, so it may be necessary to make it a little earlier and keep it warm. Pour the sauce into the top of a double boiler or into a heatproof bowl. Set it over very hot water and cover with a lid or with aluminium foil. Do not set it directly over heat or the sauce will probably spoil. If the delay before serving is longer than you anticipated and the sauce does not seem to be hot enough, set the double boiler or saucepan of hot water over very low heat. Stir the sauce while it heats through, but never allow it to boil. Take special care with Crème Anglaise to prevent curdling.

If the dessert is rather plain in appearance, spoon over a little sauce to decorate and serve the remainder in a sauceboat, bowl or jug; warming it for hot sauces, and chilling for cold. Always provide a spoon, even for sauces which pour, to enable people to control exactly how much they take.

Making Crème Anglaise

275 ml (½ pint) milk
vanilla pod or
2–3 drops vanilla essence
2 eggs
25 g (1 oz) caster sugar
5 ml (1 teaspoon) cornflour (optional)

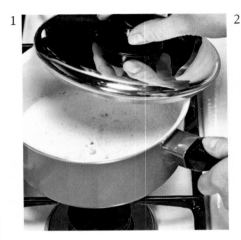

1 *Put milk in a heavy-bottomed pan and add a vanilla pod or vanilla essence. Put the pan over a medium heat and leave until bubbles appear round the edges of the milk. Remove from the heat, cover and leave to infuse.*

2 *Separate the eggs and put the yolks in a basin (use the whites for meringues). Add sugar and cornflour (if using) and beat everything together thoroughly with a wooden spoon.*

3 *If you prefer you can use 1 egg yolk and 1 whole egg and omit the cornflour. (The custard will be thinner.) Whisk the eggs thoroughly with the sugar to make sure the white is thoroughly incorporated.*

4 *Pour the hot milk in a thin, steady stream on to the eggs and sugar mixture. Stir constantly with a wooden spoon to combine the ingredients thoroughly.*

5 *Strain the egg and milk through a fine sieve either into the top of a double boiler, or into a bowl which will fit on top of a saucepan. Wash and dry the vanilla pod for use again.*

6 *Set the boiler or bowl over hot water, making sure the bottom does not touch the water. Cook over a moderate heat, stirring all the time, until the custard thickens and will coat the back of the spoon. This will probably take about 15 minutes.*

Making Rum Butter

75 g (3 oz) unsalted butter
75 g (3 oz) soft brown sugar
60 ml (4 tablespoons) dark rum
grated zest of half a lemon
squeeze of lemon juice
pinch of nutmeg

1 *Put butter in a bowl. Cream with a wooden spoon until it is light in colour and fluffy in texture (as in cake-making).*

2 *Beat in the sugar a little at a time, making sure it is thoroughly mixed and combined before adding the next spoonful. Beat until the mixture is smooth and well blended.*

3 *Beat in the rum a few drops at a time. This way the mixture will not curdle. Beat thoroughly between each addition, and continue until all the rum has been used.*

4 *Add the grated lemon zest, the squeeze of juice and a pinch of nutmeg, and beat in thoroughly. Refrigerate the sauce before serving. Serve with Christmas pudding and mince pies, or spread on biscuits in the Cumberland tradition.*

Correcting Mistakes With Sweet Sauces

What went wrong	Cause	Remedy
Lumpy sauce	The starch (cornflour or arrowroot) and liquid have not been properly blended, or the sauce has not been stirred sufficiently.	Rub the sauce through a strainer into a clean pan, or blend in an electric blender for 1–2 minutes. Reheat carefully, stirring vigorously.
Thick sauce	Incorrect proportions or the sauce has been allowed to evaporate during cooking.	Gradually beat in more *hot* liquid.
Thin sauce	If arrowroot has been used, boiling the sauce for longer than specified in the recipe.	No remedy, start again
	If custard-based, incorrect proportions or insufficient cooking	Beat one or two egg yolks in a clean bowl. Strain the custard and pour it into the egg yolk in a thin stream, stirring constantly. Reheat gently in the top of a double boiler over low heat, stirring.

Lemon Sauce

Serves 4
225 ml (8 fl oz) water
7 g (¼ oz) arrowroot
juice of 1 lemon
25 g (1 oz) sugar
5 ml (1 teaspoon) grated lemon rind
15 g (½ oz) butter, cut into small pieces

Mix together 30 ml (2 tablespoons) of the water and the arrowroot to form a smooth paste. Set aside.

Put the remaining water, the lemon juice and the sugar in a saucepan over medium heat. Cook, stirring constantly, until the sugar has dissolved. Bring the mixture to the boil.

Remove the pan from the heat and pour the syrup in a gradual stream into the arrowroot mixture, stirring constantly. Continue stirring until the mixture is thoroughly blended.

Return the sauce to the pan and bring to the boil over medium heat, stirring constantly. Boil, stirring constantly, for 1 minute.

Reduce the heat to low. Stir in the lemon rind, then whisk in the butter. Continue whisking until the butter has been incorporated and the sauce is glossy.

Serve immediately with baked and steamed puddings, hot soufflés or pancakes.

Strawberry Sauce

Serves 6
450 g (1 lb) strawberries, hulled and washed
175 g (6 oz) caster sugar
100 ml (4 fl oz) lemon juice (*see recipe*)
30 ml (2 tablespoons) Kirsch

Rub the strawberries through a strainer to make a smooth purée. Add the sugar, lemon juice to taste and the Kirsch. Stir thoroughly, until the sugar has dissolved.

Chill the sauce in the refrigerator for 2 hours before serving with ice-cream, crêpes or plain cheesecake.

Melba Sauce

Serves 4–6
450 g (1 lb) raspberries, washed
100 g (4 oz) icing sugar, sifted

Rub the raspberries through a fine strainer to make a smooth purée. Stir in the icing sugar.

Serve with ice-cream, fruit desserts and cheesecakes.

Cherry Sauce

Serves 4
100 g (4 oz) caster sugar
275 ml (½ pint) water
15 ml (1 tablespoon) redcurrant jelly
juice of ½ lemon
75 ml (3 fl oz) port or sherry
25 g (1 oz) glacé cherries, quartered

Put the sugar and water in a saucepan over medium heat. Stir constantly until the sugar has dissolved. Increase the heat and bring to the boil. Boil until the liquid is reduced by half.

Stir the redcurrant jelly, lemon juice and port or sherry into the syrup. Simmer the mixture until the jelly has dissolved completely.

Stir in the cherries and serve immediately with baked or steamed puddings or ice-cream.

Mousseline Sauce

Serves 4
1 large egg
2 extra egg yolks
65 g (2½ oz) caster sugar
30 ml (2 tablespoons) orange juice
15 ml (1 tablespoon) lemon juice
30 ml (2 tablespoons) double cream

Put the egg, egg yolks and sugar in the top of a double boiler and lightly whisk together. Add the orange and lemon juice and set the top of the boiler over the bottom placed on a low heat. Whisk for 5 minutes, or until the sauce has thickened and is hot and frothy. Remove the top of the boiler from the heat and whisk in the cream a little at a time. Pour this sauce into a warmed jug and use at once.

Madeira Sauce

Serves 4
2 eggs
3 extra egg yolks
50 g (2 oz) caster sugar
30 ml (2 tablespoons) Madeira

Beat together the eggs and the egg yolks in the top of a double boiler. When the mixture is frothy, gradually beat in the sugar and Madeira.

Set the top of the double boiler over the bottom and put on a low heat. Cook, beating constantly, until the mixture is thick and will leave a ribbon trail.

Serve immediately with plain fresh fruit or fruit salad.

Marmalade Sauce

Serves 4
45 ml (3 tablespoons) orange marmalade
15 ml (1 tablespoon) sugar
125 ml (4 fl oz) and 15 ml (1 tablespoon) water
10 ml (2 teaspoons) arrowroot
juice of ½ lemon

Mix together the marmalade, sugar and 125 ml (4 fl oz) water in a saucepan. Set over moderate heat and bring to the boil, stirring constantly. Reduce the heat to low and simmer for 5 minutes, stirring occasionally.

Mix the arrowroot to a smooth paste with 15 ml (1 tablespoon) water. Stir this into the sauce with the lemon juice and cook, stirring constantly, until the ingredients are thoroughly blended and the sauce has thickened slightly.

Serve with steamed and baked puddings.

Melba Sauce

Jam Sauce

Serves 4
60 ml (4 tablespoons) jam
grated rind and juice of 1 lemon
60 ml (4 tablespoons) sugar
275 ml (½ pint) and 15 ml (1 tablespoon) water
10 ml (2 teaspoons) cornflour

Put the jam, lemon rind and juice, sugar and 275 ml (½ pint) water in a saucepan over moderate heat. Cook, stirring constantly, until the jam has melted and the sugar has dissolved.

Remove the pan from the heat and set aside for 10 minutes.

Mix the cornflour to a smooth paste with the 15 ml (1 tablespoon) water and stir this into the jam sauce. Return the pan to the heat and bring the sauce to the boil, stirring constantly. Boil for 2 minutes.

Serve the sauce immediately with steamed puddings, baked milk puddings, pancakes or ice-cream.

Fudge Sauce

Serves 4–6
100 g (4 oz) butter
175 g (6 oz) caster sugar
50 g (2 oz) soft brown sugar
225 ml (8 fl oz) evaporated milk
15 ml (1 tablespoon) dark rum (optional)

Put the butter, caster sugar and brown sugar in a saucepan over a moderate heat. Cook, stirring constantly, until the butter has melted and the sugars have dissolved.

Stir in the evaporated milk. Increase the heat to high and boil the sauce for 5 minutes, stirring occasionally.

Remove the pan from the heat and stir in the rum. Serve the sauce immediately with ice-cream, pancakes and soufflés.

Chocolate Sauce

Serves 4–6
275 ml (½ pint) milk
15 g (½ oz) cornflour
50 g (2 oz) plain chocolate
25 g (1 oz) sugar
15 g (½ oz) butter, cut into small pieces

Mix 30 ml (2 tablespoons) milk with the cornflour to form a smooth paste. Set aside. Break the chocolate into small pieces.

Put the remaining milk, the chocolate and the sugar in a saucepan over medium heat. Cook, stirring constantly, without boiling until the chocolate has melted and the sugar has dissolved. Bring the mixture to the boil.

Remove the pan from the heat and pour the milk mixture in a gradual stream into the cornflour mixture, stirring constantly. Continue stirring until the mixture is thoroughly blended.

Return the mixture to the saucepan and bring to the boil over medium heat, stirring constantly. Boil for 3 minutes, still stirring.

Reduce the heat to low and whisk in the butter. Continue whisking until the butter has been incorporated and the sauce is glossy.

Serve immediately with ice cream or fruit or a mixture of the two.

Toffee Sauce

Serves 4–6
45 ml (3 tablespoons) rum
30 ml (2 tablespoons) chopped walnuts
15 ml (1 tablespoon) chopped angelica
15 ml (1 tablespoon) sultanas
4 maraschino cherries, chopped
15 ml (1 tablespoon) butter
30 ml (2 tablespoons) soft brown sugar
45 ml (3 tablespoons) golden syrup
10 ml (2 teaspoons) cornflour, mixed to a paste with
30 ml (2 tablespoons) water
10 ml (2 teaspoons) lemon juice
175 ml (6 fl oz) plus 30 ml (2 tablespoons) water

Combine the rum, walnuts, angelica, sultanas and cherries. Set aside for 30 minutes.

Melt the butter over moderate heat. Add the sugar and cook, stirring constantly, until it has dissolved. Add the syrup and bring the mixture to the boil. Mix the cornflour to a smooth paste with 30 ml (2 tablespoons) water and add to the sauce with the remainder of the water. Bring back to the boil, stirring.

Reduce the heat to low and simmer the mixture for 10 minutes, or until it is thick and syrupy.

Remove the pan from the heat and stir in the nut and fruit mixture and the lemon juice.

Serve immediately with ice-cream or plain cakes. Alternatively, allow it to cool and store in a screw-top jar in the refrigerator for up to 5 days.

Caramel Sauce

Serves 4–6
225 ml (8 oz) caster sugar
thinly pared rind of ½ lemon
pinch ground cinnamon
275 ml (½ pint) plus 30 ml (2 tablespoons) water
175 ml (6 fl oz) sherry

Put 175 ml (6 oz) of the sugar in a heavy-based saucepan. Add the lemon rind, cinnamon and 275 ml (½ pint) of the water. Set over medium heat and bring to the boil, stirring constantly. Reduce the heat to low and simmer for 10 minutes.

Meanwhile, put the remaining sugar and water in a pan over low heat. Cook, stirring constantly, until the sugar has dissolved. Raise the heat and boil until the syrup begins to turn brown.

Strain the contents of the first saucepan on to the caramel. Stir in the sherry and serve immediately with steamed puddings or ice-cream.

Coconut Sauce

Serves 6
100 g (4 oz) butter
100 g (4 oz) caster sugar
2 large eggs, separated
100 g (4 oz) grated coconut

Beat the butter until it is fluffy. Beat in the sugar.

Lightly beat the egg yolks together. Blend the yolks into the butter and sugar mixture. Stir in the coconut.

Whisk the egg whites until they form stiff peaks, then fold in the coconut sauce.

Transfer to a serving bowl and serve with pies and pastries.

Chocolate Sauce

Ginger Syrup Sauce

Serves 4–6
100 g (4 oz) golden syrup
small piece thinly pared lemon rind
25 g (1 oz) butter
5 ml (1 teaspoon) ground ginger
2.5 ml (½ teaspoon) lemon juice
15 ml (1 tablespoon) finely chopped, preserved ginger

Put the syrup, lemon rind, butter, ground ginger and lemon juice in a saucepan. Set over low heat and cook, stirring constantly, until all the ingredients are thoroughly blended and the sauce is thin and smooth.

Remove the pan from the heat and stir in the preserved ginger. Serve immediately, if serving with a hot pudding. Set aside to cool, if serving with ice-cream.

Index